Modelling and Decisions in Economics

Franz Ferschl

Ulrike Leopold-Wildburger,
Gustav Feichtinger, Klaus-Peter Kistner (Eds.)

Modelling and Decisions in Economics

Essays in Honor of Franz Ferschl

With 24 Figures
and 31 Tables

Physica-Verlag
A Springer-Verlag Company

Prof. Dr. Ulrike Leopold-Wildburger
Department of Statistics and Operations Research
University of Graz
Universitätsstr. 15/E3
A-8010 Graz, Austria

Prof. Dr. Gustav Feichtinger
Department of Econometrics, Operations Research
and Systems Theory
University of Technology
Argentinierstr. 8/119
A-1040 Wien, Austria

Prof. Dr. Klaus-Peter Kistner
Faculty of Economics
University of Bielefeld
Postfach 100131
D-33501 Bielefeld, Germany

Gefördert aus Mitteln der Stadt Graz und des Landes Steiermark.

ISBN 3-7908-1219-6 Physica-Verlag Heidelberg New York

Library of Congress Cataloging-in-Publication Data
Die Deutsche Bibliothek – CIP-Einheitsaufnahme
Modelling and decisions in economics: essays in honor of Frank Ferschl; with 31 tables / Ulrike Leopold-Wildburger ... (ed.). – Heidelberg; New York: Physica-Verl., 1999
ISBN 3-7908-1219-6

SPIN 10729907 88/2202-5 4 3 2 1 0 – Printed on acid-free paper

Preface

Franz Ferschl is seventy. According to his birth certificate it is true, but it is unbelievable. Two of the three editors remembers very well the Golden Age of Operations Research at Bonn when Franz Ferschl worked together with Wilhelm Krelle, Martin Beckmann and Horst Albach. The importance of this fruitful cooperation is reflected by the fact that half of the contributors to this book were strongly influenced by Franz Ferschl and his colleagues at the University of Bonn. Clearly, Franz Ferschl left his traces at all the other places of his professional activities, in Vienna and Munich. This is demonstrated by the present volume as well.

Born in 1929 in the Upper-Austrian Mühlviertel, his scientific education brought him to Vienna where he studied mathematics. In his early years he was attracted by Statistics and Operations Research. During his employment at the Österreichische Bundeskammer für Gewerbliche Wirtschaft in Vienna he prepared his famous book on queueing theory and stochastic processes in economics. This work has been achieved during his scarce time left by his duties at the Bundeskammer, mostly between 6 a.m. and midnight.

All those troubles were, however, soon rewarded by the chair of statistics at Bonn University. As a real Austrian, the amenities of the Rhineland could not prevent him from returning to Vienna, where he took the chair of statistics.

Surprisingly this was only an intermezzo as he was absorbed by the Statistics Department of the University of Munich. In the name of all contributors we want to thank Franz Ferschl for his encouragement, his friendship and his helpfulness. He is a broad scientist working not only in the field of stochastics and OR, but also on religion and philosophical issues as well as in algebraic topics. We wish him many years of health and success in his research on finite groups.

Ad multos annos!
Gustav Feichtinger
Klaus-Peter Kistner
Ulrike Leopold-Wildburger

Contents

Part 1: Decision Theory 1

Some Ideas on Economics and Ethics 3
Wilhelm Krelle

Ethics and Operations Research 29
Christoph Schneeweiss

How to Measure Risk? 39
Georg Ch. Pflug

On the Question of Speculation in Favour of or against the Euro before its Start 61
Lutz Beinsen

Resolving the Ellsberg Paradox by Assuming that People Evaluate Repetitive Sampling 83
Hans Schneeweiss

Part 2: Statistics and Econometrics 97

Maximum Likelihood Estimation for the VAR-VARCH Model: A New Approach 99
Shuangzhe Liu, Wolfgang Polasek

A Note on the Herfindahl Index of Concentration 115
Gerhart Bruckmann

A Generalization and Optimization of a Measure of Diversity 119
Helmut Beran

A Subjective Bayes Approach to the Queueing System $M/E_k/c$ 139
Harald Schmidbauer, Angi Rösch

Cooperation as the Stimulating Power for the Austrian Automobile Industry - Results of an Empirical Study 157
Carola Kratzer, Ulrike Leopold-Wildburger

Part 3: Operations Research 171

Lot Sizing and Queueing Models Some Remarks on KARMARKAR'S Model 173
Klaus-Peter Kistner

Analysis of MRP Policies with Recovery Options 189
Karl Inderfurth, Thomas Jensen

Bidding for Research Funds 229
Martin J. Beckmann

Separate versus Joint Inventories when Customer Demands are Stochastic 239
Günter Fandel, Michael Lorth

Optimal Macroeconomic Policies with and without the Monetary Instrument 255
Reinhard Neck

Dynamic Economic Models of Optimal Law Enforcement 269
Gustav Feichtinger

List of Contributors 295

Part 1:

Decision Theory

Some Ideas on Economics and Ethics

Wilhelm Krelle

Institut für Gesellschafts- und Wirtschaftswissenschaften
Universität Bonn

Abstract

In this paper we discuss the influence of ethics on the decisions of persons within the context of mutual influences of one person on another. We show that this influence may be modelled as a a Markov chain which converges to a final situation independent of the initial conditions. Different types of decisions are considered. At the end the reverse influence is considered: that of the economic development on ethics.

1 Introduction

It is a pleasure to contribute to the Festschrift in honour of Franz Ferschl at occasion of his 70. birthday. Statistics is a science where the basic concepts are subject to philosophical interpretations. Franz Ferschl was always aware of it. This may be seen from his introduction to measure theory and the theory of index numbers where he writes: "Wie kaum bei anderen Teilen der statistischen Methodenlehre zeigt sich hier, wie fließend die Grenzen zwischen einzelwissenschaftlicher und statistisch–methodologischer Argumentation ist" (Ferschl 1978, p. 141). The theory presented here depends on index numbers derived by the method of inquiries. The decision theory applied here is the same as demonstrated in his book "Nutzen– und Entscheidungstheorie" (Ferschl 1975, p. 9 ff.). Thus I may hope that Franz, my old friend and faculty collegue, enjoys this non–statistical contribution.

Ethics, where economics started from in classical antiquity, has reentered economics. There are more and more articles to be found in the literature which deal with ethical problems in a market economy (see the literature cited at the end). Thus, I think, it is time to analyze the relation of ethics and economics in general, i. e. to show where ethics influences economics (and vice versa), and how this can be taken into account in economics. Only the basic approach can be presented here. Details may be found in a discussion paper.[1]

The influence of ethics on economics is the main topic of this paper. But we shall also deal briefly with the inverse relation: the influence of economics on ethics.

Ethics is conceived as a set of moral evaluations. A moral evaluation is an immaterial reward or punishment of a certain size connected with a certain perceived or real act of a person which — if positive — comprises respect, esteem, reverence and the like by others and by the person himself, and — if negative — contempt, disdain, breaking off relations and the like by others and/or pricks of conscience by the person himself. Often these reactions of the society or of the "super–ego" to an act of a person is of much greater importance for the person than any sort of physical reward or punishment. But be that as it may: we assume that with each decision of a person which is of ethical importance[2] there is a "moral evaluation" connected with it. We explain the origin and the change of these moral evaluations and their influence on economics (this is the main topic of this paper), and vice versa: the influence of economics on these moral evaluations.

In the whole paper we assume that a person is able to state his evaluation of a certain phenomenon numerically on a scale of discrete numbers, e.g. as $-\bar{z}, -\bar{z}+1, \ldots, 0, 1, 2, \ldots, +\bar{z}, \bar{z}$ an integer ≥ 1, where a valuation of $-\bar{z}$ means the largest possible dislike, 0 means: no judgment or indifference, and $+\bar{z}$ means the largest possible appreciation. Of course, the grading may be coarse ($\bar{z}$ may be a small, positive number). Such grading is done permanently in politics and economics, also at the university level.

2 Classification of Private Decisions

We divide all situations where a moral evaluation may appear into four large groups:

---

[1]see: Krelle, Economics and Ethics, Disc. Paper No. B–441 (1998), Sonderforschungsbereich 303, Universität Bonn, Adenauerallee 24–42, D-53113 Bonn

[2]There are many acts without ethical importance, e.g. whether I like apples or pears. For these acts the corresponding morality figure is zero.

1. Private decision problems in personal life,

2. Public issues of the general political and economic order and of the current policy,

3. Behavior in different economic situations,

4. Decision to work as entrepreneur or not.

We shall deal in detail with situation 1. The other topics may be treated accordingly, they will be only sketched here. Details may be found in the discussion paper mentioned in note 1. Thus we start with situation 1.

We assume that there are h possible private situations of moral importance with which the person may be confronted (see Table 1). We call them B_1 , ... ,B_h .[3] In each of these situations the person has two possible decisions: a "good" one B_{i1} and a "bad" one B_{i2}, $i = 1, \dots, h$, where "good" or "bad" is determined by law or (if the law is silent) by the ethics which the majority of the population accepts.[4] In many cases the economic and the moral evaluation of a decision of a person run parallel, in others not. E.g. when passing by a store which exhibits some of its merchandise openly outside the shop the person may not touch it (the good act) or may steal (the bad act). The figures $G_{i1}^{(p)}, G_{i2}^{(p)}$ in Table 1 indicate the immediate economic advantage or disadvantage to the person p caused by the decision B_{i1} or B_{i2}, respectively; in our example: $G_{i1}^{(p)} = 0$ (if one does not steal, one does not have an economic advantage by not touching the merchandise), but $G_{i2}^{(p)} > 0$: the value of the loot for the thief is positive.

The figures $M_{i1}^{(p)}, M_{i2}^{(p)}$ in Table 1 connected with the decisions B_{i1}, B_{i2} constitute the moral evaluation of these decisions by person p. The $G_{ij}^{(p)}$ and $M_{ij}^{(p)}$ in Table 1 refer to a specific person p and are in general different from person to person. The following two columns in Table 1 refer to the set of all persons in the society. v_{i1} indicates the proportion of all persons who, if confronted with problem i, would choose the good alternative B_{i1}, the proportion $v_{i2} = 1 - v_{i1}$ would choose the bad alternative B_{i2} . ß$_i$ in the next column is the frequency with which the problem B_i occurs in the society. The

[3]If one is content with a crude approximation one could identify the h situations of moral importance for a person with the classification in criminal statistics, see e. g. the "Hauptdeliktsgruppen" in the Statistical Yearbook for the FRG, 1995, p. 376. But our theoretical concept goes much further.

[4]This ordering is a matter of convenience of notation and has no importance with regard to the substance.

$\bar{v}_{i1}$ in the following column in Table 1 are equal to the figures v_{i1} and may be called the *morality rates* for the different decision problems.[5] The $\bar{v}_{i2}$ are the *observed criminal rates.* They are the product of $ß_i$ and v_{ij}: $\bar{v}_{ij} = ß_i v_{ij}$.

The second–last column shows the elasticities of real GDP with respect to $\bar{v}_{i2}$: e. g. $\epsilon_{Y,\bar{v}_{12}} = \frac{\partial Y}{\partial \bar{v}_{12}} \cdot \frac{\bar{v}_{12}}{Y}$; it shows by which percentage GDP per capita changes if $\bar{v}_{12}$ (i. e. the criminal rate in problem i) is changed by 1%. This measures the economic consequences of deciding $B_{12}, \ldots, B_{h2}$. Of course, other measures (e.g. the effect on the distribution of income) may also be taken into account.

The last column of Table 1 gives the total valuation $V_{ij}^{(p)}$ of a decision B_{ij} by person p (thus the column is really a matrix of N columns if there are N persons in the society. The same applies for all other figures with an upper index (p).). Since valuations are crude estimations we admit only positive or negative integers as valuation figures. We shall derive these valuations later (see equations (1) and (2) below).

Now we come to the first columns of Table 1 . There are $m+1$ possible punishments in the society described by $S_0, S_1, \ldots, S_m$, where $S_0 = 0$ means no punishment and S_m the highest possible punishment. Given the judicial system, the size and efficiency of the police force and the number of places in the prisons, there are probabilities $w_{ij} = (w_{ij,0}, \ldots, w_{ij,m})$, $w_{ij,\mu} \geq 0$, $\sum_{\mu=0}^{m} w_{ij,\mu} = 1$, connected with each decision B_{ij}, $i = 1, \ldots, h$, $j = 1, 2$. A crime may go unpunished, i.e. $w_{i2,0} > 0$. Most criminals think they will not be caught. If $S_0, \ldots, S_m$ are stated in the same units (e.g. in monetary units or in "utils") we may form the punishment expectation connected with decision B_{ij}:

$$E(S_{ij}) = \sum_{\mu=0}^{m} w_{ij,\mu} \cdot S_\mu$$

The next column represents the subjective expectation of punishment $H_{ij}^{(p)}$ by person p which in most cases will deviate from the mathematical expectation. This explains the basic definitions and interrelations as illustrated in Table 1.

[5]The v_{ij} are theoretical figures. Actually, only the proportion $ß_i$ of the population is confronted with problem B_i. The figure $\bar{v}_{i1}$ is estimated for $\beta_i = 1$: it gives the hypothetical proportion of "good" decisions if ***all*** people were confronted with problem B_i. The figure $\bar{v}_{i1}$ has no impact on economics, but is relevant for ethics.

3 Private Decisions

As mentioned above, the immediate advantage or disadvantage of a decision B_{ij} may be evaluated by a person as G_{ij}[6], $i = 1, \ldots, h$, $j = 1, 2$. For instance, in the case of a burglary G_{ij} is the value of the loot. But there are probabilities w_{ij} of being caught and punished later, and there is an immaterial "loss of moral capital" M_{ij} (negative in this example) connected with the immoral act B_{i2}.

For simplicity we assume that the punishments start in the next period and stay the same in each future period. Then each alternative B_{ij} is connected with an immediate advantage G_{ij} and with probabilities $w_{ij} = (w_{ij,0}, w_{ij,1}, \ldots, w_{ij,m})$ of future punishments $S_0, S_1, \ldots, S_m$. Let the future be discounted by the person by a rate $d \geq 0$. Then, assuming additivity and neutral behavior with respect to risk and assuming a moral evaluation of zero, the decision B_{ij} is evaluated by the person as

$$\tilde{V}_{ij} = G_{ij} - E(S_{ij}) \cdot \sum_{t=1}^{\infty} (\frac{1}{1+d})^t = G_{ij} - E(S_{ij}) \cdot h,$$

where $E(S_{ij}) = \sum\limits_{k=0}^{m} w_{ij,k} \cdot S_k$ is the mathematical expectation of punishment and
$h = \frac{1}{d} \geq 0, h = 0, 1, 2, \ldots, \infty$, is the "economic horizon" of the person.[7] Now the moral remuneration or punishment M_{ij} comes in. Thus we finally get for the evaluation V_{ij} of a decision B_{ij} by the person p:

$$V_{ij}^{(p)} = n.i.(\alpha_{ij,1}^{(p)} \cdot G_{ij}^{(p)} + \alpha_{ij,2}^{(p)} \cdot H_{ij}^{(p)} + \alpha_{ij,3}^{(p)} \cdot M_{ij}^{(p)}),$$

where $H_{ij}^{(p)} = E(S_{ij}) \cdot h^{(p)}$ is the subjective expectation of punishment

and n.i. means: next integer. (1)

---

[6] The G_{ij}, M_{ij} and S_{ij} have to be measured in the same units, e.g. in money or in "utils".

[7] These are simplifying assumptions in order to keep the expressions simple. If the punishments S_{ij} were only imposed for h periods we would get

$$\tilde{V}_{ij} = G_{ij} - E(S_{ik})[1 - (\frac{1}{1+d})^h] \cdot \frac{1}{d}.$$

If the punishments were different in time we would get

$$\tilde{V}_{ij} = G_{ik} - d \cdot \sum_{t=1}^{h} E(S_{ik,t})(\frac{1}{1+d})^t.$$

But these are unnecessary complications in this context.

The $\alpha^{(p)}_{ij,k}$, $k = 1, \dots, 3$, are subjective weights for the values G, H and M, with $0 \leq \alpha^{(p)}_{ij,k}$ and $\sum_{k=1}^{3} \alpha^{(p)}_{ij,k} = 1$. The weights depend on the personal characteristics of the person, which are taken as given here. For G, H, M and α only finitely many values are admissible, e. g. all integer values between $-\tilde{z}$ and $+\tilde{z}$ for G, H, M, $\tilde{z}$ a positive integer, and $\frac{\tilde{z}_k}{\tilde{z}}$ for $\alpha^{(p)}_{ij,k}$, $\tilde{z}$ and $\tilde{z}_k$ non-negative integers, where $\tilde{z}_k \leq \tilde{z}$ and $\sum_{k=1}^{3} \tilde{z}_k = \tilde{z}$. The upper index p indicates that this figure is "private" to the person, i.e. different from person to person; the figure $E(S_{ij})$ is common knowledge.

The person p chooses that decision $B^{(p)}_{ij}$ which is most attractive for him, namely that with the maximum value of $V^{(p)}_{ij}$:

$$B^{(p)}_{ij} \leftarrow \max\,(V^{(p)}_{i1}, V^{(p)}_{i2}), \qquad j \in \{1, 2\}, \tag{2}$$

We may infer from equation (1):

1. The larger the M_{ij}, i.e. the clearer and the stiffer the moral rules are, the more likely is a behavior according to these rules.
2. A larger economic horizon (or: a smaller future discount rate) leads, as usual, to more moral decisions in the case where G_{ij} and M_{ij} are inversely related.
3. Higher punishments for crimes and deviations from moral behavior yield less crimes in general, i.e. if $h > 0$.
4. Usually moral laws do not contradict criminal laws, i.e. for all $M_{ij} > 0$ we have $E(S_{ij}) = 0$. Conflicts arise if $E(S_{ij}) > 0$ for $M_{ij} > 0$.
5. For finite $E(S_{ij})$ and finite h and M_{ij} there always exists a number G_{ij} such that V_{ij} is positive and the largest among all V_{i1}, V_{i2}. This means: since there are almost no limits for evaluations of a situation by different persons, there will always be persons which take any possible action. From the individual point of view: everything is possible. We are, however, not interested in individual behavior but in the behavior of large groups of people.

Table 1 illustrates the assumptions on private decisions and their consequences. In the relevant cases we have

$$G_{i1} < G_{i2} \quad \text{and } M_{i1} > M_{i2}.$$

If G_{ij} and M_{ij} run parallel and $E(S_{i1}) = 0$ there is no moral problem, we are in the best of all worlds as far as moral behavior is concerned. One should try to find a political, social and economic order where this comes true. But this does not seem possible for all issues.

4 Ethical Standards and the Determination of Moral Evaluations of a Decision

Equation (1) shows the determinants of the evaluation of a decision by a person p. These are: the immediate economic advantage $G_{ij}^{(p)}$ (which follows from the specific decision), the mathematical expectation $E(S_{ij})$ of being punished if the decision is illegal (this expectation is treated as common knowledge), the size $h^{(p)}$ of the economic horizon (specific for each person), and the moral evaluation $M_{ij}^{(p)}$ of the decision by person p. We want to explain the moral evaluations $M_{ij}^{(p)}$. First, there is an interdependence of moral judgments within each society. Value judgments are discussed and transfered from person to person either personally or by the information system. Thus, in principle, everyone is influenced by the value judgments of everyone else though usually only to a relatively small amount so that one keeps one's convictions by and large for a longer time and changes only slowly (as a rule).

But there are also philosophies (including theologies and ideologies) from which moral standards can be derived. The word "philosophy" has to be interpreted in the broadest sense. It also includes economic theories with implications for optimal behavior. Thus Marxism is a "philosophy" in this sense, and Keynesianism or neoclassical economics as well. They influence the "ethical standards", i.e. the evaluation of personal decisions, also the evaluation of collective decisions (to be treated later). The philosophies are passed on in the form of books, by the teaching in schools, by tradition etc. These philosophies are fixed and do not change with time[8]. They influence the evaluations of persons but are not in turn influenced by these evaluations. Usually many philosophies with different moral standards for each possible decision exert their influence in a society. It might happen that a decision B_{i1} which is best from the economic point of view is bad from the point of view of a certain philosophy k.

We assume that each philosophy k postulates or favours ethical standards

$$\bar{M}^{(k)} = (\bar{M}_{11}^{(k)}, \bar{M}_{12}^{(k)}, \dots, \bar{M}_{h1}^{(k)}, \bar{M}_{h2}^{(k)}),$$

i. e. each possible decision B_{ij} is morally evaluated by a positive or negative figure $\bar{M}_{ij}^{(k)}$ or, if the philosophy is silent or indifferent in this issue, by

[8]This is a simplification, of course. The interpretation of philosophies may change, and new philosophies may arise. But here we consider the simplest case.

$\bar{M}_{ij}^{(k)} = 0$. These evaluations may be rather different in the different philosophies (e. g. entrepreneurship may be positively evaluated in one philosophy and discriminated as exploitation in another). These "ethical standards" $\bar{M}_{ij}^{(1)}, \ldots, \bar{M}_{ij}^{(K)}$ (if there are K philosophies) influence (in general) each person directly or indirectly (via other persons). These relations may be modeled as a Markoff chain. This means that the moral evaluation $M_{ij,t}^{(p)}$ of a decision M_{ij} by person p in period t is to a proportion $p_{ij,p}^{(p)}$ determined by his own moral evaluation in the period before and with other proportions $p_{ij,p}^{\nu}$ by the moral evaluation of other persons ν, $\nu = 1, \ldots, N$, and again with other proportions $\overline{p}_{ij,p}^{\kappa}$ by the moral evaluation of a philosophy κ. Let there be N persons and K doctrines in the society. Then we assume:

$$(M_{ij,t}^{(1)}, \ldots, M_{ij,t}^{(N)}, \bar{M}_{ij}^{(1)}, \ldots, \bar{M}_{ij}^{(K)}) =$$

$$(M_{ij,t-1}^{(1)}, \ldots, M_{ij,t-1}^{(N)}, \bar{M}_{ij}^{(1)}, \ldots, \bar{M}_{ij}^{(K)}) \cdot P_{ij}, \quad i = 1, \ldots, h, \quad j = 1, 2,$$

where

$$P_{ij} = \begin{pmatrix} p_{ij,1}^{(1)} & \cdots & p_{ij,N}^{(1)} & 0 & \cdots & 0 \\ \vdots & & \vdots & & & \vdots \\ p_{ij,1}^{(N)} & \cdots & p_{ij,N}^{(N)} & 0 & \cdots & 0 \\ \overline{p}_{ij,1}^{(1)} & \cdots & \overline{p}_{ij,N}^{(1)} & 1 & \cdots & 0 \\ \vdots & & \vdots & & & \vdots \\ \overline{p}_{ij,1}^{(K)} & \cdots & \overline{p}_{ij,N}^{(K)} & 0 & \cdots & 1 \end{pmatrix}, \tag{3}$$

$$\text{and } p_{ij,\mu}^{(\nu)} \geq 0, \overline{p}_{ij,\nu}^{(\kappa)} \geq 0 \text{ and } \nu = 1, \ldots, N, \quad \mu = 1, \ldots, N,$$

$$\text{and } \sum_{\nu=1}^{N} p_{ij,\mu}^{(\nu)} + \sum_{\kappa=1}^{K} \overline{p}_{ij,\mu}^{(\kappa)} = 1.$$

This system converges to $\bar{M}_{ij}$ with:

$$\bar{M}_{ij} := (\tilde{M}_{ij}^{(1)}, \ldots, \tilde{M}_{ij}^{(N)}, \bar{M}_{ij}^{(1)}, \ldots, \bar{M}_{ij}^{(K)}) \text{ and } \bar{M}_{ij} = \bar{M}_{ij} \cdot P_{ij}.$$

The solution of this system of equations gives the value $\tilde{M}_{ij}^{(\nu)}$ of the final moral evaluation of a decision B_{ij} by each person ν. It depends on the influence of the philosophies $1, \ldots, K$ and of the convictions of other people.

The convergence values $\bar{M}_{ij}$ may be written as follows.[9] Let $x = (y, z)$ be

[9] I thank Dr. Christopeit for the following calculations.

the columm vector

$$x = \begin{pmatrix} y \\ z \end{pmatrix} = \begin{pmatrix} x_1 \\ \vdots \\ x_m \\ x_{m+1} \\ \vdots \\ x_n \end{pmatrix} = \begin{pmatrix} M_{ij}^{(1)} \\ \vdots \\ M_{ij}^{(N)} \\ \bar{M}_{ij}^{(1)} \\ \vdots \\ \bar{M}_{ij}^{(K)} \end{pmatrix} \text{ and } Q = P' = \begin{pmatrix} Q_0 & Q_1 \\ O & I \end{pmatrix},$$

$$\text{where } Q_0 = \begin{pmatrix} p_{11} & \cdots & p_{m1} \\ \vdots & & \vdots \\ p_{1m} & \cdots & p_{mm} \end{pmatrix}, \quad Q_1 = \begin{pmatrix} p_{m+1,1} & \cdots & p_{n1} \\ \vdots & & \vdots \\ p_{m+1,m} & \cdots & p_{nm} \end{pmatrix}$$

$O =$ the $(n-m) \times m$ null matrix and

$I =$ the $(n-m) \times (n-m)$ unit matrix

The stationary solution:

$$y = Q_0 y + Q_1 z$$

yields $y = (I - Q_0)^{-1} Q_1 z$, i. e. all stationary solutions are:

$$x = \begin{pmatrix} (I - Q_0)^{-1} Q_1 z \\ -------- \\ z \end{pmatrix}, \quad z \in R^{n-m},$$

and for all initial values $x_0' = (y_0', z_0')$ we have

$$\lim_{t \to \infty} x_t = \begin{pmatrix} (I - Q_0)^{-1} Q_1 z_0 \\ -------- \\ z_0 \end{pmatrix} = \begin{pmatrix} y \\ z_0 \end{pmatrix}$$

independent of the initial values y_0'. Thus the asymptotic values of the moral convictions in a population depend essentially on the philosophies which are valid in the society, but also on the transition probabilities given in the matrix Q_0, i. e. on the mutual influence that the persons exert on each other — but not on the initial conditions of the personal moral values. If governments have some influence on the information system (influence on journals, books, radio, television) they will endeavor to reduce the influence (i. e. the $\overline{p}_{ij,\nu}^{\kappa}$) of all philosophies κ which the leading group does not like and to increase the influence of a philosophy it likes (e. g. a certain religion or a certain philosophy like Marxism). We do not model this explicitly in the present approach.

5 The Length of the Economic Horizon, the Relative Frequencies of Personal Decisions, and the Morality or Criminality in a Society

Besides depending on $M_{ij}^{(p)}$ the value $V_{ij}^{(p)}$ of a decision B_{ij} depends on the subjective expectation of punishment $H_{ij}^{(p)} = E(S_{ij}) \cdot h^{(p)}$. The mathematical expectation $E(S_{ij})$ is given to the individual person. But $H_{ij}^{(p)}$ is also a function of the economic horizon $h^{(p)}$ of the person p. We assume that the length of the foresight follows a relatively stable distribution in the society: relatively few people live only from day to day (i. e. the length of their horizon is zero), relatively more have a bit more foresight, but above a certain size the relative number of persons with rather large foresight declines. The relative frequencies of personal decisions v_{i1} are:

$$v_{i1} = \frac{\#(p|V_{i1}^{(p)} \geq V_{i2}^{(p)})}{N}, \quad N = \#(p), \tag{4}$$

where N is the number of persons in the society. v_{i1} is the relative number of persons which in a situation B_i would choose B_{i1}, and accordingly

$$v_{i2} = 1 - v_{i1} = \frac{\#(p|V_{i1} < V_{i2})}{N}$$

the relative number of persons which would choose B_{i2}. If our theory of decision is (at least approximately) right, the v_{i1} or v_{i2} may be derived from the personal distributions of the values of $G_{ij}^{(p)}, H_{ij}^{(p)}, M_{ij}^{(p)}$ and the $\alpha_{ij,k}^{(p)}, k = 1, \ldots, 3$ which determine the valuation $V_{ij}^{(p)}$ of the decision B_{ij}, see equation (1). We have already derived the development of $M_{ij}^{(p)}$ if the initial conditions $M_{ij,0}^{(1)}, \ldots, M_{ij,0}^{(N)}$ are given for all persons p, or in other words: if the personal distribution of the M_{ij} in period 0 are known. The same applies for the distributions of $G_{ij}^{(p)}, H_{ij}^{(p)}$ and $\alpha_{ij}^{(p)}$. For simplicity, we assume constancy of these distributions.

The internal situation of a society as far as personal morality is concerned may be reflected by the vector

$$\mathcal{M} = (v_{11}, v_{21}, \ldots, v_{h1})$$

of the proportions of persons acting according to the normal rules. This vector may be called the basic degree of "personal morality" in the society. Conversely, the vector

$$\mathcal{K} = (v_{12}, v_{22}, \ldots, v_{h2})$$

indicates the basic degree of criminality. From the criminality vector $(v_{12}, v_{22}, \ldots, v_{h2})$ we may infer the frequency of violations of moral and criminal laws. Let $\beta = (\beta_1, \beta_2, \ldots, \beta_h)$ be the average number of decision problems of the kind $B_1, \ldots, B_h$ per year which a person will be confronted with,[10] or in other words: the frequency of occurence of the choice problem B_i. Let $N_{i2} = v_{i2} \cdot N$ be the number of persons who in situation B_i would choose the bad alternative B_{i2}, where N = the number of persons in the society. Then the observed number $\overline{N}_{i2}$ of violations of moral obligations or of the criminal laws is given by the vector

$$\overline{N_{\bullet 2}} = (\overline{N}_{12}, \overline{N}_{22}, \ldots, \overline{N}_{h2}), \quad \text{where} \quad \overline{N}_{i2} = \beta_i \cdot v_{i2} \cdot N, \quad i = 1, \ldots, h. \tag{5}$$

$\overline{N}_{\bullet 2}$ may be called the *actual criminality.* We define $\overline{V} = (\overline{v}_{12}, \ldots, \overline{v}_{h2})$ as the *vector of criminal rates* in the society, where $\overline{v}_{i2} = \frac{\overline{N}_{i2}}{N} = ß_i \cdot v_{i2}$ is the relative number of persons taking the "bad" decision B_{i2}. It may be called the *observed criminal rate* for problem B_i and may be found in the criminal statistics. The vector

$$\overline{N}_{\bullet 1} = (\overline{N}_{11}, \overline{N}_{21}, \ldots, \overline{N}_{h1}), \text{where } \overline{N}_{i1} = v_{i1} \cdot N,$$

gives the number of persons who would choose the "good" decision if confronted with problem B_i, and $\overline{v}_{i1} = \frac{\overline{N}_{i1}}{N} = v_{i1}$ may be called the *morality rate* in the society with respect to problem B_i. It is not found in the statistics, and it has no direct influence on economics: if all $\overline{v}_{i1} = 0$ (the society consists only of criminals) this would not have any direct influence on economics if situation B_i where crimes could be committed did not exist ($\beta_i = 0$). E. g. if private property could be guarded perfectly there would be no theft. Thus the $\overline{v}_{i1} = v_{i1}$ are of economic interest only if $\beta_i > 0$ and then in the form of $v_{i2} = 1 - v_{i1}$.

6 Private Valuations of Collective Issues

Now we come to the second type of moral evaluations. Besides these private problems which lead to a decision of a person, there are issues where the judgment of a person is required. This refers to all public issues where the person as a member of the society is involved though he may not be among the members of the leading group which decides on the issues. One could differ between issues referring to the *basic political and economic order* of

[10]For simplicity we assume that the probability of being confronted with problem B_i is equal for all persons.

the society and issues with respect to *current political and economic problems* within this basic order, but for simplicity we lump them together. We enumerate all possible basic and current political and economic issues concerning the society and the economy as a whole by $B_{h+1}, B_{h+2}, \dots, B_k$ (k a very large number), and the possible decisions for each of these issues by $B_{i1}, \dots, B_{iz}$, $i = h+1, \dots, k$ (see Table 2). The realized situation may be distinguished as the first alternative; e.g. in the situation $B_i, i = h+1, \dots, k$, the valid rule (depending on a former decision) is B_{i1}; possible changes are $B_{i2}, \dots, B_{iz}$. The vector $(B_{h+1,1}, \dots, B_{l1})$ indicates the *basic political and economic order* or *the constitution* valid for the period considered. Correspondingly, we have *current political and economic problems* $B_{l+1}, \dots, B_k$ and again z possible alternatives $B_{i1}, \dots, B_{iz}$, $i = l+1, \dots, k$, for each of these problems. Each alternative B_{ij} is defined by an exact description of the state of the society if this alternative is realized. In the discussion paper mentioned in note 1 an expample for the definition of $B_{i1}, \dots, B_{iz}$, $i = h+1, \dots, k$ is presented. Each alternative is also characterized by the vector of possible punishments in case somebody violates this rule. Different punishments define different alternatives.

We only consider the probability distribution $w_{ij} = (w_{ij,0}, \dots, w_{ij,m})$ contained in a finite set W of probability distributions. Let us assume that there are T probability distributions in this set. This guarantees the finiteness of the number z of alternatives. Table 2 illustrates this approach: the probabilities of being punished if one violates the rule described by the alternative B_{ij} are listed there. From the probabilities of being punished follows the mathematical expectation $E(S_{ij})$ of punishment (supposed to be common knowledge), from this, given the economic horizon $h^{(p)}$ of person p, follows the subjective probability of punishment $H_{ij}^{(p)}$, see equation (1).

A person who evaluates a possible state of the society will as a rule also consider his personal situation in this state which we call $G_{ij}^{(p)}$ (his income, his influence in the society, his reputation, ..., see Table 2). Few people will be objective enough to refrain from this and only consider the moral value $M_{ij}^{(p)}$ and the economic evaluation E_{ij} of this state which is provided by economists in the form of GDP per capita and other indices. Now we can determine the total valuation $V_{ij}^{(p)}$ of the social situation B_{ij} by a person p. We assume the simplest case: $V_{ij}^{(p)}$ is a weighted average of $G_{ij}^{(p)}, M_{ij}^{(p)}$ and

E_{ij}:

$$V_{ij}^{(p)} = n.i.\left[\alpha_1^{(p)} \cdot G_{ij}^{(p)} + \alpha_2^{(p)} M_{ij}^{(p)} + \alpha_3^{(p)}) E_{ij}\right], \; \alpha_k^{(p)} \geq 0, \; \sum_{k=1}^{3} \alpha_k^{(p)} = 1,$$

$$n.i. = \text{next integer}, \quad i = h+1, \dots, k; \quad j = 1, \dots, z. \tag{6}$$

The weights $\alpha^{(p)}$ will be different from person to person. Not always the best economic solution is preferred. We shall assume that the α_1, α_2, with $\alpha_i \geq 0$, $\sum_{i=1}^{2} \alpha_i \leq 1$, are taken from a finite set of distributions, and that the distributions of the α_i are relatively stable, such that for these distributions a similar but multi–dimensional graph arises as for h. In this manner all public issues are evaluated by all members of the society,[11] and this is the basis for the social decision process which will be dealt with in the next section.

From equation (6) it follows that the evaluation $V_{ij}^{(p)}$ of a public state by person p depends on his own position $G_{ij}^{(p)}$ in this state, on his moral evaluation $M_{ij}^{(p)}$ and on the economic situation E_{ij} in this state (the possible punishments if one acts against the order B_{ij} is irrelevant for the evaluation of the order itself). The moral valuation $M_{ij}^{(p)}$ of the alternative j of a public issue i is (as for the evaluation of private decisions) determined by the influence of other people's valuations and by the influence of doctrines of philosophy.[12] We assume again a Markoff chain as in equation (3):

$$M_{ij,t} = M_{ij,t-1} \cdot P_{ij}, \tag{7}$$

where $M_{ij,t} = (M_{ij,t}^{(1)}, \dots, M_{ij,t}^{(N)}, \bar{M}_{ij}^{(1)}, \dots, \bar{M}_{ij}^{(K)})$ and P is a transition matrix as in (3), but now $i = h+1, \dots, k$, $j = 1, \dots, z$, N = number of persons in the society, K = number of doctrines.

The $G_{ij}^{(p)}$ are the valuations of a social state B_{ij} by a person p given his prospective position in the society. $G_{ij}^{(p)}$ depends on the personal characteristics of a person which we do not consider here in detail. But we may assume

[11]Of course, no person will be able to consider all the alternatives. Only few of them are known and evaluated positively or negatively. In our approach this means: for the great majority of issues the valuation of a person will be zero: no judgment.

[12]The meaning of $M_{ij}^{(p)}, i = h+1, \dots, k$, is a bit different from the meaning of $M_{ij}^{(p)}, i = 1, \dots, h$, which relates to personal decisions and could be called "conscience". $M_i, i = h+1, \dots, k$, refers to states of the society and could be called the "intuitive ethical evaluation" of this state.

that there is a rather stable personal distribution of these characteristics which leads to a rather stable personal distribution of the $G_{ij}^{(p)}$.

The E_{ij} are the values which the economic profession would attach to a decision B_{ij}. The main indicator would be the GDP per capita, discounted to the present, but also other economic indicators (like distribution of income) may be considered. There would be no unanimity among economists, but a reasonable agreement among the group of the "mainstream" economists may be assumed.[13] This economic valuation E_{ij} is taken to be common knowledge. In judging one possible decision j for problem i, all the other decisions E_{kl} are held constant. Of course, the economic value E_{ij} depends also on these other decisions. We take E_{ij} as exogenous. Thus we need the personal distribution of the initial conditions $M_{ij,0}^{(p)}$ and of the values $G_{ij}^{(p)}$ and E_{ij}. As in the case of private decisions they may be obtained by asking all persons in the society (or a representative sample) to state their valuation of G_{ij} and M_{ij} and E_{ij} respectively on an integer scale between $-\bar{z}$ and $+\bar{z}$, and to state their weights $\alpha_k^{(p)}$ for G_{ij}, M_{ij} and E_{ij}. This allows one to estimate the total valuation $V_{ij}^{(p)}$. Alternatively, the persons may be asked directly to indicate their valuation of B_{ij} on a scale $-\bar{z} \ldots + \bar{z}$. In principle each person has to value all possible states of the society. Of course, in most cases the valuation will be zero, i. e. no judgment. But the really relevant alternatives are often much debated, and many persons have an outspoken preference for one or another public order.

Since the alternative which is realized always gets the number one, the actual order is given by

$$\overline{\mathcal{O}} = (B_{h+1,1}, \cdots, B_{k,1}).^{14}$$

The political and economic order is decided by the leading group (see next section). Their decisions on all public issues constitute the political and economic order $\mathcal{O}$ of the next period t. A specific order $\mathcal{O}_t$ is a vector of all

[13]If one takes the reports of the German Board of Economic Advisers to the ministry of commerce (Wissenschaftlicher Beirat beim Bundesministerium für Wirtschaft) or of the German Council of Economic Experts (Sachverständigenrat) into account, one finds a large degree of agreement on the economic assessment of different situations. But if the economic profession really disagrees and if non–economists think they know things better - which happens rather often - the economic valuation E_{ij} becomes a personal value $E_{ij}^{(p)}$.

[14]The time sequence is as follows. In period t the political and economic order $\mathcal{O}_{t+1}$ is determined. This is valid for period $t+1$ and the following periods, if it is not changed. The personal decisions $B_{ij}(t)$ in period t are taken on the basis of the political and economic order of that period.

these decisions:

$$\overline{\mathcal{O}}_t = (B_{h+1,\zeta_1}, B_{h+2,\zeta_2}, \dots, B_{k,\zeta_k})$$

where $\zeta_i \in \{1, \dots, z\}, \quad i = 1, \dots, k.$

7 Collective Decisions

Up to now we have considered only personal decisions and personal valuations which may have effects on other people but are valid only for that person. Now we shall turn to decisions which are valid for the whole society. As a rule, they are taken by a relatively small group of people (or by a small number of groups of people, the relations between them being fixed by the constitution or by some other convention). As in the case of private valuations we could differentiate between decisions taken by this group with respect to the basic political and economic order (issues $h+1, \dots, l$) and with respect to current issues within this order (issues $l+1, \dots, k$). But in this article we shall, for simplicity, lump these two types of decisions together. If there were a dictator p^* (the leading group consists of one person), the decisions would be easily determined: for each issue B_i the decision $B_{i\zeta}$ is chosen for which $V_{i\zeta}^{(p^*)}$ is maximal. But usually there is a group decision. There is a whole range of literature on the problem of the existence of a social preference ordering.[15] In this article we assume measurability and interpersonal comparability of preferences – surely restrictive assumptions, but not unreasonable ones in our context.[16]

In this case we can assign a certain relative weight $g_i^{(p^*)}$ to each person p^* (who is member of the leading group) with respect to the issue i which indicates his (or her) influence within the group. Then by informal compromising

[15]For a survey see e.g. Krelle (1968), p. 85 ff.

[16]In our context these assumptions are not so strange as it is sometimes depicted in the literature. For many parts of economics one does not need these restrictive assumptions. But for other purposes one needs them. E.g. the normal utilization of public polls depends on them , and (to my knowledge) nobody has objected to this until now. E.g. the Institut für Demoskopie Allensbach each year asks a representative sample of the German population: Sehen Sie dem neuen Jahr mit Hoffnungen oder Befürchtungen entgegen? It offers four answers: “Mit Hoffnungen, mit Befürchtungen, mit Skepsis, Unentschieden“ and forms the difference of the percentage of answers of this year compared to those of the last year, which implies measurable and interpersonal comparable preferences. Of course, there will be a certain degree of uncertainty connected with these figurs; we disregard this here.

within the leading group (assumed to have N^* members) a valuation

$$\overline{V}_{ij} = \sum_{p^*=1}^{N^*} g_i^{(p^*)} \cdot V_{ij}^{(p^*)}, \quad g_i^{(p^*)} \geq 0, \quad \sum_{p^*=1}^{N^*} g_i^{(p^*)} = 1 \tag{8}$$

of a decision B_{ij} emerges, $i = h+1, \ldots, k$, $j = 1, \ldots, z$.

If the capacity of compromising and reaching a decision within the leading group were unlimited and if there were no difference in the decision process between basic decisions on the general political and social order and current and more short term decisions within this order, the political and economic order $\mathcal{O}_{+1}$ of the next period would be determined by

$$B_{i\zeta} \Leftarrow \max(\overline{V}_{i1}, \ldots, \overline{V}_{iz}) \quad \text{for all } i = h+1, \ldots, k. \tag{9}$$

But the capacity of processing issues is limited, and decisions on the basic political and economic order are usually much more difficult than decisions on the current policy. But we disregard this difference here. We may assume that in one period only a small number γ of issues can be treated and solved by the leading group, and these are the *most urgent* ones. *Most urgent* are those, where the possible new state $B_{i\zeta}$ gives a value $\overline{V}_{i\zeta}$ which in the opinion of the leading group is very much larger than the value $\overline{V}_{i1}$ of the present state. This idea is elaborated in the discussion paper mentioned in note 1. It limits the number of issues which can be dealt with in one period. After that equation (8) determines the decision. In the same discussion paper a theory on the determination of the persons which form the leading group and on their influence within this group is given. But we do not go into these details here.

8 The Direct Influence of Ethics on Normal Economic Decisions

The cases that we have considered hitherto are those where a failure of complying with the rules yields a punishment of one kind or another. But the normal economic decisions in the field of consumption, investment, exports, imports, portfolio composition etc. are not of this kind. There is a broad field of admissible lawful decisions, limits as far as the law is concerned are rather wide. But ethics is not silent in these cases: it influences the economic decisions directly.

Let there be economic situations $B_{k+1}, \ldots, B_n$ of the kind in the economy where a person p (or a household h in the case of consumption and portfolio decisions and an entrepreneur u in the case of production, employment and investment decisions) has the decision alternatives $B_{i1}, \dots, B_{iz}$, see Table 3. The person p has intuitive preferences for each alternative which he puts into the form of a valuation $G_{ij}^{(p)}, -\bar{z} \leq G_{ij}^{(p)} \leq +\bar{z}$, $G_{ij}^{(p)}$ an integer, $i = k+1, \dots, n, j = 1, \dots, z$. The reasons can be very different, resulting from the personal charateristics of the person or household. The same economic situation may be judged very differently by different persons . We do not go into these psychological details but take the $G_{ij}^{(p)}$ as given.

There are K philosophies in the society which evaluate the different alternatives from their point of view. E. g. a person is free to use his income according to his preferences. But the Christian doctrine says that a rich man should give a part of his income to the poor. Thus if this religion is known and accepted in the population, the person knows the moral evaluation $M_{ij}^{(p)}$ of his possible decisions. In addition, there is an economic evaluation E_{ij} independent of the characteristics and morality of the person which follows from the basic aim of economics: to procure the highest possible GDP per capita now and in the future.[17] Economics as a rule valuates an increase of investment at the cost of consumption positively (up to a certain point).

As in the case of evaluating public issues (see equation (6)) we assume that the final valuation $V_{ij}^{(p)}$ of the alternative B_{ij} by a person p is a weighted average of these three different valuations:

$$V_{ij}^{(p)} = n.i.[\alpha_1^{(p)} G_{ij}^{(p)} + \alpha_2^{(p)} M_{ij}^{(p)} + \alpha_3^{(p)} E_{ij}^{(p)}],$$

$$\alpha_k^{(p)} \geq 0, \quad \sum_{k=1}^{3} \alpha_k^{(p)} = 1, \; i = k+1, \dots, n. \tag{10}$$

The remarks as to the $\alpha_k^{(p)}$ made in connection with equations (1) and (6) also apply here. The $G_{ij}^{(p)}$ and $E_{ij}^{(p)}$ are exogenous in this context, but the $M_{ij}^{(p)}$ are determined endogenously as in equations (3) and (7):

$$M_{ij,t} = M_{ij,t-1} \cdot P_{ij}, \tag{11}$$

where $M_{ij,t} = (M_{ij,t}^{(1)} \cdots M_{ij,t}^{(N)}, \bar{M}_{ij}^{(1)} \cdots \bar{M}_{ij}^{(K)})$ amd P_{ij} is a transition matrix as in equation (3), but $i = k+1, \dots, n, j = 1, \dots, z$; there are N persons in the society and K relevant philosophies.

The person selects that decision which maximizes his "overall" valuation $V_{ij}^{(p)}$:

$$B_{ij}^{(p)} \leftarrow \max(V_{i1}^{(p)}, \dots, V_{iz}^{(p)}), \tag{12}$$

[17] This is a very simplified statement. But we do not want to go into details here.

as in equations (3) and (9). As is obvious from equations (10) to (12), ethical considerations may play an important role. The size of this influence depends on the weight $\alpha_2^{(p)}$ which the person gives to his ethic convictions as well as on those ethic convictions which are transferred to the person from available ethical systems $1, \ldots, K$ and on the influence of these systems on the person which is represented by the transition matrix P.

In the discussion paper quoted in note 1 this approach has been applied in the case of consumption decisions of households and of production, employment and investment decisions of entrepreneurs, but we do not go into these details here. The same applies to the application of this approach to the choice of a person between self–employment and employment by others.

9 The Influence of Economics on Ethics

Up to now we have only considered the influence of ethics on economics and have found that there are many influences on almost all economic decisions. The opposite influence is more long–term and not so obvious, but nevertheless quite marked if one considers the development of ethics during the centuries. In this section we shall use a simplified model of decision making which, after some redefinition of the variables, may cover the different cases analysed in the foregoing sections. We assume now, that the valuation $V_{ij}^{(p)}$ of a choice B_{ij} in a situation B_i, $i = 1, \ldots, n$, $j = 1, \ldots, z$, is a weighted average of the personal valuation $G_{ij}^{(p)}$ of person p, of the moral weight $M_{ij}^{(p)}$ carried by the decision B_{ij} of person p, and of an economic valuation E_{ij} which we take to follow from economics and business administration and are contained in textbooks or expert opinions and are common knowledge. The economic valuation E_{ij} is supposed to reflect the long term well–being of all persons in the society. Thus the valuation of a decision B_{ij} by person p is

$$V_{ij}^{(p)} = \alpha_{i1}^{(p)} G_{ij}^{(p)} + \alpha_{i2}^{(p)} M_{ij}^{(p)} + \alpha_{i3}^{(p)} E_{ij}, \quad \alpha_{ik}^{(p)} \geq 0, \quad \sum_{k=1}^{3} \alpha_{ik}^{(p)} = 1,$$

similar as in equation (10), but not identical.

Assume that person p has chosen B_{ij^*}, because

$$V_{ij^*}^{(p)} \Leftarrow max[V_{i1}^{(p)}, \ldots, V_{iz}^{(p)}], \quad j^* \in \{1, \ldots, z\},$$

but $M_{ij}^{(p)}$ and E_{ij} run opposite, i. e. if E_{ij} is high, $M_{ij}^{(p)}$ is low and vice versa, or $M_{ij}^{(p)} < E_{ij}$. If there were a philosophy which yields a moral valuation

$M_{ij}^{(p)} = E_{ij}$, i. e. which justifies the economic valuation also as a result of ethical reasoning, and the person would accept this valuation, then the person p would reach a result which he valuates higher. Let $M_{ij}^{(p)} = E_{ij}$, then the evaluation of B_{ij} is:

$$\overline{V}_{ij}^{(p)} := \alpha_{i1}^{(p)} G_{ij}^{(p)} + (\alpha_{i2}^{(p)} + \alpha_{i3}^{(p)}) E_{ij} > V_{ij}^{(p)},$$

$$\text{and} \qquad V_{ij^{**}}^{(p)} \Leftarrow max \quad [\overline{V}_{i1}^{(p)}, \ldots, \overline{V}_{iz}^{(p)}] > V_{ij^{*}}^{(p)}.$$

If one acts in the economically best way with a good conscience, one is more satisfied than if one were to act in that way with a bad conscience. Thus, if the difference between $V_{ij^{**}}^{(p)}$ and $V_{ij^{*}}^{(p)}$ becomes too large and the consequences of economically "bad" decisions are visible to all, a new philosophy $K+1$ will develop which declares what is economically "good" as also being "good" from the moral point of view: if $V_{ij^{**}}^{(p)} - V_{ij^{*}}^{(p)} \geq \overline{V}_{ij}$ (a threshold value) for a majority of persons p, we can be pretty sure that a new ethics $K+1$ will arise where $\overline{M}_{ij}^{K+1} \approx E_{ij}$, $\overline{M}_{ij}^{K+1}$ = moral valuation of decision B_{ij} by the new philosophy $K+1$. In this way the economic progress of the society is guaranteed, but only in the very long run. According to the Markoff chain procedure of extending moral values in a society, it takes (in general) quite a lot of time, till the new valuations will spread out in the society. Nations which preserve their old platform of moral values will stay more and more behind in economic performance compared to those that adapt it, and thus we may infer that in the very long run economics codetermines ethics: there is an interdependence of the two spheres.

10 Conclusions

This article has shown why philosophies, or if one wants to be impolite: ideologies, have an important task in the society: to coordinate and control all important economic decisions in the long run – together with other determinants, of course. In the short run their influence may be hardly visible since the moral valuation of economic decisions is to a large degree due to traditional evaluations; only slowly the influence of ethics asserts itself. The importance of philosophies may be seen in the difficulties when changing from a planned to a market economy, especially in Russia, but also in the new states of Germany, the former GDR. One speaks of "mental barriers" ("Grenzen in den Köpfen") which makes the transition especially difficult (among other things, of course). The moral values in the population are to an important extent incompatible with those necessary in a market economy (instead of relying one's his own resources, one waits to be ordered; instead of confidence and loyalty to others and to the government, there is breaking of contracts, cheating the government, fraud, corruption, etc. which do not seem to affect the conscience and are not punished in many cases, at least in Russia).

For the functioning of a market economy it is of great importance to strengthen the influence of philosophies which form the ethical basis of a free society: those who favor honesty, reliability, respect for others, aid for people in need etc. , work in favor of others, willingness to take over responsibilities and risks and reliance on one's own forces. In the paper it is shown how and where in the economic world these forces influence economic decisions. Like air they are almost ubiquitous and perhaps therefore almost neglected in neoclassical economics. The method employed here has also allowed us to connect economics with political science and law and to show the origin and influence of criminal acts. The paper starts there because this gives a simple idea of the whole approach.

To implement this aproach one would have to consider groups of persons with similar personal characteristics, define industries, introduce the government, the monetary system and foreign countries and close the model. But this would be the topic of another paper.

Table 1: Decision Table; Private Ethical Problems for Individuals[1)]

Situation	Decision	possible punishments $S_0 = 0$	S_1	…	S_m	Math. expectation of punishment	Subjective expectation of punishment	Immediate advantage for person p	Moral valuation by person p	Proportion of persons choosing B_{ij}	Frequency of occurrence of B_i	Morality rate, criminal rate, resp.[2)]	Elasticity of GDP with respect to $\overline{v}_{ij}$	Total valuation by person p
situation 1: B_1	"good" decision B_{11}	$w_{11,0}$	$w_{11,1}$	…	$w_{11,m}$	$E(S_{11})$	$H_{11}^{(p)}$	$G_{11}^{(p)}$	$M_{11}^{(p)}$	v_{11}	β_1	$\overline{v}_{11}$		$V_{11}^{(p)}$
	"bad" decision B_{12}	$w_{12,0}$	$w_{12,1}$	…	$w_{12,m}$	$E(S_{12})$	$H_{12}^{(p)}$	$G_{12}^{(p)}$	$M_{12}^{(p)}$	v_{12}		$\overline{v}_{12}$	$\epsilon_{Y,\overline{v}_{12}}$	$V_{12}^{(p)}$
⋮														
situation h: B_h	B_{h1}	$w_{h1,0}$	$w_{h1,1}$	…	$w_{h1,m}$	$E(S_{h1})$	$H_{h1}^{(p)}$	$G_{h1}^{(p)}$	$M_{h1}^{(p)}$	v_{h1}	β_h	$\overline{v}_{h1}$		$V_{h1}^{(p)}$
	B_{h2}	$w_{h2,0}$	$w_{h2,1}$	…	$w_{h2,m}$	$E(S_{h2})$	$H_{h2}^{(p)}$	$G_{h2}^{(p)}$	$M_{h2}^{(p)}$	v_{h2}		$\overline{v}_{h2}$	$\epsilon_{Y,\overline{v}_{h2}}$	$V_{h2}^{(p)}$

[1)]This includes decisions to act against moral and civil laws as well as decisions to act against the public order.–We assume that all probability distributions $w_{ij} = (w_{ij,0}, w_{ij,1}, \dots, w_{ij,m})$ are taken from a finite set W of probability distributions. The situations $B_1, \dots, B_h$ depend on the general political and social order and the actual political and economic decisions of the government, which we collect in the vector $\bar{O}$ (to be explained later). Thus $B_1(\bar{O}), \dots, B_h(\bar{O})$.

[2)]The observed criminal rate $\overline{v}_{i2} = v_{i2} \cdot \beta_i$ may be found in the criminal statistics. The morality rate $\overline{v}_{i1}$ is defined as $\overline{v}_{i1} = v_{i1}$.

Table 2: Private Valuations of Collective Issues

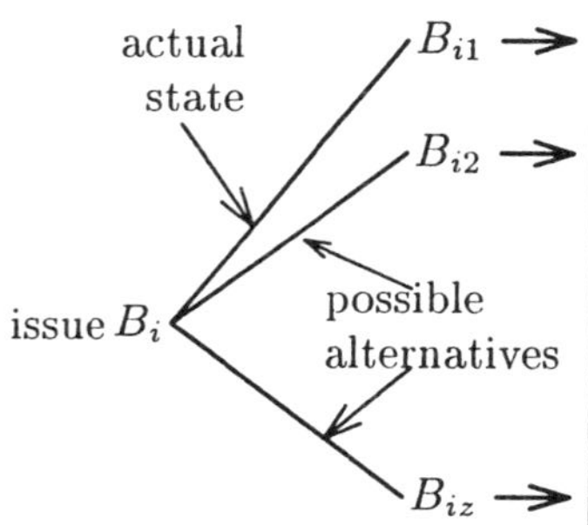

	punishments $S_0 = 0$	S_1	$\cdots$	S_m	Math. expectation of punishment	Subjective expec. of punishment by person p	Personal advantage of person p	Moral valuation by person p	Economic valuation	Total valuation by person p	relative number of persons who prefer B_{ij} [1].
B_{i1} →	$w_{i1,0}$	$w_{i1,1}$	$\cdots$	$w_{i1,m}$	$E(S_{i1})$	$H_{i1}^{(p)}$	$G_{i1}^{(p)}$	$M_{i1}^{(p)}$	E_{i1}	$V_{i1}^{(p)}$	v_{i1}
B_{i2} →	$w_{i2,0}$	$w_{i2,1}$	$\cdots$	$w_{i2,m}$	$E(S_{i2})$	$H_{i2}^{(p)}$	$G_{i2}^{(p)}$	$M_{i2}^{(p)}$	E_{i2}	$V_{i2}^{(p)}$	v_{i2}
	$\vdots$	$\vdots$	$\vdots$	$\vdots$	$\vdots$	$\vdots$	$\vdots$	$\vdots$	$\vdots$	$\vdots$	$\vdots$
B_{iz} →	$w_{iz,0}$	$w_{iz,1}$	$\cdots$	$w_{iz,m}$	$E(S_{iz})$	$H_{iz}^{(p)}$	$G_{iz}^{(p)}$	$M_{iz}^{(p)}$	E_{iz}	$V_{iz}^{(p)}$	v_{iz}

$i = h+1, \ldots, k$

[1] $v_{ij} \geq 0, \sum_{j=1}^{z} v_{ij} = 1$

Table 3: Decision Table; Normal Economic Problems

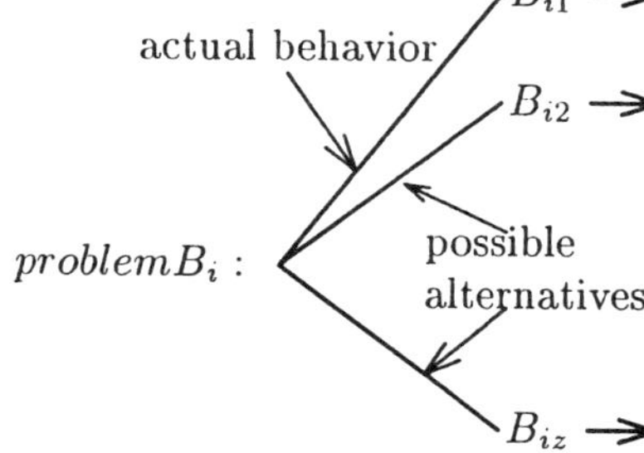

	Personal advantage to person p	Moral valuation by person p	Economic valuation	Total valuation by person p
$B_{i1} \rightarrow$	$G_{i1}^{(p)}$	$M_{i1}^{(p)}$	E_{i1}	$V_{i1}^{(p)}$
$B_{i2} \rightarrow$	$G_{i2}^{(p)}$	$M_{i2}^{(p)}$	E_{i2}	$V_{i2}^{(p)}$
	$\vdots$	$\vdots$	$\vdots$	$\vdots$
$B_{iz} \rightarrow$	$G_{iz}^{(p)}$	$M_{iz}^{(p)}$	E_{iz}	$V_{iz}^{(p)}$

$i = k+1, \ldots, n$

References

[1] Becker, Gary S.: Crime and Punishment: An Economic Approach, *Journal of Political Economics*, vol. 76, 1968, S. 169–217

[2] Becker, Gary, S.: Altruism, Egoism, and Genetic Fitness: Economics and Sociobiology, *Journal of Economic Literature* , vol. 14, 1976, p. 817-826;

[3] Bergstrom, Stark: How Altruism can Prevail in an Evolutionary Environment, *American Economic Review*, vol. 83/2, 1993, p. 149-155

[4] Bester, Helmut / Güth, Werner: Is Altruism Evolutionary Stable?, Center for Economic Research, Tilburg University, *Disc. Paper Nr. 94103*, 1994

[5] Cameron, Samuel: The Economics of Crime Deterrence: A Survey of Theory and Evidence, *Kyklos*, vol. 41, 1988, S. 301–323

[6] Ehrlich, Isaac: Crime, Punishment, and the Market for Offenses, *Journal of Economic Perspectives*, vol. 10, 1996, S. 43–67

[7] Engel, Gerhard: Wirtschaftsethik und pragmatische Moralskepsis. Zum Vorrang der Empiric vor der Ethik, in: Aufderheide, D. und Dabrowski, M. (Hrsg.), *Wirtschaftsethik und Moralökonomik. Normen, soziale Ordnung und der Beitrag der Ökonomik*, Berlin (Duncker und Humboldt), 1997, S. 71–120

[8] Engelhardt, Werner Wilhelm: Ökonomische Denktraditionen, Ökonomismus versus Ethik und die kulturellen Aufgaben der Zukunft, in: Elsner, Wolfram / Engelhardt, Werner Wilhelm / Glastetter, Werner (Hrsg.), *Ökonomie in gesellschaftlicher Verantwortung*, Festschrift zum 65. Geburtstag von Siegfried Katterle, Berlin (Duncker und Humboldt,1998, S. 19-43)

[9] Ferschl, Franz: "Nutzen– und Entscheidungstheorie. Einführung in die Logik der Entscheidungen", Opladen (Westdeutscher Verlag), 1975

[10] Ferschl, Franz: "Deskriptive Statistik", Würzburg–Wien (Physica–Verlag), 1978

*This is just a selection of references. For a more complete list of references, see the discussion paper mentioned in note 1

[11] Gaertner, Wulf: *Wirtschaftsethische Perspektiven IV*, Schriften des Vereins für Sozialpolitik Band 228/IV, Berlin (Duncker und Humboldt), 1998 (vgl. auch Teil I-III, 1994-1996)

[12] Güth, Werner: *Do Banks Crowd in or out Business Ethics — An Indirect Evolutionary Analysis*, Discussion Paper 40, SFB 373, Humboldt-Universität at Berlin, 1998

[13] Hammerstein, Peter / Selten, Reinhard:*Game Theory and Evolutionary Biology*, Ch. 28 in: Handbook of Game Theory, Vol. 2 (ed.: Aumann and Hart), Elsevier Science, 1994, p. 929-993

[14] Höffe, Otfried (Hrsg.): *Einführung in die utilitaristische Ethik*, München (Beck), 1975

[15] Höffe, Otfried: *Lexikon der Ethik*, 5. Aufl., München, 1997

[16] Homann, Karl: Die Rolle ökonomischer Überlegungen in der Grundlegung der Ethik, in: Helmut Hesse (Herausg.), *Wirtschaftswissenschaft und Ethik, Schriften des Vereins für Socialpolitik*, N.F. Bd. 171, Berlin (Duncker & Humblot) 1988, S. 218

[17] Homann, Karl: Sinn und Grenze der ökonomische Methode in der Wirtschaftsethik, in: Aufderheide, D. und Dabrowski, M. (Hrsg.), *Wirtschaftsethik und Moralökonomik. Normen, soziale Ordnung und der Beitrag der Ökonomik*, Berlin (Duncker und Humboldt), 1997, S. 11–42

[18] Koller, Peter: Rationales Entscheiden und moralisches Handeln, Kap. IX in: Julian Nida-Rümelin (Herausg.), *Praktische Rationalität*, Berlin (De Gruyter), 1993 S. 281-311

[19] Krelle, Wilhelm: Latent Variables in Econometric Models, *Discussion-Paper B-104*, SFB 303, Bonn, 1988

[20] Krelle, Wilhelm: Entwicklung und Aufrechterhaltung moralischer Standards, in: Immenga/Möschel (Hrsg.), *Festschrift für Ernst-Joachim Mestmäcker zum 70. Geburtstag*, Baden-Baden, 1996, S. 227–241

[21] Krelle, Wilhelm: *Ökonomische Grundlagen der Ethik*, Discussion Paper No. B-428, SFB 303, Rheinische Friedrich-Wilhelms-Universität Bonn, März 1998

[22] Lorenz, Konrad: *Das sogenannte Böse*, München, dtv, 17. Aufl. 1992

[23] Rabin, Matthew: Incorporating Fairness into Game Theory and Economics, *American Economic Review*, vol. 83/5, 1993, p. 1281-1302

[24] Wieland, Wolfgang: Verantwortungsethik als Spielart des Utilitarismus, in: *Akademie–Journal*, Mitteilungsblatt der deutschen Akademie der Wissenschaften, Nr. 1/98, S. 37-40

Ethics and Operations Research

Christoph Schneeweiss

University of Mannheim
Email:schneeweissbwl.uni-mannheim.de

1 Introduction

What has Operations Research to do with ethics? Or, more generally, what has science to do with ethics? Should not science be free or at least intellectually be separable from moral norms as Max Weber [Weber] postulated? Indeed, being aware that Operations Research (OR) may be identified as the science of formal decision making, these questions are of particular significance for this discipline. Formal decision making has, in a very general way, to do with norms, and these norms are not simply exogenously given but essential objects of investigation.

One might therefore even ask: "What are the implications of OR with respect to ethics?" Or, in more operational terms: "Are the concepts of general systems theory, and more specifically, those of OR, appropriate to investigate ethical questions?"

As is well-known, ethics is usually defined as the science of moral norms. Morality, on its part, may be understood as the totality of all rules of a society to differentiate between "good and evil". These rules are deemed to be essential for the viability of a society. They provide a certain security and often enjoy a broad societal acceptance. Some of these rules are codified by law, particularly those that are easy to scrutinize.

Usually, one associates with moral behavior those actions that are banned by society but which are not or not yet punished or punishable by codified law. Typical examples for ethical issues are genetic manipulations or medical experiments with human beings, and the production of poison gas or nuclear weapons. But not only in the domain of the natural sciences one has ethical questions, in business administration, too, such questions arise. Think of the general problem of cheating, the free rider problem or untruthfulness as a marketing instrument.

Obviously, looking at the *applications* of Operations Research, planning problems will often touch questions of moral concern as it is the case for other sciences as well. In what follows, we do not intend to discuss moral conflicts of a particular kind, rather we are aiming to investigate more conceptual questions concerning the interrelation between ethics and OR. In doing so, our starting point will be the general decision (or planning) process which seems to be rich enough to discuss some important methodological questions of ethics, such as

- How do moral norms interfere with the decision process for a particular problem?
- What is the relationship between moral norms and rationality?
- How to deal with the problem of changing moral norms?

2 The Decision Process and its Ethical Implications

Operations Research as a pure science provides general insights and develops techniques and rules about modeling, optimization, and implementation. This general expertise may then, in a specific setting, be applied to real-life problems using in an interdisciplinary way, 'applied knowledge' of various other disciplines. Hence, as most sciences, Operations Research consists of a pure and an applied direction. As to the discussion of ethical questions, two scenarios seem to be of particular interest:

1. Short term effects, i.e., direct violations of moral norms, and
2. Long term effects, i.e., decisions (or better: omissions) which in the long run imply violations of moral norms.

The first scenario will be met more on the applied side of OR, whilst the second one touches more basic questions of research strategies and is of crucial significance for a science like Operations Research that has as its object the decision process itself. Both scenarios will be discussed as specific configurations within the general decision process.

2.1 The General Decision Process

As mentioned before, the general decision process comprises all three major activities of OR, i.e., modeling a problem, generating a solution, and implementing the generated plan. In abstract terms the process may be understood as a sequence of decision models of which the pertaining decision fields and criteria are undergoing a permanent learning process. In this process several persons may be involved and the problem to be solved may change over time. Hence the decision process is to be discussed within a multi-person, multi-criterion, dynamic setting with asymmetric information and various hierarchical interdependencies. One of the key notions for the discussion to follow may be seen in the fact that *the decision process is at the same time a goal seeking and a goal observing process.* Operations Research, as a pure science, is analyzing this process and is particularly providing optimization techniques to contribute to its efficiency. Moreover, through its modeling techniques, it provides methods to construct preference systems. On the other hand, via an analyst or consultant, Operations Research as an applied science is part of the decision process and thus is - at least partially - responsible for keeping moral norms. Since, for the subsequent discussion, a deeper understanding of some of the main features of the general decision process turns out to be crucial, let us illustrate this process somewhat further.

A decision process describes all stages, from an initial stimulus via various operationalizations up to a solution and its implementation. It is evolving in cycles of the type as illustrated in Fig. 1. Each cycle is defined by a description of the 'problem' to be solved ('Model'), by a 'Solution', and a 'Discrepancy' (DIS) which provides the decision maker with some idea of how far apart the present solution is from the solution he is desiring. If a discrepancy is still existing, the decision maker has to select a new cycle (through his 'Governing Process'). In particular, he has to decide whether he should change his preferences and especially his aspiration levels. Thus, obviously, depending on the kind of cycles one is selecting, the decision process is simultaneously a goal observing and a goal seeking process. (For a much deeper discussion of the general decision process, see [Schneeweiss (1987) or Schneeweiss (1992)].)

Using the general structure of the decision process to analyze ethical problems, one may identify moral norms with special aspiration levels which need not only be observed but, simultaneously, may be allowed for change. It clearly shows that the solution of a particular real-life problem might give rise to question the validity of certain moral norms and might even give rise to change these norms for future decision processes.

Particularly, in Section 3, we will continue this discussion on a more fundamental basis. For this general discussion, it should be clear that aspiration levels and (moral) constraints of the decision field can be very general quantities. Thus a prescribed decision rule, e.g., can of course be considered as a moral norm.

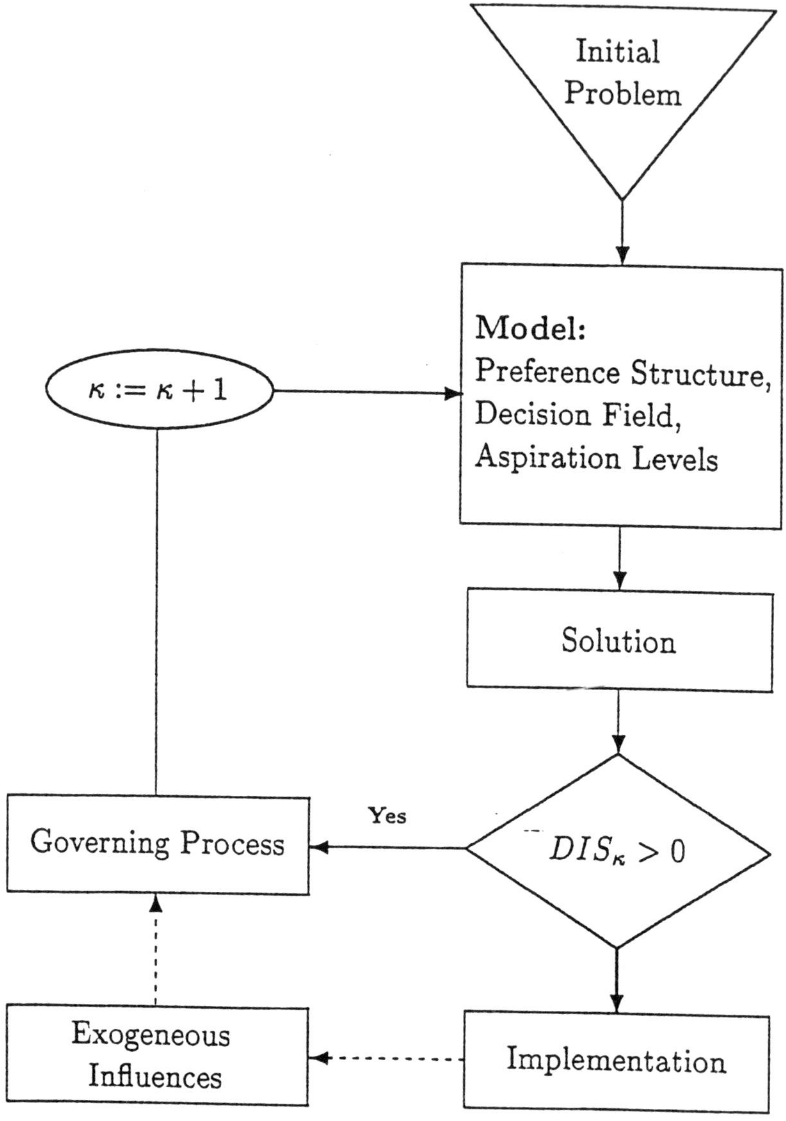

Fig. 1: Main Features of the General Decision Process

2.2 Short Term and Long Term Scenarios

Let us come back to the two scenarios mentioned before. They may be considered as being associated with the goal observing (1) and the goal seeking (2) aspect of the Operations Research decision process. Let us deal with scenario 1 first.

(1) Scenario 1, short term effects - goal observation

As any member of a society, Operations Research as an institution is compelled to observe moral norms. This seems to be obvious for day to day applications and is no specific problem of Operations Research but of those who apply it. Thus, professional groups like applied statisticians or the various associations of engineers possess an ethic committee which guarantees their clients a morally fair treatment.

Ethical questions become far more intricate, however, if moral norms are *not yet settled or contradict to other moral norms*. Concerning these questions, let us content ourselves with only two remarks:

1. Not settled or contradictory moral norms have to be discussed within its particular context. What can be demanded from a science like Operations Research, however, is that it makes every effort to support the search for appropriate solutions and to explore their possible implications. In particular, it should employ its multi-person, multi-criterion decision techniques.
2. Coming back to the postulate of Max Weber [Weber] mentioned in the introduction, ethical considerations should be separated from the subject under investigation or should at least be made explicit. The decision process proves to be especially appropriate to discuss such questions. As mentioned before, one might formulate moral norms as additional goals or as aspiration levels within a multi-criterion decision problem. We return to this point in the next section.

(2) Scenario 2, long term effects - goal seeking

Considering Operations Research as a *pure* science, one has not primarily the problem of not observing moral norms but far more the question of omissions that might imply non-moral behavior. This is an extremely intricate problem which points to the center of a science of decision making. Moral norms usually are conservative rules. They give society a certain security and focus on elementary human needs. Some of these rules, however, are subject to substantial change. Hence, in considering long term involvements, science, and in particular Operations Research, has to analyze moral rules themselves.

To elucidate the problems that might occur consider an omission which deliberately avoids a conflict with given moral norms. Assume further that this omission implies, at a future point in time, a catastrophy which necessitates to break traditional norms. Clearly, these traditional norms will then be sacrificed in view of the pressures inherent in the situation and no immorality would be involved. Hence only the cognizant scientist knows that he or she acted immorally.

These highly involved questions may again be discussed within the framework of the decision process. As explained before, the planning process may be considered as a learning process. This means that the decision fields are permanently changing and that preferences are to be adapted. This adaptation is caused on the one hand by the history of the process, i.e., by the experience one has gained thus far and on the other hand by external re-evaluations or the presumption of a possible change. A science of the decision process has to consider all these possibilities and has thoroughly to explore all possibilities in a given situation.

With these general remarks we arrive at a point which brings ethics and a decision science like Operations Research even closer together.

3 Ethics and Rationality

Obviously, since ethics discusses problems of discerning between "good and evil", it describes part of the preferences of a society and certainly has an impact on the criteria of the decision process. The relationship between ethics and the analysis of the decision process, however, turns out to be much more fundamental than one might suppose and cannot simply be described by extending the decision process by an additional criterion in the frame of a moral norm. The key question is indeed rationality. Under which conditions might the decision process be considered to be rational?

Usually rationality has to do with welfare, i.e., with the welfare of the present and future generations. To achieve a rational solution, the decision process must have in mind the welfare of all parties involved. In its comprehensive meaning, this is of course almost impossible. Arrow's famous 'impossibility theorem' [Arrow] and the impossibility of 'rationally' aggregating ordinal data [Arrow/Raynaud] reveal some of the principle difficulties. In particular, it shows that one has to be content with a less arbituous notion of rationality that that being usually employed in formal decision analysis: Within available resources, one has to explore all decision fields and criteria which might increase the well-being of the particular decision maker and of further parties concerned. Since the decision process is a goal seeking process, rationality cannot be defined in obeying certain goals. Thus one has to be satisfied with a "process or discourse rationality" (e.g., see [Habermas], [Ulrich]), which says that all activities are rational that follow logical arguments and obey commonly accepted rules of discourse. Indeed, this postulate is not too far from general considerations in ethics, and in particular from Kant's categorial imperative [Kant]. Thus, ethics and the analysis of the general (discourse) rationality of the decision process are closely related: *rationality involves ethics and ethics might be discussed within a general discourse rationality.*

However, rationality and moral norms are, of course, not identical. Let us stress only three points:

(1) Moral norms are primarily concerned with the conservation of existing (morally accepted) societal rules. Hence those actions are deemed as favorable that defend these rules which are felt to be indispensible. Activities which simply increase welfare (without breaking moral norms) are not considered as being of ethical relevance but would simply be viewed as being rational. The same holds for activities which might affect a moral status in the far reaching future. Rationality would have to consider these aspects as well. Hence moral norms are simple and often all too simple rules of a society bound to here and now, i.e., they are often simple aspiration levels assigned to only one cycle of the decision process that do not consider the entire development of the process in the future.

(2) Typical for many moral norms is their highly personal character. Deep emotions are often associated affecting the whole personality. Thus, a simple rationality concept as that of the "homo economicus" [e.g., Bernoulli rationality] would by no means be capable of capturing this far more general and comprehensive aspect of moral norms. Usually, however, Operations Research will have to do with less personal ethical questions. As an example think of the modern problem of sustainability. Planning a society's sustainable development implies activities which at least do not negatively effect the well-being of future generations and of socially discriminated groups. Hence, sustainability might be used to define more precisely in which kind of ethical problems OR might generally be involved.

(3) Ethical postulates and general rationality postulates differ also in the comprehensiveness of their content. Rationality has to consider not only ethical postulates but the particular problem one has to solve. To reconcile these two types of criteria, again the decision process gives a hint. One might adopt a two-stage consideration [Schneeweiss (1987), Sec. 6]. In a first stage, within a rather general framework, one would specify certain ethical norms which would then have to be observed on the lower level of the specific decision problem at hand. Thus this

two-stage representation decouples the (ethical) normative rationality from the instrumental or purposive rationality ("Zweckrationalitt") and allows the lower stage considerable freedom.

It should be clear, however, that ethical norms as additional criteria components do not only have an impact on the lower stage criteria but also on its decision field, or, more generally, on the *whole process of finding a decision.* Thus, the entire decision process finally grounds in moral postulates and cannot be discussed without considering ethical questions, and it is exactly in this context one should interpret Max Weber's postulate of a value-free science.

4 Conclusions

Within this short discourse on ethics and Operations Research, we emphasized that Operations Research is particularly concerned with ethical questions. These questions do not only arise in applying Operations Research to real-world problems but are a constituating part of OR as a normative science. Withdrawing to a position of a very general notion of rationality, ethics and the analysis of rationality are not too far apart. As a prerequisite, both for ethical considerations and for the general concept of rationality, the decision process is required to be thoroughly explored within an "oppression free" discourse [Ulrich], i.e., all possible scenarios and decisions should be considered and all their possible consequences should in principle be known by all parties being involved.

Thus, the hitherto rather general considerations may result in some concrete desiderata. These desiderata ultimately result from the (moral) postulate of taking into account a general concept of rationality which considers the observation and the possible change of moral norms. Thus follwing this general concept of rationality, all the following suggestions put a particular problem into a more comprehensive perspective.

(1) Extend the scope of time.

This particularly implies that the long term consequences of proposed decisions should be analyzed, having as an important effect that Operations Research should extend its activities from the operational to the strategic level.

(2) Extend the space of decision variables.

This requirement tends into the same direction as the extension of the scope of time. Not only the problem at hand should be considered, but all possible 'side effects' as well.

For a typical example that combines (1) and (2) consider the so-called rebound effect. For Operations Research the rebound effect says that saving certain resources in applying specific planning procedures often has as a consequence that having removed this one bottleneck other resources will be exploited even more. Obviously, the decision problem had been formulated within a too narrow perspective, and hence does not follow the postulate of general rationality.

(3) Extend the cultural perspective.
This postulate primarily has to do with the multi-person character of the planning and implementation process. Particularly the claim of OR to be applicable for a multi-cultural society calls for its further extension into the field of distributed decision making.

(4) Extend the language of description.
Obviously, in extending the perspectives of a planning problem, one often has to incorporate other than decision analytic descriptions. Hence, more general languages are necessary and, what is of crucial importance, in order to follow general rationality, these levels have to be connected with each other. Hierarchical planning might provide some general ideas how such an integration of different levels of description could be performed (e.g., see [Schneeweiss (1999)]).

Considering proposals (1) to (4), ethical considerations necessitate at least an enhancement of a problem's perspectives. This results in a re- search strategy that expands OR from the operational, one person analytic paradigme to a more strategic, multi-person and less analytic stage of description. To provide efficient tools for this important step proves to be a major challenge for Operations Research.

Developing instruments to analyze complex situations and hence to be able to observe moral norms proves not only to be an essential postulate for OR as an area of research but for OR as an institutionalized science as well. Operations Research as an institution is responsible for the content of the education within its discipline. The ethical perspective finally results in the claim that education in OR should provide a comprehensive view of a problem's solution which particularly takes into account all parties being involved and affected.

References

Arrow, K.J. (1963). "Social Choice and Individual Values". 2nd ed., New York.

Arrow, K.J., Raynaud, H. (1986). "Social Choice and Multicriterion Decision Making". MIT Press, Cambridge, London.

Habermas, J. (1981). "Theorie des kommunikativen Handelns". 2 Bände, Frankfurt.

Kant, I. (1987). "Critique of Judgement". Hackett Publ. Comp. Indianapolis.

Schneeweiß, Ch. (1987). "On a formalization of the process of quantitative model building". In: European Journal of Operational Research 29, pp 24-41.

Schneeweiß, Ch. (1992). "Planung 2: Konzepte der Prozeß- und Modellgestaltung". Springer, Berlin, Heidelberg, New York.

Schneeweiß, Ch. (1999). "Hierarchies in Distributed Decision Making". Springer, Berlin, Heidelberg, New York.

Ulrich, W. (1983). "Critical Heuristics of Social Planning. A New Approach to Practical Philosophy". Bern, Stuttgart.

Weber, M. (1973). "Der Sinn der 'Wertfreiheit' der soziologischen und ökonomischen Wissenschaften". In: Gesammelte Aufsätze der Wissenschaftslehre, 4. Aufl., Tübingen.

How to Measure Risk?

Georg Ch. Pflug

Institute of Statistics and OR
IIASA and University of Vienna, Austria

Abstract

In financial optimization, the future distribution of wealth is projected by methods of statistical estimation and simulation. For making decisions, different wealth distributions have to be compared and the optimal has to be chosen. In this paper we discuss methods of assignining measures for risk (which are to be minimized) and measures for safety (which are to be maximized) to wealth distributions. Some properties of the presented measures are shown.

1 Introduction

Decision making in finance is decision making under uncertainity: The outcome of today's decision depends on quantities (like future asset prices, interest rates or exchange rates), which are not known yet. The usual approach to deal with this uncertainity is to represent these quantities by a stochastic model. As a consequence, the outcome of the decision (e.g. the future wealth) is a random variable.

Stochasticity of the objective adds a new dimension to the decision making process: Whereas deterministic problems are characterized by costs, returns or wealth as real numbers, these quantities are random distributions in stochastic problems. It is the possible random variability which adds the *risk dimension* to the problem.

A natural question is therefore how to measure the risk dimension. This is a question of descriptive statistics. A first, simple answer could be to measure value by a location measure and risk by a dispersion measure of the underlying distribution.

However, we will consider combined measures of value (location) and risk (dispersion) in this paper and study some of their properties. Combined measures can be seen as good candidates for objective functions for financial optimization.

More precisely, we call *risk measure* $\mathcal{R}$ a functional of the distribution of wealth, which risk averse decision makers try to minimize, and *safety measure* $\mathcal{S}$ a functional which they maximize. By setting $\mathcal{R} = -\mathcal{S}$ we can always switch between risk and safety measures.

Let W a random wealth variable and let $G(x) = \mathbb{P}(W \leq x)$ be its distribution. We require that a risk (or safety) measure depends on the random varable W only through its distribution G, but we use alternatively the notation $\mathcal{R}(W)$ and $\mathcal{R}(G)$.

Sometimes, we do not consider the random wealth W, but random costs Y, but everything, which is formulated for wealth, can be formulated for costs by setting $W = -Y$. A decision maker wants to maximize $\mathcal{S}(W)$ or $\mathcal{S}(Y)$ and minimize $\mathcal{R}(W)$ or $\mathcal{R}(Y)$.

Let $\mathcal{G}$ be the family of all probability distribution functions on $\mathbb{R}$. We define safety measures and risk measures as real (or extended real) valued functions on $\mathcal{G}$.

We will consider the following operations for distribution functions:

(i) Translation T_x:
$$[T_xG](u) = G(u - x)$$

(ii) Scaling S_x:
$$[S_xG](u) = G(u/x)$$

(iii) Convolution $G_1 * G_2$:
$$[G_1 * G_2](u) = \int G_1(u - v)\, dG_2(v)$$

Moreover, we consider the *generalized convolution set*

$$\begin{aligned} G_1 \otimes G_2 \quad = \quad & \{ \text{ the set of all distributions of } X_1 + X_2, \\ & \text{such that } X_1 \text{ is distributed according to } G_1 \text{ and} \\ & X_2 \text{ is distributed according to } G_2, \text{ but the joint} \\ & \text{distribution is otherwise arbitrary } \}. \end{aligned}$$

Notice that the convolution $G_1 * G_2$ is contained in $G_1 \otimes G_2$.

We also introduce some preference relations on $\mathcal{G}$:

- Stochastic dominance of order k

$$G_1 \prec_{SD(k)} G_2$$

iff

$$G_1^{(k)}(u) \geq G_2^{(k)}(u) \qquad \text{for all } u,$$

where $G^{(k)}$ is defined recursively by

$$\begin{aligned} G^{(1)}(u) &= G(u) \\ G^{(k)}(u) &= \int_{-\infty}^{u} G^{(k-1)}(v)\, dv. \end{aligned}$$

- Monotonic dominance of order k

$$G_1 \prec_{MD(k)} G_2$$

iff

$$\int \psi(u)\, dG_1(u) \leq \int \psi(u)\, dG_2(u)$$

for all $\psi \in M^{(k)}$. Here $M^{(k)}$ is the familiy of all functions, which are monotonic of order k (A function ψ is called monotonic of order k, if its k-th derivative is nonnegative).

It is well known, that $G_1 \prec_{SD(1)} G_2$ is equivalent to $G_1 \prec_{MD(1)} G_2$. $G_1 \prec_{MD(2)} G_2$ is also known under the names of Bishop-de Leeuw ordering or Lorenz dominance. The relation $G_1 \prec_{SD(2)} G_2$ is equivalent to

$$\int \psi(u)\, dG_1(u) \leq \int \psi(u)\, dG_2(u)$$

for all monotonic, concave functions ψ. We prove here the last statement: Since $\int_{-\infty}^{x} G(u)\, du = \int_{-\infty}^{\infty} [x-u]^+\, dG(u)$, one sees that $G_1 \prec_{SD(2)} G_2$ is equivalent to $\int_{-\infty}^{\infty} \psi(u)\, dG_1(u) \leq \int_{-\infty}^{\infty} \psi(u)\, dG_2(u)$ for all functions of the form $\psi(u) = \sum_k (-\alpha_k)[x_k - u]^+ + \beta_k$, with $\alpha_k \geq 0$. These functions are dense in the set of all concave, monotonic functions.

For more properties of $\prec_{SD(2)}$ see Ogryczak [9].

We give now some definitions of properties for safety (risk) measures. For convenience, some properties are defined for risk measures and some are defined for safety measures. By setting $\mathcal{S} = -\mathcal{R}$ every definition for $\mathcal{R}$ translates to a definition for $\mathcal{S}$ and vice versa.

(1.1) Definitions.

(i) The risk measure $\mathcal{R}$ is called *translation-equivariant*, if for every constant c

$$\mathcal{R}(T_c G) = \mathcal{R}(G) + c.$$

(ii) The risk measure $\mathcal{R}$ is called *subadditive*, if

$$\mathcal{R}(G) \leq \mathcal{R}(G_1) + \mathcal{R}(G_2),$$

for every $G \in G_1 \otimes G_2$. For safety measures, the analogous property is called *superadditive.*

(iii) The risk measure $\mathcal{S}$ is called *positively homogeneous*, if for all $\lambda > 0$

$$\mathcal{R}(S_\lambda G) = \lambda \mathcal{R}(G).$$

(iv) The safety measure $\mathcal{S}$ is called *isotonic* w.r.t. the order relation $\prec$, if

$$G_1 \prec G_2 \text{ implies that } \mathcal{S}(G_1) \leq \mathcal{S}(G_2).$$

(For risk measures, the second inequality is reversed).

(v) The risk measure $\mathcal{R}$ is called *generalized convolution convex*, if

$$\mathcal{R}(S_{1/2}G) \leq \frac{1}{2}[\mathcal{R}(G_1) + \mathcal{R}(G_2)]$$

for every $G \in G_1 \otimes G_2$. (For safety measures, the analogous property is generalized convolution concavity).

(vi) The risk measure $\mathcal{R}$ is called *convex* in G, if

$$\mathcal{R}(\frac{1}{2}(G_1 + G_2)) \leq \frac{1}{2}(\mathcal{R}(G_1) + \mathcal{R}(G_2)).$$

Notice that homogeneity together with subaddiditvity (superadditivity) implies convexity (concavity).

Risk measures which are generalized convolution convex, exhibit the following property: If the wealth variable is linear in the decision vector x, i.e. if W can be written as $W = x \cdot W_1 + W_2$, then $x \mapsto \mathcal{R}(x \cdot W_1 + W_2)$ is a convex function in x, which is the crucial property for minimization.

To each risk measure we associate the level sets

$$\mathcal{A}_{\mathcal{R}}(c) = \{G : \mathcal{R}(G) \leq c\}.$$

Level sets are interpreted as "acceptance sets" for the decision making process: After having chosen a level c, we accept all distributions with risk smaller than this level (or with safety larger than this level).

The notion of acceptance sets is due to Artzner, Delbaen, Eber and Heath [2].

(1.2) Definition.

Let $\mathcal{A}$ be a set of distribution functions (the acceptance set). We associate to $\mathcal{A}$ a risk measure $\mathcal{R}_{\mathcal{A}}$ by defining

$$\mathcal{R}_{\mathcal{A}}(G) = \inf\{x : T_x G \in \mathcal{A}\}.$$

The risk measure defined on the basis of an acceptance set $\mathcal{A}$ has the following interpretation: Which price x should by paid to the decision maker to make the distribution G acceptable to him? Evidently, higher prices reflect higher risks.

Before discussing the relation between acceptance sets and risk measures, we introduce some important properties for acceptance sets.

(1.3) Definitions.

The set $\mathcal{A}$ of distribution functions is called

(i) a *positive cone*, if $G \in \mathcal{A}$ and $\lambda > 0$ imply that $S_\lambda G \in \mathcal{A}$.

(ii) *translation invariant*, if $G \in \mathcal{A}$ and $x \geq 0$ imlpy that $T_x G \in \mathcal{A}$;

(iii) *convex*, if $G_1 \in \mathcal{A}$, $G_2 \in \mathcal{A}$ implies that $\frac{1}{2}(G_1 + G_2) \in \mathcal{A}$;

(iv) *closed under generalized convolutions*, if $G_1 \in \mathcal{A}$, $G_2 \in \mathcal{A}$ implies that $G \in \mathcal{A}$ for all $G \in G_1 \otimes G_2$;

(v) *generalized convolution convex*, if $G_1 \in \mathcal{A}$ and $G_2 \in \mathcal{A}$ $S_{1/2}G \in \mathcal{A}$ for all $G \in G_1 \otimes G_2$.

Properties of risk measures and properties of the corresponding acceptance sets are related:

(1.4) Proposition.

If $\mathcal{R}$ is positively homogeneous, then $\mathcal{A}_{\mathcal{R}}(0)$ is a positive cone. Conversely, if $\mathcal{A}$ is a positive cone, then $\mathcal{R}_{\mathcal{A}}$ is positively homogeneous.

Proof. Let $\mathcal{R}$ be positively homogeneous and let $G \in \mathcal{A}_{\mathcal{R}}(0)$, i.e. $\mathcal{R}(G) \leq 0$. Then $\mathcal{R}(S_\lambda G) \leq 0$ for $\lambda > 0$, i.e. $S_\lambda G \in \mathcal{A}_{\mathcal{R}}(0)$. Conversely, if $\mathcal{A}$ is a positive cone, then

$$\begin{aligned}\mathcal{R}_{\mathcal{A}}(S_\lambda G) &= \inf\{x : T_x S_\lambda G \in \mathcal{A}\} \\ &= \inf\{x : S_\lambda T_{x/\lambda} G \in \mathcal{A}\} \\ &= \lambda \inf\{y : T_y G \in \mathcal{A}\} \\ &= \lambda \mathcal{R}_{\mathcal{A}}(G).\end{aligned}$$

□

The natural question, whether we can go back and forth between the risk measures and their level (acceptance) sets is answered by the following two propositions.

(1.5) Proposition.

If $\mathcal{R}$ is translation-equivariant, then

$$\mathcal{R}_{\mathcal{A}_{\mathcal{R}}(0)} = \mathcal{R}.$$

Proof.

$$\begin{aligned}\mathcal{R}_{\mathcal{A}_{\mathcal{R}}(0)}(G) &= \inf\{x : T_x G \in \mathcal{A}_{\mathcal{R}}(0)\} \\ &= \inf\{x : \mathcal{R}(T_x G) \leq 0\} \\ &= \inf\{x : \mathcal{R}(G) - x \leq 0\} \\ &= \mathcal{R}(G)\end{aligned}$$

□

(1.6) Proposition.

$$\mathcal{A} \subseteq \mathcal{A}_{\mathcal{R}_{\mathcal{A}}}(0).$$

If $\mathcal{A}$ is a translation invariant and closed w.r.t. weak topology, then

$$\mathcal{A}_{\mathcal{R}_{\mathcal{A}}}(0) = \mathcal{A}.$$

Proof. Let $G \in \mathcal{A}$. Then $T_0 G \in \mathcal{A}$ and therefore $\inf\{x : T_x G \in \mathcal{A}\} \leq 0$. This implies that $G \in \mathcal{A}_{\mathcal{R}_{\mathcal{A}}}(0)$. Conversely, let $G \in \mathcal{A}_{\mathcal{R}_{\mathcal{A}}}(0)$ and suppose that $\mathcal{A}$ is a weakly closed and translation invariant. Let $x^* = \inf\{x : T_x G \in \mathcal{A}\} \leq 0$. Then, by the closedness, $T_{x^*} G \in \mathcal{A}$ and therefore $G = T_{-x^*} T_{x^*} G \in \mathcal{A}\}$. □

Convexity translates from risk measures to level (acceptance) sets in the following way:

(1.7) Proposition.

If $\mathcal{R}$ is convex [generalized convolution-convex] then $\mathcal{A}_{\mathcal{R}}(c)$ is convex [generalized convolution-convex] for all levels c. Conversely, if $\mathcal{A}$ is generalized convolution-convex, then $\mathcal{R}_{\mathcal{A}}$ is generalized convolution-convex. If $\mathcal{A}$ is closed under generalized convolutions, then $\mathcal{R}_{\mathcal{A}}$ is subadditive.

Proof. If $\mathcal{R}$ is convex (in whatever sense), then so are its level sets. Conversely, let $\mathcal{A}_{\mathcal{R}}(c)$ generalized convolution convex for all c. Let W_1 resp. W_2 be two wealth variables and let $x_1 = \mathcal{R}(W_1)$, $x_2 = \mathcal{R}(W_2)$. Then, for all $\epsilon > 0$, the distribution of $x_1 + \epsilon + W_1$ and $x_2 + \epsilon + W_2$ are in $\mathcal{A}$ and therefore the distribution of $\frac{1}{2}[x_1 + x_2 + 2\epsilon W_1 + W_2]$ is in $\mathcal{A}$ and hence $\mathcal{R}(\frac{1}{2}(W_1 + W_2)) \le \frac{1}{2}(\mathcal{R}(W_1) + \mathcal{R}(W_2))$. A similar argument proves the last assertion. □

(1.8) Definition. (Artzner, Delbaen, Eber, Heath [2])

The risk measure $\mathcal{R}$ is called *coherent*, if it is translation-invariant, subadditive, positively homogeneous and isotonic w.r.t. $\prec_{SD(1)}$.

(1.8) Proposition.

(i) If $\mathcal{R}$ is coherent, then $\mathcal{A}_{\mathcal{R}}(0)$ is a closed positive translation invariant cone, which is closed w.r.t. generalized convolutions.

(ii) If $\mathcal{A}$ is a closed positive, translation invariant cone, which is closed w.r.t. generalized convolutions, then $\mathcal{R}_{\mathcal{A}}$ is coherent.

Proof. (see [2]). □

2 Classes of risk-measures

There are many proposals for risk-measures in the literature. We review here some of these proposals and discuss their properties. Not all statements are formally proved. The omitted proofs are simple and left to the reader.

2.1 Linear measures

Linear safety measures are linear in the distribution function G. They are of the form

$$\mathcal{S}(G) = \int U(v)\, dG(v).$$

If U is some monotone function, interpreted as utility, then these measures are called *von Neumann-Morgenstern* measures. They were intensively studied by Arrow and (independently) Pratt, who related the curvature of the utility function U to the risk aversion.

Special cases are

- the power utility
$$U(v) = \frac{v^\gamma}{\gamma};$$
- the logarithmic utility
$$U(v) = \log(v);$$
(Notice that $\lim_{\gamma \to 0} \frac{u^\gamma - 1}{\gamma} = \log u$)
- the excess value
$$\mathcal{S}(G) = \int_t^\infty v \, dG(v);$$
- the excess probability
$$\mathcal{S}(G) = 1 - G(t),$$
where t is some fixed threshold amount.

These measures have thc following properties: They are

- not translation-equivariant (unless $U(v) = v$)
- subadditive, if U is subadditive
- concave, even linear in G
- generalized convolution-concave, if U is concave
- not homogeneos (unless $U(v) = c \cdot v$)
- isotonic w.r.t $\prec_{MD(k)}$, if $U \in M^{(k)}$; isotonic w.r.t. $\prec_{SD(2)}$, if U is monotonic and concave.

2.2 Linear/quadratic measures

These are linear/quadratic in the distribution function G, typically

$$\mathcal{S}(G) = \int v \, dG(v) - \delta \int \int h(v-u) \, dG(u) \, dG(v)$$

where h is a convex, symmetric function. Here and in the following, δ denotes a factor of risk aversion, which reflects the risk perception of the decision maker.

Examples are

- the *Markowitz value* ($h(u) = u^2$)

$$\begin{aligned}\mathcal{S}(G) &= \int v \, dG(v) - \delta \int \int (v-u)^2 \, dG(u) \, dG(v) \\ &= \text{Expectation } - 2\delta \cdot \text{ Variance} .\end{aligned}$$

- *Yitzhaki's measure* ($h(u) = |u|$)

$$\begin{aligned}\mathcal{S}(G) &= \int v \, dG(v) - \delta \int \int |v-u| \, dG(u) \, dG(v) \\ &= \text{Expectation } - \delta \cdot \text{ Gini-coefficient} .\end{aligned}$$

These measures are

- translation-equivariant
- subadditive, if g is subadditive
- concave
- generalized convolution-concave
- not homogeneous, unless h is homogeneous
- not isotonic in general.(However, Yitzhaki's measure is isotonic w.r.t. $\prec_{MD(2)}$).

2.3 Expectation/dispersion measures

$$\mathcal{S}(G) = \int v \, dG(v) - \delta \int h[v - \int u \, dG(u)] \, dG(v)$$

where h is some convex function with $h(0) = 0$. Since we may rewrite $\mathcal{S}(G)$ as

$$\mathcal{S}(G) = \int G^{-1}(v)\, dv - \delta \int h(G^{-1}(v) - \int G^{-1}(u)\, du)\, dv,$$

we see that these risk measures are concave in G^{-1}.

These measures are

- translation-equivariant
- subadditive
- not concave in G
- generalized convolution-concave
- not homogeneous (unless h is homogeneous)
- not isotonic in general.

Examples for the functions h are $h(u) = ([u]^+)^2$, $h(u) = ([u]^-)^2$ and $h(u) = [u]^+$, leading to
the *upper semivariance*

$$\mathrm{Var}^+(G) = \int [(v - \int u\, dG(u))^+]^2\, dG(v),$$

the *lower semivariance*

$$\mathrm{Var}^-(G) = \int [(v - \int u\, dG(u))^-]^2\, dG(v)$$

and the *mean lower absolute deviation*

$$\mathrm{MLAD}(G) = \int [(v - \int u\, dG(u))^-]\, dG(v),$$

which is half of the *mean absolute deviation*

$$\mathrm{MAD}(G) = \int |v - \int u\, dG(u))|\, dG(v),$$

since

$$\begin{aligned} &\int [v - \int u\, dG(u)]^+\, dG(v) + \int [v - \int u\, dG(u)]^-\, dG(v) \\ = &\int |v - \int u\, dG(u)|\, dG(v). \end{aligned}$$

and

$$\begin{aligned}&\int [v-\int u\,dG(u)]^+\,dG(v)-\int [v-\int u\,dG(u)]^-\,dG(v)\\ =\;&\int [v-\int u\,dG(u)]\,dG(v)=0.\end{aligned}$$

$\mathrm{Var}^-(G)$ and MLAD(G) measure the negative deviation of the wealth from its mean, which is the critical and dangereous deviation.

The Markowitz mean/variance measure belong to the previous, but also to this group of measures.

Related measures are

$$\mathcal{S}(G)=\int v\,dG(v)-\delta h^{-1}\Big(\int h([v-\int u\,dG(u)]^-)\,dG(v)\Big) \qquad (1)$$

where h is strictly monotonic and convex.

Setting e.g. $h(u)=u^2$ we get

$$\mathcal{S}(G)=\int v\,dG(v)-\delta\;\mathrm{Std}^-(G)$$

where Std^- is the *lower semi-standard-deviation*

$$\mathrm{Std}^+(G)=\sqrt{\mathrm{Var}^-(G)}$$

and setting $g(u)=u$, we get

$$\mathcal{S}(G)=\int v\,dG(v)-\delta MLAD(G).$$

These measures are

- translation-equivariant
- subadditive
- not concave
- generalized convolution concave
- not homogeneous unless if $h(u)=u^\gamma$
- isotonic w.r.t. $\prec_{SD(2)}$, if $\delta\le 1$

Isotonicity w.r.t. $\prec_{Sd(2)}$ for the special case of $h(u) = u$ and $h(u) = u^2$ was shown by Ruszczynski and Ogryczak ([15]). We show here a more general result:

(2.1) Proposition.

If h is monotone, convex, differentiable and $u \mapsto h' \circ h^{-1}(u)$ is concave, then $\mathcal{S}$ given by (1) is isotonic w.r.t. $\prec_{SD(2)}$ for $0 \le \delta \le 1$.

Proof.

We begin with showing that for all random variables Z and $b \ge 0$

$$h^{-1}\{(\mathbb{E}(Z)\} \le h^{-1}\{\mathbb{E}(h(Z-b))\} + b. \tag{2}$$

By assumption

$$\mathbb{E}(h'[h^{-1}(W)]) \le h'(h^{-1}[\mathbb{E}(W)])$$

for every random variable W. Setting $W = h(Z-a)$ we get

$$\begin{aligned} \mathbb{E}(h'(Z-a)) &\le h'(h^{-1}[\mathbb{E}(h^{-1}(Z-a))]) \\ &= [(h^{-1})'(\mathbb{E}(h^{-1}(Z-a)))]^{-1} \end{aligned}$$

which can be written as

$$\frac{\partial}{\partial a}(-h^{-1}[\mathbb{E}(h(Z-a))]) \le 1. \tag{3}$$

Integrating (3) from $a = 0$ to $a = b$ we get

$$h^{-1}\{(\mathbb{E}(Z)\} - h^{-1}\{\mathbb{E}(h(Z-b))\} \le b$$

and (2) is proved.

In order to show the main assertion, let $G_1 \prec_{SD(2)} G_2$ and let $W_1 \sim G_1$, $W_2 \sim G_2$. We know that $\mathbb{E}(W_1) \le \mathbb{E}(W_2)$ and since $u \mapsto -h([u - \mathbb{E}(W_1)]^-)$ is monotonic and concave,

$$\mathbb{E}(h([W_1 - \mathbb{E}(W_1)]^-)) \ge \mathbb{E}(h([W_2 - \mathbb{E}(W_1)]^-)).$$

Therefore, using (2) and the inequality $[u+b]^- \ge [u]^- - b$ we get

$$\begin{aligned} & \mathbb{E}(W_1) - \delta h^{-1}\{\mathbb{E}(h([W_1 - \mathbb{E}(W_1)]^-))\} \\ \le\; & \mathbb{E}(W_1) - \delta h^{-1}\{\mathbb{E}(h([W_2 - \mathbb{E}(W_1)]^-))\} \\ =\; & \mathbb{E}(W_1) - \delta h^{-1}\{\mathbb{E}(h([W_2 - \mathbb{E}(W_2) + \mathbb{E}(W_2) - \mathbb{E}(W_1)]^-))\} \\ \le\; & \mathbb{E}(W_1) - \delta h^{-1}\{\mathbb{E}(h([W_2 - \mathbb{E}(W_2)]^- - [\mathbb{E}(W_2) - \mathbb{E}(W_1)]))\} \\ \le\; & \mathbb{E}(W_1) - \delta h^{-1}\{\mathbb{E}(h([W_2 - \mathbb{E}(W_2)]^-))\} + \delta[\mathbb{E}(W_2) - \mathbb{E}(W_1)] \\ =\; & (1-\delta)\mathbb{E}(W_1) + \delta\mathbb{E}(W_2) - \delta h^{-1}\{\mathbb{E}(h([W_2 - \mathbb{E}(W_2)]^-))\} \\ \le\; & \mathbb{E}(W_2) - \delta h^{-1}\{\mathbb{E}(h([W_2 - \mathbb{E}(W_2)]^-))\}. \end{aligned}$$

□

An alternative risk measure can be based on the notion of the Minkowski-gauge $\|Z\|_h$ of a random variable (see [12]).

(2.2) Definition.

Let h be a convex, monotonic function on $\mathbb{R}^+$ with $h(0) = 0$. For a random variable Z, the Minkowski-gauge is defined as

$$\|Z\|_h = \inf\{a : \mathbb{E}[h(\frac{|Z|}{a})] \leq 1\}.$$

It is easy to see that the Minkowski-gauge is homogeneous ($\|\lambda Z\|_h = |\lambda| \cdot \|Z\|_h$) and fulfills the triangle inequality ($\|Z_1 + Z_2\|_h \leq \|Z_1\|_h + \|Z_2\|_h$). Special cases are:

- $h(u) = u$:
$$\|Z\|_h = \|Z\|_1 = \mathbb{E}[|Z|];$$
- $h(u) = u^2$:
$$\|Z\|_h = \|Z\|_2 = \sqrt{\mathbb{E}[Z^2]};$$
- $h(u) = u^p$:
$$\|Z\|_h = \|Z\|_p = \mathbb{E}^{1/p}[|Z|^p]].$$

Based on the Minkowski-gauge, we may define the safety measure

$$\mathcal{S} = \mathbb{E}(W) - \delta\|[W - \mathbb{E}(W)]^-\|_h \tag{4}$$

which generalizes the MLAD and the lower-semi-standard deviation measures.

(2.3) Proposition.

The safety measure $\mathcal{S}$ given by (4) is subaddiditve and isotonic w.r.t. $\prec_{SD(2)}$ for $0 \leq \delta \leq 1$.

Proof.

Let us first show the subadditivity of $\|[W - \mathbb{E}(W)]^-\|_h$.

Let W_1 and W_2 be two random variables. W.l.o.g. we may assume that both have expectation zero. By $[W_1 + W_2]^- \leq W_1^- + W_2^-$ we get using the triangle inequality

$$\|[W_1 + W_2]^-\|_h \leq \|W_1^- + W_2^-\|_h \leq \|W_1^-\|_h + \|W_2^-\|_h.$$

Notice that subadditivity implies the generalized convolution-concavity, since $\|\cdot\|_h$ is homogeneous.

In order to show the second assertion, let $G_1 \prec_{SD(2)} G_2$ and let $W_1 \sim G_1$, $W_2 \sim G_2$. Let $a = \|[W_1 - \mathbb{E}(W_1)]^-\|_h$, i.e. $\mathbb{E}(h([W_1 - \mathbb{E}(W_1)]^-)) = a$. We know that $\mathbb{E}(W_1) \leq \mathbb{E}(W_2)$ and since $u \mapsto -h(\frac{[u-\mathbb{E}(W_1)]^-}{a})$ is monotonic and concave,

$$1 = \mathbb{E}(h(\frac{[W_1 - \mathbb{E}(W_1)]^-)}{a}) \geq \mathbb{E}(h(\frac{[W_2 - \mathbb{E}(W_1)]^-}{a})),$$

whence

$$\begin{aligned} a &\geq \|[W_2 - \mathbb{E}(W_1)]^-\|_h \\ &\geq \|[W_2 - \mathbb{E}(W_2)]^- + \mathbb{E}(W_1) - \mathbb{E}(W_2)\|_h \\ &\geq \|[W_2 - \mathbb{E}(W_2)]^-\|_h + \mathbb{E}(W_1) - \mathbb{E}(W_2) \end{aligned}$$

and an arguing similar as in the proof of Proposition (2.1) we get

$$\begin{aligned} & \mathbb{E}(W_1) - \delta\|[W_1 - \mathbb{E}(W_1)]^-\|_h = \mathbb{E}(W_1) - \delta \cdot a \\ \leq\; & \mathbb{E}(W_1) - \delta\|[W_2 - \mathbb{E}(W_2)]^-\|_h + \delta\mathbb{E}(W_2) - \delta\mathbb{E}(W_1) \\ \leq\; & \mathbb{E}(W_2) - \delta\|[W_2 - \mathbb{E}(W_2)]^-\|_h \end{aligned}$$

□

Summarizing, we see that the safety measures of type (4) exhibit the following properties: They are

- translation-equivariant
- subadditive
- not concave
- generalized convolution concave
- homogeneous
- isotonic w.r.t. $\prec_{SD(2)}$, if $0 \leq \delta \leq 1$

In contrast to the just discussed one-sided measures, the two-sided measures

$$\mathcal{S} = \mathbb{E}(W) - \delta\|W - \mathbb{E}(W)\|_h$$

are not isotonic w.r.t. $\prec_{SD(2)}$. They are however

- translation-equivariant
- subadditive
- not concave
- generalized convolution concave
- homogeneous
- isotonic w.r.t. $\prec_{MD(2)}$.

An important example in this class is

$$\mathcal{S}(G) = \int v \, dG(v) - \delta \sqrt{\mathrm{Var}(G)}.$$

2.4 Inverse-linear risk measures

These are linear in the inverse distribution function (quantile function) $G^{-1}(t)$. An example is *Yaari's index* ([16])

$$\mathcal{R}(G) = \int_{-\infty}^{\infty} g(G(u)) \, du = \int_0^1 g(u) \, dG^{-1}(u)$$

for some monotonic function g.

An important example is the *value at risk*, i.e. the $1 - \alpha$-quantile $G^{-1}(1 - \alpha)$.

These measures are

- translation-equivariant
- not subadditive in general
- not concave in G (but linear in G^{-1})
- not generalized convolution concave
- not homogeneos (unless g is homogeneos)
- isotonic w.r.t. $\prec_{SD(1)}$ (which is equivalent to $\prec_{MD(1)}$.

Since these measures are not generalized convolution convex, the associated decision problem is typically nonconvex. Although there is some interest from practitioners to optimize e.g. values at risk, the associated nonconvex and even nonsmooth optimization problems are very difficult to handle.

Convexity is a basic property also for the vector risk approach treated in the next section.

3 Risk functions for vectors

Unlike individuals, governments as decision makers have to consider the whole vector of individual losses $\mathbf{Y} = (Y_1, \ldots, Y_N)$ and to take the aspect of equity and fairness in risk distribution in account.

Suppose that x is a decision variable for the government. For instance think of the share of expenditures for road safety and for cancer prevention. Then $\mathbf{Y} = \mathbf{Y}(x)$ is a function of x and we need an instrument to decide which x is optimal under a given preference structure. As we will show, there is an antagony between *social risk* and *individual risk* and the balance between the two is a fundamental issue in public policy.

If $\mathcal{R}(Y)$ is any generalized convolution convex risk function, then we may define the *social risk* as $S_{\mathcal{R}}(\mathbf{Y}) := \mathcal{R}(\frac{1}{N}\sum_{i=1}^N Y_i)$ and the *individual risk* as $I_{\mathcal{R}}(\mathbf{Y}) := \frac{1}{N}\sum_{i=1}^N \mathcal{R}(Y_i)$. Because of convexity,

$$I_{\mathcal{R}}(\mathbf{Y}) \geq S_{\mathcal{R}}(\mathbf{Y})$$

and we define the unfairness as

$$U_{\mathcal{R}}(\mathbf{Y}) = I_{\mathcal{R}}(\mathbf{Y}) - S_{\mathcal{R}}(\mathbf{Y}) \geq 0.$$

As an example, let $\mathcal{R}$ be the Markowitz mean/variance measure $\mathcal{R}(Y) = \mathbb{E}(Y) + \delta \operatorname{Var}(Y)$, which is generalized convolution convex.

We have

$$I_{\mathcal{R}}(\mathbf{Y}) = \frac{1}{N}\sum_{i=1}^N \mathbb{E}(Y_i) + \frac{\delta}{N}\sum_{i=1}^N \operatorname{Var}(Y_i);$$

$$S_{\mathcal{R}}(\mathbf{Y}) = \frac{1}{N}\sum_{i=1}^N \mathbb{E}(Y_i) + \delta \operatorname{Var}(\frac{1}{N}\sum_{i=1}^N Y_i);$$

and the *unfairness*

$$U_{\mathcal{R}}(\mathbf{Y}) = \delta\frac{1}{2N^2}\sum_{i\neq j} \operatorname{Var}(Y_i - Y_j).$$

For a proof of the last assertion, let $c_{ij} = \operatorname{Cov}(Y_i, Y_j)$. Then

$$\begin{aligned} NU_{\mathcal{R}}(\mathbf{Y}) &= \frac{\delta}{N}\sum_{i,j}[c_{ii} + c_{jj} - c_{ij} - c_{ji}] \\ &= \delta\sum_{i=1}^N c_{ii} - \frac{\delta}{N}\sum_{i,j} c_{ij} \end{aligned}$$

$$
\begin{aligned}
&= \delta \sum_{i=1}^{N} \operatorname{Var}(Y_i) - \frac{\delta}{N} \operatorname{Var}(\sum_{i=1}^{N} Y_i) \\
&= N I_{\mathcal{R}}(\mathbf{Y}) - N S_{\mathcal{R}}(\mathbf{Y}).
\end{aligned}
$$

Example. Let Y_i be independent Bernoulli variables with $\mathbb{P}(Y_i = 1) = 1 - \mathbb{P}(Y_i = 0) = p$. Then

$$
\begin{aligned}
S_{\mathcal{R}}(\mathbf{Y}) &= p + \frac{\delta}{N} p(1-p), \\
I_{\mathcal{R}}(\mathbf{Y}) &= p + \delta p(1-p) \\
U_{\mathcal{R}}(\mathbf{Y}) &= \delta \frac{N-1}{N} p(1-p).
\end{aligned}
$$

On the other hand, if Y_1 is defined as above and $Y_i = Y_1$ for $i = 2, \ldots, N$, then the marginal distribution and hence the componentwise risks are the same as before, but

$$
\begin{aligned}
S_{\mathcal{R}}(\mathbf{Y}) &= I_{\mathcal{R}}(\mathbf{Y}) = p + \delta p(1-p), \\
U_{\mathcal{R}}(\mathbf{Y}) &= 0.
\end{aligned}
$$

We may now define the preference relation $\prec$ called vector dominance.

(3.1) Definition.

The loss vector $\mathbf{Y}_1$ dominates the loss vector $\mathbf{Y}_2$ (in symbol $\mathbf{Y}_1 \prec \mathbf{Y}_2$, if

$$
\begin{aligned}
S_{\mathcal{R}}(\mathbf{Y}_1) &\leq S_{\mathcal{R}}(\mathbf{Y}_2) \\
I_{\mathcal{R}}(\mathbf{Y}_1) &\leq I_{\mathcal{R}}(\mathbf{Y}_2) \\
U_{\mathcal{R}}(\mathbf{Y}_1) &\leq U_{\mathcal{R}}(\mathbf{Y}_2)
\end{aligned}
$$

Notice that a linear function $\beta_1 S_{\mathcal{R}}(\mathbf{Y}) + \beta_2 I_{\mathcal{R}}(\mathbf{Y})$ is compatible with vector dominance, if $\beta_1 \geq \beta_2$ and $\beta_2 \geq 0$.

Figure 1 illustrates this preference relation.

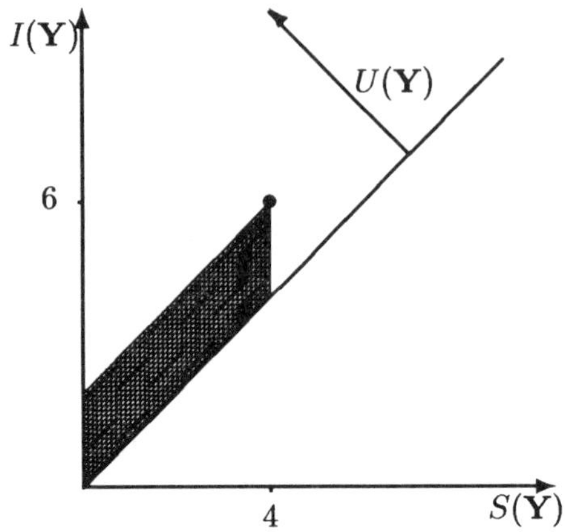

Figure 1: The social risk $S_{\mathcal{R}}(\mathbf{Y})$, the individual risk $I_{\mathcal{R}}(\mathbf{Y})$ and the unfairness $U_{\mathcal{R}}(\mathbf{Y})$. The shaded area shows the risk vectors, which dominate the vector $S_{\mathcal{R}} = 4, I_{\mathcal{R}} = 6$.

We may easily show that mutual insurance reduces unfairness. For simplicity, consider an insurance, where the fraction α of the individual loss is reimbursed by all others. The loss vector $\mathbf{Y} = (Y_1, \ldots, Y_N)$ is changed by this contract to

$$\tilde{\mathbf{Y}} = (\alpha Y_1 + (1-\alpha)\bar{Y}, \ldots, \alpha Y_N + (1-\alpha)\bar{Y}),$$

where $\bar{Y} = \frac{1}{N}\sum_{i=1}^N Y_i$. We get

$$\begin{aligned} U_{\mathcal{R}}(\tilde{\mathbf{Y}}) &= \frac{1}{N}\sum_{i=1}^N \mathcal{R}(\alpha Y_i + (1-\alpha)\mathcal{R}(\bar{Y}) - \mathcal{R}(\bar{Y}) \\ &\leq \frac{1}{N}\sum_{i=1}^N [\alpha\mathcal{R}(Y_i) + (1-\alpha)\mathcal{R}(\bar{Y})] - \mathcal{R}(\bar{Y}) \\ &= \alpha\frac{1}{N}\sum_{i=1}^N \mathcal{R}(Y_i) - \alpha\mathcal{R}(\bar{Y}) \\ &= \alpha U_{\mathcal{R}}(\mathbf{Y}) \end{aligned}$$

As one sees, the unfairness reduces at least by the factor α. For $\alpha = 1$, i.e. for total loss sharing, the unfairness is 0.

4 Conclusions

We have presented concepts and properties of measures for safety and risk for wealth and cost distributions. Unlike in [2] our mesures depend only on the distribution functions and not on the underlying probability space. They are descriptive and capture the necessary compromise between location and dispersion measures.

Among all presented measures, the following two have most attractive properties: The mean/MAD-measure:

$$\mathcal{S}(G) = \int v\, dG(v) - \frac{\delta}{2} \int |v - \int u\, dG(u)|\, dG(v)$$

and the mean/lower-semi-standard-deviation measure:

$$\mathcal{S}(G) = \int v\, dG(v) - \delta \sqrt{\int ([v - \int u\, dG(u)]^-)^2\, dG(v)}.$$

Both are special cases of the more general Minkowski-gauge functional measures. Recall that these measures are translation-equivariant, homogeneous, generalized convolution convex and isotonic w.r.t. $\prec_{SD(2)}$. Notice also that these measures can equivalently be described by acceptance sets, but are not coherent in the sense of [2]. Coherence in their sense requires the isotonicity w.r.t. $\prec_{SD(1)}$, but these measures are isotonic w.r.t. $\prec_{SD(2)}$ – an equally important property.

The mean/variance measure

$$\mathcal{S}(G) = \int v\, dG(v) - \delta \int ([v - \int u\, dG(u)])^2\, dG(v)$$

exhibits similar properties as the mean/MAD or the mean/lower-semi-standard-deviation measure except that it is not positively homogeneous and not isotonic w.r.t. $\prec_{SD(2)}$.

It exhibits however the following rather attractive risk accumulation property: Suppose that the risk measures of W_1 and W_2 are known. What is the risk of $W_1 + W_2$? In case of the mean/variance measure, only one additional number, namely the correlation between W_1 and W_2 has to be given for calculating the risk of the sum. In all other cases, the cumulative risk depends on the complete joint distribution function of W_1 and W_2, making the analysis of accumulated risks cumbersome.

However, for some classes of typical wealth (cost) distributions, a small number of parameters may be sufficient to calculate cumulative risks also for other risk measures. More research in this direction is needed.

References

[1] Arrow K.J. (1971): Essays in the theory of risk-bearing. Markham, Chicago

[2] Artzner Ph., Delbaen F., Eber J.-M., Heath D. (1998): Coherent measures of risk. Preprint

[3] Ferschl F. (1985): Deskripive Statistik. Physica Verlag (in German)

[4] Fishburn P.C. (1980): Stochastic Dominance and Moments of Distributions. Mathematics of Operations Research 5, 94 – 100

[5] Huang C.-F., Litzenberger R. (1988): Foundations of Financial Economics, Prentice Hall, Englewood Cliffs, New Jersey

[6] Jia Jianmin, Dyer J. (1996): A Standard Measure of Risk and Risk-value Models. Management Science 42, (12), 1691 – 1705

[7] Konno H., Yamazaki H. (1991): Mean Absolute Deviation Portfolio Optimization Model and its Applications to Tokyo Stock Market. Management Science 37, 519 – 531

[8] Markowitz, H.M. (1952): Portfolio selection. Journal of Finance 7, 77 - 91

[9] Ogryczak W. (1998): Stochastic dominance relation and linear risk measures. 23rd Meeting of the EURO Working group on Financial Modelling, Cracow, Poland

[10] Pflug G. Ch. (1998): Risk reshaping contracts and stochastic optimization. Central European Journal of Operations Research and Economics 5, (3 - 4), 205 – 230

[11] Pratt J. (1964): Risk aversion in the small and in the large. Econometrica 32, 122 – 136

[12] Rao R.R., Ren Z.D. (1991): Theory of Orlicz spaces. Marcel Dekker, New York

[13] Rejda, George E. (1992): Principles of Risk Management and Insurance. Harper Collins, New York

[14] Ritchie Bob (1993): Business risk management. Chapman and Hall, London

[15] Ruszcynski A., Ogryczak W. (1997): From Stochastic Dominance to Mean-Risk Models: Semideviations as Risk Measures. IR-97-027, IIASA, Laxenburg, Austria

[16] Yaari, Menhem E. (1986):. Univariate and multivariate comparisons of risk aversion: a new approach. Essays in honor of Kenneth J. Arrow, Vol. III. (W. Heller, R. Starr, D. Starrett eds.). Cambridge University Press

[17] Yitzhaki S. (1982): Stochastic Dominance, Mean Variance and Gini's Mean Difference. The American Economic Review 72, 178 – 185

On the Question of Speculation in Favour of or against the Euro before its Start

Lutz Beinsen*

University of Graz

Abstract

The transition of the European Currency System to a common currency offers an opportunity for the study of speculation in foreign exchanges. There are many reasons for speculative activities in the transition to the Euro. Speculation, as a matter of motives, can only indirectly be observed, that is to say by the statistical evaluation of the behaviour of exchange markets. Five examples are tested which are based on the proposition that the presence of speculation is eventually revealed in certain residuals. Another approach is the comparison of the variances of exchange rate estimates which does not lead to clear results. Finally, the evaluation of random walk estimations reveals a trend of increasing efficiency of certain foreign exchange markets.

1. Introduction

The decision to introduce a common currency for the member states of the European Union was mainly a political one. For politicians it may seem quite natural that a common currency belongs to a common market. The idea dates back to the Hague summit conference of 1969 when the heads of the governments of the member states decided to let elaborate a gradual plan for the development of an economic and currency union. The result was the Werner Plan (1971) which, in the face of the breakdown of the world monetary system, could not be realised at that time[1]. After the "currency snake" starting in 1972 and the European Monetary System starting in 1979, a stepwise transition to a currency union[2] was agreed on in the frame of the Maastricht Treaty. But for the members of the European Union the membership in the currency union, named European

*The Author is indebted for discussions and hints to Johann Kellerer, Heinz D. Kurz and Ulrike Leopold-Wildburger.

[1] Weindl (1994), p. 324.

[2] ibid., pp. 330 ff.; Gandolfo (1995), pp. 429 ff.

Monetary Union (EMU) was not compulsory. Some members of the former, Great Britain, Sweden and Denmark, indeed refused to become members of the latter (whereas Greece failed to fulfil the criteria of participation). They are obviously not convinced of the advantages of a common currency.

On the other hand there is also a disagreement on theoretical grounds whether the European Union is a kind of optimum currency area[3]. Therefore we may expect that on the foreign exchange markets some traders speculate in favour of the "Euro", parking their funds in one of the most stable currencies of the European Monetary System (EMS), while others speculate against the new currency, or, at least choose a stable outside currency in order to wait and to first observe the performance of the Euro. Like the early seventies, after the breakdown and the following reorganisation of the Bretton Woods system, these years are an interesting time to pursue the possible trail of speculation and of its effects.

In this study it is examined whether foreign exchange speculation in the context of the transition to the Euro can be identified during the last years. Since speculation is not directly observable, some indirect measurement concepts are tried out. As the Euro does not yet exist, of course, it must be replaced by some currency of the European Monetary System. The idea is that speculation in favour of or against the Euro must take EMS currencies as a substitute. For this purpose the German mark was chosen, as one of the strongest prospective member currencies. Investors who speculate in favour of the Euro are assumed to choose a long position (more assets than debts) in the German mark. Speculators against the Euro are supposed to prefer a short position (more debts than assets) in this currency.

In section 2 it is asked why speculation with regard to the introduction of the Euro was to be expected. In section 3 we discuss five empirical estimates following different measurement concepts which refer to theoretical determinants of exchange rates. Section 4 considers the question whether the efficiency of the random walk of some currencies inside and outside the EMS has changed. In Section 5 summarising conclusions are drawn.

2. Reasons for Bull and Bear Speculation in the Euro

Let us start with the question why bull speculation (long position) in the Euro, or in the German mark or in another stable presumable member currency as a substitute, could sensibly be expected. One argument is that the Euro bloc will certainly be one of the most stable currency areas in the world. This follows not only from the "construction" represented by the institutional rules of the Maastricht treaty, i.e. mainly article 109a ff. and especially the regulations

[3] Krugman/Obstfeld (1996), pp. 631-634.

concerning the independence of the European Central Bank (ECB). The treaty also established price stability as the principal objective according to article 105 (1). A philosophy of a beggar-thy-neighbour-policy or, more general, of an active currency policy, using the external value of the Euro as a means of demand management, does not fit into this environment. One can also argue that a basket currency like the Euro will in general be more stable than the weaker of its member currencies because the basket is nothing else but a weighted average of weak and strong currencies. Therefore a movement into the stronger member currencies can be expected.

If all payments hitherto carried out in the former own currencies of the EMU-members will be settled in Euro, this will mean a much more than proportionate increase in the use of one single European currency because the Euro replaces twelve former currencies. Consequently central-banks outside the EMU will have to keep much more liquidity in Euro than in any other single European currency before. This will be a remarkable simplification of the foreign exchange reserve management.[4] If there is a certain amount of liquidity to be hold in Euro it will prove practical for the central-banks outside the EMU to use the Euro also for their mutual payments like it is done with the US-dollar[5]. Indeed, we suppose that, to a certain degree, the Euro will take over the role of the dollar as an international transactions and reserve currency. This means that not only the (outside) export and import and capital transactions of the nearly 300 million people of the EMU member countries but also payments among third countries will be carried out in Euro. The market share of the US-dollar in international transactions will consequently decrease, and there will be an additional demand for Euro and a corresponding appreciation at least during the time while Euro funds are accumulated by foreign central banks.

Last but not least it has to be realised that the sheer quantity of Euro units will simply be a many times bigger quantity of money than any of the former single currencies alone. This means that it will be much more difficult for the speculators in foreign exchanges to destabilise the Euro than it was before with regard to the single currencies. This should lead speculators rather to speculate with the bulls (like the ECB) than with the bears.

If we turn now to the reasons of speculation against the Euro the first very simple but convincing argument says that there is necessarily no experience[6] with the currency policy of the European Central Bank (ECB) and the corresponding stability behaviour of the Euro. For risk averse people this is enough reason to

[4] Giovannini (1991), p. 98, the need for reserves in high-powered money will considerably decrease.
[5] Giovannini (1991), pp. 94 ff., 98 f.
[6] This can be seen as a matter of „reputation“ which the German „BuBa“ (Bundesbank) has, but the European Central Bank has not. See e.g. Krugman/Obstfeld (1996), p. 619.

hold their funds in other stable currencies and first observe the Euro for some time. Of course, there are not so many stable currencies outside the EMU, but the Swiss franc is a case in point.

Secondly, though the Euro may prove more stable than some of the former single currencies of the members it is still an open question whether it will be a bit weaker or similarly stable as the most stable currencies like the Dutch guilder, the German mark, the French franc, the Austrian schilling. The future monetary policy of the European Central Bank will be the result of a decision board, the members of which are from different member countries with different attitudes towards inflation[7]. Doubts are admitted that they all think the lowest rate of inflation is the best.

Thirdly, the criteria of participation were useful in attaining a minimum level of monetary and financial discipline[8] of the successful candidates most of which have had to pass some years of austerity. But now, after attaining the main objective, that is to say the membership in the EMU, the general ambition for stability may be somewhat less pronounced than before. The pact for stability was designed to guarantee a continuous concern for discipline in economic policy. In this regard the question arises whether the penalties agreed on have strong enough effects. The convergence criteria come close to establishing the conditions for an optimum currency area, but since they are not equally fulfilled by the EMU members[9] and since exchange rates are no longer available as an instrument of EMU-internal foreign economic policy, the question is whether resulting tensions will be fought by expansionary policies which finally lead to a depreciation of the Euro. This possibility is still supported by the fact that the trade unions within the EMU show extremely different attitudes ("cultures") towards strike, the toughest strikers being presumably found in France, whereas Austria is at the opposite extreme. At least it would be a surprise if such different conditions would vanish by aggregation.

After the last German election to the federal parliament in autumn 1998, the resulting transition of the power to rule from the coalition of Christian-Democratic and Liberal to Social-Democratic and Green Parties ("red-green coalition") followed similar changes from conservative to socialist parties or to social-democratic parties or coalitions in other member countries in recent years. This led to a great majority of left-wing-dominated governments of the EMU members and paved the way for the announcement of more socially-oriented economic policies of these countries and for plans of a full-employment initiative on EU-level. True, a corresponding programme which is operational in substance has not yet been presented, but soon it became clear that the objective of price

[7] See Gandolfo (1995), p. 408.
[8] For severe critique see Gandolfo (1995), p. 434.
[9] Österreichisches Institut für Wirtschaftsforschung (1998), Monatsberichte, H. 4, p. 235.

stability lost in importance relative to the objective of full-employment. The German Bundesbank understood this as an attack on monetary stability.

Another argument refers to the fact that there was a devaluation criterion but no balance of payments equilibrium criterion of participation. Indeed some countries carried over considerable external balances or deficits, respectively, into the EMU without any clear idea how to cope with this problem in the future. Austria for instance accumulated deficits of the balance on current account of a bit less than ATS 250 milliards[10] between 1994 and 1998 with no observable tendency for a reversal. Besides, all candidates with the exception of Finland, France and Luxembourg failed the public debt criterion. The council, however, didn't follow the literal content of the Maastricht Treaty but preferred the "political" interpretation that all candidates (with the exception of Greece) met the criteria. The public deficit criterion was officially met by all candidates (except Greece) but not in all cases on a lasting basis because the causes of the deficits were not sufficiently cured[11]. The latter two points can be seen as a weakness of the system on which the foreign exchange markets are expected to react.

The "1 Euro = 1 ECU" rule of the Madrid Council in 1995 means that the closing rate of the ECU on 31 December 1998 is the opening rate of the Euro on the first market day in 1999. This kind of transition from ECU to Euro leaves no room for policy considerations in order to avoid the influence of accidental factors ("shocks") present on 31 December 1998 to be perpetuated in the Euro on 3 January 1999. As Obstfeld[12] points out, since the currency basket looses its validity in stage 3 and no other numéraire is defined, we have to suppose that the 1:1 rule must be true in any member currency. This implies that the bilateral conversion ratios at the beginning of stage 3 must equal the bilateral market rates at the end of stage 2. When thus "temporary shocks will be frozen forever" increased exchange rate volatility is to be expected whereby stabilising speculation will be discouraged[13].

3. Empirical Results Following Different Measurement Concepts

a) How to identify speculation in reality

It is a well-known problem that what is speculation and what is professional or commercial action is a matter of motives and motives cannot directly be observed. Hence we must construct an artificial distinction between speculative

---

[10] Oesterreichische Nationalbank (1998): Statistische Monatshefte, H. 12, p. 110.
[11] Österreichisches Institut für Wirtschaftsforschung (1998), Monatsberichte, H.4, p. 236.
[12] Obstfeld (1998), p. 981.
[13] ibid., p. 984.

and non-speculative actions. This is an uncomfortable task because we cannot make any judgements on speculation if we have no safe comparison with a situation without speculation. In other words, we very often must be aware that speculation may be omnipresent but we don't know to what extent. If we observe a situation with increasing price volatility one might be tempted to attribute this to speculation. But who can say whether price volatility without speculation would not even be higher? Speculation may be destabilising or stabilising. We speak of destabilising speculation if speculation increases the price volatility or the variance or the standard deviation of a price, and of stabilising speculation in the opposite case. We understand speculation as a purchase of a certain quantity of some speculative commodity (or money or other asset) for the sole purpose of making profits from the later sale of the same quantity of this commodity[14].

In what follows attempts are made to gain some insight into the question of speculative activities by different ways to look at the variances, standard deviations and residuals, respectively.

b) The speculative residual in the covered interest parity

If speculation cannot directly be distinguished from non-speculative foreign exchange transactions one can still try to find an indirect identification. A possible way is to theoretically determine and empirically estimate an exchange rate that would exist without speculation and then compare it with the actual exchange rate. The first attempt is to consider the deviation of the forward exchange rate from the estimated covered interest parity, i.e. the residual of the estimation, as a measure of the influence of speculation. The idea, originating from Canterbery[15], behind this approach is that the covered interest parity is a risk-free and therefore speculation-free solution. In other words, if great deviations of the actual exchange rate from the covered interest parity can be observed there must be considerable speculation in this market. The explanation is that these deviations mean chances for earning money by arbitrage transactions and if such chances are not exploited the supposed reason is the presence of speculation. Otherwise professional exchange dealers would instantly close the gap between the swap rate and the interest parity up to a very small percentage.

The equilibrium condition of the forward exchange market is correctly represented in the regression equation

$$(1)\quad \left(\frac{e^{T3M}}{e}-1\right)_t = \alpha\ (i-i^*)_t + u_t$$

[14] These are the usual assumptions in the speculation literature.

[15] Canterbery (1974), p. 182.

where e^{T3M} = 3 month forward rate, e = spot rate, α = coefficient, i = short term interest rate, * = foreign, t = time index, u = error term. The terms in parentheses are the swap rate on the left-hand side and the interest parity on the right-hand side. The estimation result for the swap rate was[16]:

Example 1

Variable	Coefficient	Std.Error	t-value	PartR²
ZdayDiffD_U	0.0023846	0.00022887	10.419	0.7950

R^2 = 0.79496 \sigma = 0.00411705 DW = 2.20
29 observations

The endogenous variable is the German mark/US-dollar (DEM/USD) swap rate and the only exogenous variable ZdayDiffD_U is the difference of the daily interbank rates of interest of Germany and of the US, respectively. The standard error of the coefficient is less than 10 percent of the latter (t-value more than 10) and therefore significant, the value of sigma is very low, and this estimation explains nearly 80 percent of the variance of the swap rate. The t-value and the low sigma indicate that there is hardly any room left for a speculative residual. The graphical presentation in Figure 1 also shows that the differences between the calculated and the actual values of the swap rate are very small. The conclusion is that, with high probability, there was no remarkable speculation in the transition to the Euro, at least not in the German mark/US-dollar relation.

The same principal idea as in the first estimation can be used in logarithmic form

$$(2)\quad \ln e_t^T = \alpha_0 + \alpha_1 \ln e_t + \alpha_2 (i - i^*)_t + u_t$$

This equation, of course, is neither identical to (1) nor strictly derived from (1), but it permits to follow the same theoretical background, namely that if the forward rate is determined to a very high degree by the elements of covered interest arbitrage such that there is practically no space left for other influences, we can deny the presence of speculation. In the opposite case the existence of speculation would have to be accepted. The estimation, including a constant, gives example 2:

---

16 The econometric estimations (OLS) were carried out with the soft ware of Doornik/Hendry, Give Win (1996) and PcGive 9.0 (1997). The annual and the quarterly data are from OECD Statistical Compendium ed. 01#1998 (CDRom). Monthly data are from Reuters/Siemens, Vienna; day-to-day exchange rates and their end-of-month and end-of-quarter values, respectively, are taken from the Internet service OANDA, Olsen & Associates, Inc.

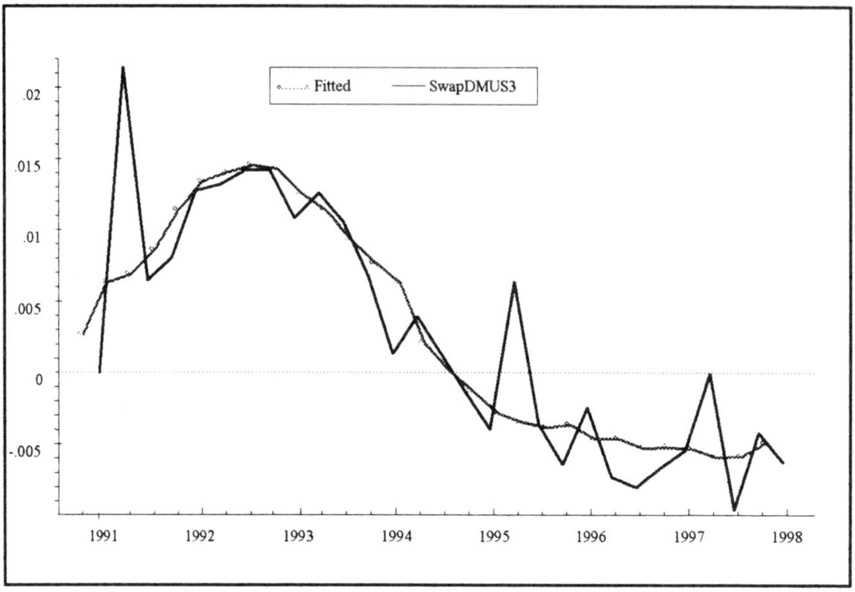

Figure 1
The swap rate estimated as a function of the interest differential.
The figure shows the actual and the calculated swap rate.

Example 2

Variable	Coefficient	Std.Error	t-value	PartR²
LDMUSDK	0.99732	0.010349	96.366	0.9972
ZdayDiffD_U	0.0023423	0.0002548	9.193	0.7647
Constant	0.0015768	0.0047914	0.329	0.0041

$R^2 = 0.997356$ $F(2,26) = 4903.5$ [0.0000] \sigma = 0.00421951 DW = 2.21
29 observations
with LDMUSDK = log of the German mark/US-dollar spot rate

The endogenous variable is the three month German mark/US-dollar forward rate (in logs), the exogenous variables are the corresponding spot rate (DEMUSDK in logs) and the difference of German and US daily interbank interest rates (ZdayDiffD_U). The above regression explains 99.7 percent of the forward rate, the standard errors of the coefficients are very small and small, respectively, corresponding to high t-values. Only the constant is insignificant. The F-test is significant, the sigma is very low, there is no marked autocorrelation of the error terms and the latter are very small. Using the same equation for one three month forecast of the forward rate the forecast error is 1.78298 DEM/USD (forecast forward rate) minus 1.78090 DEM/USD (actual forward rate) which gives a relative forecast error of 0.00168. This, indeed, leaves no space for speculators to earn money.

Since the constant proved insignificant in example 2 the estimation was repeated without a constant term. This furnished the following values:

<u>Example 3</u>

Variable	Coefficient	Std.Error	t-value	PartR²
LDEMUSDK	1.0007	0.0017902	558.962	0.9999
ZdayDiffD_U	0.0023362	0.00024990	9.349	0.7640

$R^2 = 0.999927$ \sigma = 0.00414925 DW = 2.22
29 observations

This result is even better than the previous one. The t-value of the second coefficient is only slightly better, but that of the first coefficient is more than five times the value before. The equation explains nearly 100 percent of the variance, the sigma is very low again, the DW is roughly right, and the residuals are very small. The otherwise nearly incredible partial R^2 value of the coefficient of the spot rate confirms the widespread observation of the very tight connection between spot and forward rate. Using now this equation for a three month forecast one receives a relative forecast error of 0.00149, which is less than one sixth of one percent and it supports the view that speculative activity in the German mark/US-dollar realm is highly improbable for the last decade.

c) The speculative residual after allowance for "fundamentals"

A widely used approach in determining empirically what can be considered as a theoretically correct interpretation of the exchange rate is the monetary theory of the exchange rate. This approach starts from the quantity theory of money with the money demand functions[17]

(3.a) $$\frac{M^d}{P} = \alpha_0 Y^{\alpha_1} e^{\alpha_2 i}$$ (3.b) $$\frac{M^{*d}}{P^*} = \alpha_0 Y^{*\alpha_1} e^{\alpha_2 i^*}$$

[17] See e.g. Gandolfo (1995), p. 394, with different symbols.

with M^d = quantity of real money demand, P = price level, Y = aggregate real income (GDP), α = constant coefficients, * = foreign, e = exp. Equation (3.a) is divided by (3.b), solved for P/P*, and transformed to logs. This gives the theoretical equation

$$(4)\quad \ln P - \ln P^* = -\alpha_2(\ln Y - \ln Y^*) + \alpha_3(i - i^*) + (\ln M - M^*)$$

or, in a simpler notation with lower case letters for logs (except i):

$$(4')\quad p - p^* = (m - m^*) - \alpha_2(y - y^*) + \alpha_3(i - i^*)$$

The above is in the first line a relative price level equation and not necessarily an exchange rate equation. But if we believe in the purchasing power parity (PPP) theory it becomes an exchange rate equation, what means that the exchange rate e (as the price of foreign in terms of home currency) is determined by the relation[18]

$$(5)\quad e = (m - m^*) + \alpha_2(y - y^*) - \alpha_3(i - i^*)$$

The theory leading to equation (5) is still considered as a modern approach, although it is a well-known fact that the PPP theory did not prove very successful as a basis of empirical estimation[19]. As empirical studies during the past twenty years have shown, PPP is established only in the long run and maybe in the very long run, but it is almost always failing in the short run[20]. Despite its plausible basis there are many good reasons[21] why international price relations adapt only very slowly to the long run equilibrium values so that the short run failure of PPP theory is no big surprise[22]. With regard to empirical estimation this means that we cannot expect a very good fit of the right-hand side to the left-hand side of (5). Nevertheless, this approach is presented whenever the theoretical fundamentals of exchange rates are asked for, as it is the case when a theoretically justified, speculation-free value of the exchange rate has to be determined[23]. Besides, the monetary approach, after being transformed to an estimation equation and from an empirical point of view, is not too far from the portfolio approach to the exchange rate insofar as both have the first three right-hand terms in common whereas the

---

[18] This is practically the standard equation of the monetary theory of the exchange rate, see e.g. Levich (1985), p. 1008; Frankel (1983), p. 88; Meese/Rogoff(1983), p. 5; Obstfeld/Stockmann (1985), p. 966 with the additional introduction of tastes.

[19] See, e.g., Frenkel (1981), passim; Rogoff (1996), passim; Taylor (1995), p. 20; Dornbusch (1993), p. 47.

[20] Rogoff (1996), p. 654.

[21] Gandolfo (1995), pp. 379 ff.

[22] In an evaluation of empirical studies Gandolfo (1995), pp. 399 f (also p. 393) pleads for comprehensive macroeconometric models as the only chance to attain superior results.

[23] Kohlhagen (1979), p. 332.

portfolio approach in addition tries to capture some form of risk and the effects of news[24]. In this sense equation (5) was used as a basis of the following estimation.

Example 4

Variable	Coefficient	Std. Error	t-value
LDiffM2DUS	0.030453	0.013119	2.321
LDiffYDUS	-0.29537	0.043343	-6.815
ZdayDiffD_U	0.0089002	0.0039552	2.250

R^2 = 0.982533 \sigma = 0.0642212 DW = 0.937
quarterly data, 30 observations

The endogenous variable is the log of the spot rate; the exogenous variables are LDiffM2D_US for the difference of the logs of the M2 quantities of money (i.e. reserves plus day-to-day deposits plus time deposits) in Germany and in the US, LDiffYD_US for the difference of the logs of the German and the US gross domestic product, ZdayDiffD_U for daily interbank interest differentials as before. The explained percentage of the variance is high, the sigma is low, the signs of the coefficients correspond to the theoretical expectation, the coefficients are significant at the 5%-level. But the first and third t-value are not very satisfactory insofar as the sign is just confirmed but nothing more. Only the coefficient of the relative income variable is satisfactorily high. The DW suggests some autocorrelation of the error terms. The overall result is that a theoretically based estimation has been determined, but that the statistical test values of the equation are not so high as to exclude by themselves other non-theoretical, say speculative influences, notwithstanding that the latter are not confirmed either.

Besides the above equation (which is in a certain sense a kind of "natural product" of theory) many others were tested, especially with regard to different lags, different notions of the quantity of money, interest rates for different terms, and different transformations of the variables. But the results of these attempts were worse[25] – as concerns the signs, the significance and/or the R^2.

Quite a number of other estimations derived from the same theoretical background were run with monthly data, as before with a variety of lags, different definitions of money, different interest rates, and different transformations of the variables. The best result with respect to theory is given below.

[24] Gandolfo (1995), pp. 396 f.

[25] But not generally worse than the results presented by Kohlhagen (1979), p. 334.

Example 5

Variable	Coefficient	Std.Error	t-value
LdiffM1DUS	0.4896	0.01938	2.5263
LDiffYDUS	-0.1137	0.06589	-1.7256
ZDiff1JDUS	0.1032	0.01688	6.1137
Zdiff10JDUS	- 0.2448	0.03415	7.168

$R^2 = 0.996489$ \sigma = 0.0346115 DW = 1.01
26 observations, monthly data, sample 1996 (7) to 1998 (8)

The endogenous variable is again the log of the spot rate; the exogenous variables are LdiffM1DUS for the German/US quantity of money differential (day-to-day money, i.e. M1, in logs), LDiffYDUS for the German/US gross domestic product differential (in logs) as above, ZDiff1JDUS for one year government bond yield differentials and Zdiff10JDUS for 10-year government bond yield differentials between Germany and the US. The R^2 is high, the sigma low, the signs are right, but the significance is a problem. Good t-values for the interest differentials are accompanied by a just sufficient value of the relative money quantities and a just insufficient value for the income differential. Viewed from the original theoretical perspective it is surprising that the interest differentials should have more influence on the price ratio than the income differential. But when we replace the price differential by the exchange rate this may easily be in order. The opposite signs of short-term and long-term bonds are largely in correspondence with theoretical considerations and other empirical work[26]: higher short-term bond yields in Germany (positive sign) cause a devaluation of the German forward mark which works similarly on the German spot mark (positive sign)[27]. Higher long-term yields in Germany (positive sign) cause increasing demand for the German currency and, consequently, its revaluation (negative sign).

A general remark on a principal shortcoming of this approach for the purpose of empirical estimation is in place. From beginning on the solution of the ratio of the home and foreign money market equilibria by the use for the relative home and foreign price levels is - in an empirical understanding - so indirect that it needs a deep trust in this theory[28]. Furthermore, the price level ratio is replaced by

---

[26] See the short outline with Meese/Rogoff (1983), p. 5 and Gandolfo (1995), p. 397.

[27] The explanation for the parallel influence on forward and spot rates is nothing else but the aforementioned widely observed tight connection between these rates.

[28] That is to say, if we trust in the theory of money demand implied above, we have to trust to the same degree in all mathematically correct transformations of the basic equation for the demand of money. But a good econometric performance of the basic equation does not guarantee an equally good econometric performance for all mathematically correct transformations. In other words, it is difficult enough to attain good empirical results for

the (spot) exchange rate, on the basis of another theory with a poor empirical performance. Finally, the statistical qualities of the estimate depend on whether both theories together represent sufficient empirical truth. Consequently, the results leave plenty of room for speculative activities, but simpler explanations are also possible.

d) Judgements by variance

When we say that speculation may increase or decrease the volatility of prices then the question arises whether this is a one-to-one causality so that we can conclude from observed changes in volatility on the presence of speculation. This is not generally true of course, since there can be many non-speculative reasons for any development of volatility. The situation is different if we are able to attribute a certain partition of the variance either to commercial or to speculative transactions. There are no clear guidelines for modelling speculation but as we saw in the last section economic theory offers explanations which determine exchange rates in the absence of speculation, e.g. the monetary theory. Once the theoretical approach, referring to the so-called "fundamental" determinants, is clear, the corresponding theoretical variance can be calculated and compared to the actual variance of the exchange rate, the residual variance being attributed to speculation[29]. The explanation is as follows.

Consider the price equation

$$(6) \quad P_t = \alpha X_t + \beta P_t^e + u_t$$

where P_t is the price variable, X_t a variable (or a set of variables) following from economic theory relating to P_t, P_t^e a variable (or a set of variables) representing the speculative influence on P_t, u_t the error term, α, β coefficients, t = time. Eliminating the influence of speculation (and omitting the subscripts t for matter of simplicity) leads to

$$(7) \quad \ddot{P} = P - \beta P^e = \alpha X + u$$

---

equations (3) but may be much more difficult in the case of equations (4) and (5). To believe in equations (3) means to believe in a certain form of the quantity theory of money. But to believe in equation (5) means to believe in purchasing power parity theory. Empirically this is quite a different question albeit it is mathematically implied already in equations (3).

[29] This is obviously implied in equations (3) and (4) with Kohlhagen (1979), pp. 324 f, who strongly recommends this method: "In order to correctly determine whether or not speculation destabilizes the exchange rate (...), one must show what the rate would have been in the absence of speculation." Ibid., p. 322.

with $\tilde{P}$ as the hypothetical price variable prevailing in the absence of speculation.

The especially interesting thing in this approach and the reason why it was, among other procedures, chosen here, is the circumstance that the variances of P as well as that of $\tilde{P}$ can separately be calculated and compared without knowing anything about the character and specification of speculation[30]. The latter is a critical point. One problem is that in the empirical estimation a very good approximation to the fundamentals is needed first, in order to be sure that the variance of the error term is assigned correctly to the variance of the endogenous variable and that the difference between the variances of the observed and of the calculated endogenous variable does not capture the influence of some, falsely left-out, fundamental variable. However, it is a real surprise that Kohlhagen includes an explicit speculation variable in his own model of the exchange market[31]. Why should we calculate the difference of the variances of the actual and of the speculation-free exchange rate, respectively, if we can directly estimate the influence of speculative activities? Actually, it seems to be just the advantage of variance comparison that it enables us to circumvent the difficult specification of speculation[32]. Another weakness is, though, that this method will nearly always conclude either destabilising or stabilising speculation but only at the very knife edge of matching variances will it state "no speculation".

Assuming independence between the error term and the exogenous variables (covariance = zero) the variance of P and the variance of $\tilde{P}$ can be separated to a sum of the single variances so that the total variance of the price variable consists of the variance of the fundamental determinants, the variance of the speculation term, the variance of the error term and the covariance of the fundamental and the speculation term:

(8) $\sigma_P^2 = \sigma_X^2 + \sigma_{P^e}^2 + \sigma_u^2 + 2\alpha\beta Cov(X, P^e)$

with σ_P^2 = variance of P, $\sigma_{\tilde{P}}^2$ = variance of X, σ_X^2 = variance of X,

$\sigma_{P^e}^2$ = variance of P^e, σ_u^2 = variance of u.

The separate variance of the fundamental term is

(9) $\sigma_{\tilde{P}}^2 = \sigma_X^2 + \sigma_u^2$

---

[30] See footnote 29.

[31] Kohlhagen (1979), p. 333; he also argues in favour of the specification of a speculation term, ibid., pp. 322 f, 331.

[32] Especially the significance of the coefficients of the speculative variable is, with one exception, very low, ibid., p. 334. So, at least in this case, the value of the information content of the speculation term can be questioned.

with $\sigma_{\tilde{P}}$ = variance of $\tilde{P}$. The difference of (9) minus (8)

$$(10)\quad \sigma_P^2 - \sigma_{\tilde{P}}^2 = \sigma_{P^e}^2 + 2\alpha\beta Cov(X, P^e)$$

is applied as a criterion of destabilising speculation in the case of

$$\sigma_P^2 > \sigma_{\tilde{P}}^2$$

or stabilising speculation in the case of

$$\sigma_P^2 < \sigma_{\tilde{P}}^2$$

The σ for the variance of the (unknown) true probability distribution has to be replaced, of course, by the calculated variance S of the sample distribution which is derived by strict analogy with (8), starting from the definition of the (calculated) variance:

$$S_P^2 = \frac{1}{n-1}\sum (P - \bar{P})^2 = \frac{1}{n-1}\sum [\alpha(X - \bar{X}) + \beta(P^e - \bar{P}^e) + u]^2$$

This, after some calculations, gives the exact analogues to equations (8), (9) and (10) with S instead of σ. This concept was applied to the empirical estimations presented in the five examples above, the results being summarised in Table 1.

Table 1

Comparison of the variances of actual and estimated exchange rates
Exchange rate estimates based on fundamental determinants

Example	S_P^2	$S_{\tilde{P}}^2$	$S_P^2 - S_{\tilde{P}}^2$
1	0.000073105	0.000055450	0.000017655
2	0.006330571	0.006466888	- 0.000136316
3	0.00633057	0.00650911	- 0.00017854
4	0.00543269	0.00051000	0.00492269
5	0.00537546	0.00225213	0.00312333

Although in example 1, the estimation of the swap rate in absolute values, the residuals were very small, mostly below one percent and for longer periods not much more than one half percent of the swap rate, the comparison of the variances shows in the fourth column that in principle there may have been some destabilising speculation. However, with a 1 only in the fifth decimal this was so faint that it rather confirms the former view of “no speculation”.

The examples 2 and 3 (calculated in logs) render visible a certain stabilising speculation relating to the forward rate. With a view to the very good fit of the spot rate and the interest parity in the corresponding estimates the speculative

influence can hardly be supposed to have been very strong (little room for a speculative residual), but the differences of the variances show eight to ten times the value of line 1. Therefore the presence of speculation, at least at a low level, cannot be fully denied.

The examples 4 and 5, referring to the estimation of the spot rate on the basis of its fundamental determinants, show differences in the variances of, roughly speaking, 10 to 20 times of the two previous examples and give thereby a remarkable hint on destabilising speculation. In a sense this has to be accepted simply as the result of the method chosen, but some caution is in order because the statistical qualities of the fourth and fifth example are evidently poorer than in the first three examples. This procedure certainly needs further investigation as concerns the method proper.

4. Random Walk Considerations

In empirical forecasting it happens very often that the hypothesis of "no change" does best. This so-called random walk hypothesis showed in many studies such a good performance in exchange rate forecasting that even the question was raised whether better forecasts can be found which are able to earn more money in the exchange market. The answer was after all in the affirmative[33] but only after overcoming considerable difficulties. This was reason enough why the random walk was tried out also in this study.

A constant sequence of 60 monthly exchange rate data, starting from February 1990, was used to estimate a one month forecast of the spot exchange rate, the first forecast for February 1995. Then the sequence of data was shifted one month ahead, now starting in March 1990, to estimate the next forecast for March 1995.

This procedure was repeated up to the last forecast for November 1998. The estimations were carried out for the spot rates of German mark per US-dollar, French franc per US-dollar, Swiss franc per US-dollar, German mark per French franc, German mark per Swiss franc and French franc per Swiss franc.

[33] Gandolfo (1995), pp. 393, 400.

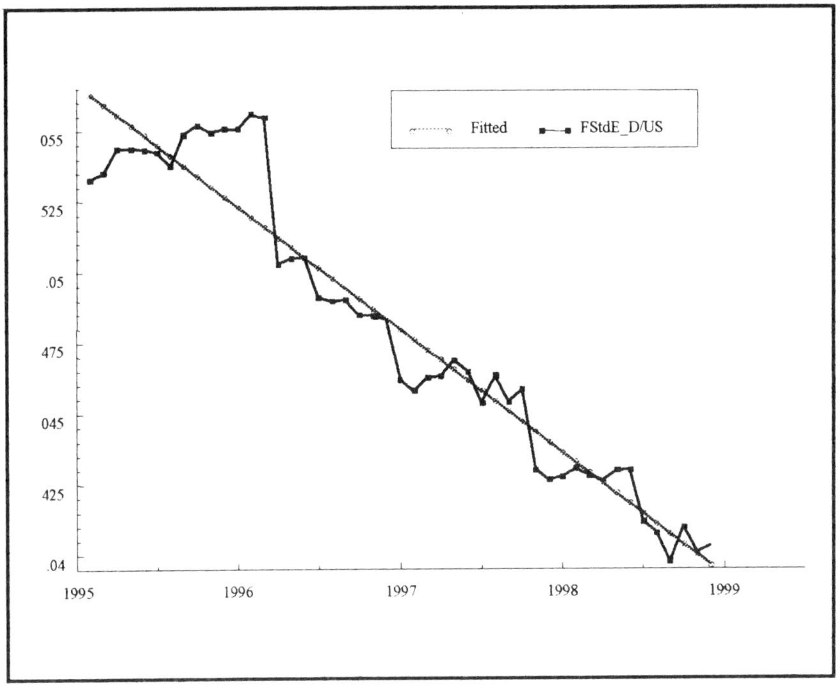

Figure 2
Trend of one-step forecast standard deviations of the DEM/USD spot rate

The actual forecasts as well as the statistical test values were rather good, at least so good that it would very difficult to attain better results with estimations based on the theoretical fundamentals of the exchange rate. But the objective was not to make very good forecasts but to find out whether the statistical output of the forecasts unveils signs of the presence of speculation. Time-dependent changes in the forecast quality would suggest that speculators are at work provided there are no other plausible reasons which can be explained by special developments of the commercial transactions. The behaviour of the forecast standard errors informs on the development of market efficiency. Consequently, using the forecast standard errors of the previous-mentioned random walk forecasts as a new database, simple trend regressions were run for the different currency relations. The results are shown in Table 2 and summarised in Table 3.

As can be seen from Table 2 a negative trend of high significance exists in the forecast standard errors of the DEM/USD and the CHF/USD relations. This means that the efficiency of these exchange markets has increased during the last four years before the transition of the Euro. It suggests that there was stabilising

Table 2
Estimated trends in the forecast standard errors of the random walk forecasts

Exchange rate	Constant	t-value	Trend coefficient	t-value	R^2
DEM/USD	0.078720	60.417	- 0.00036177	-23.899	0.926969
FRF/USD	0.18607	75.242	- 0.000053831	-1.367	0.9816
CHF/USD	0.071117	53.749	- 0.000285510	-18.457	0.885618
DEM/FRF	0.0019534	52.195	0.00000074	0.553	0.00674
DEM/CHF	0.014092	32.358	0.00000049	0.095	0.00021
FRF/CHF	0.0037278	23.912	- 0.000004195	-2.301	0.10744

speculation at work, a bull speculation which need not be carried out only by professional speculators but can be supported also by outright transactions in the framework of commercial trade and, of course, by the banking system. At first sight it is a bit surprising that the principally same development in the FRF/USD relation is so much weaker and after all not significant. This may be due to the

Table 3
Trends in the standard deviations of one-step forecasts of exchange rates

	DEM	FRF	USD	CHF
DEM		no trend	significant negative trend	no trend
FRF			negative trend not significant	Weak negative trend of low significance
USD				Significant negative trend

fact that the Banque de France had so much less time than the German Bundesbank to build up "reputation" , insofar being a matter of long-run trust. Whereas the efficiency of the DEM/CHF was not increased, the Swiss franc shows a similar behaviour as the German mark. The overall result of these estimations is that there certainly was no kind of destabilising speculation in the last years. Otherwise it should have been observable in one of the above currency relations.

5. Conclusions

The transition period to the Euro is an interesting opportunity to study speculation. There are many reasons why foreign exchange speculation could have taken place in this phase, but it is difficult to find out because speculation, as a matter of motives, can only indirectly be observed. Three econometric estimates, based on the relations between forward rates, spot rates and interest parities, indicate that in the forward market actually no room was left for speculative residuals. Two other estimates which used the theoretical ('fundamental') determinants of the spot rate as exogenous variables, i.e. the quantity of money differentials, the income differentials and the interest parity, showed that speculation may have been present - without telling us anything more. This was in principle confirmed by a comparison of the variances, a method which presumably needs further research. It points to stabilising or no speculation, respectively, in forward exchanges and destabilising speculation in the spot exchanges. All this was studied only in the German mark/US-dollar relation, using quarterly data.

Finally, the evaluation of random walk estimations, namely one-step forecasts with a moving set of 45 monthly data in the currency relations among US-dollar, German mark, French franc and Swiss franc (with quite good statistical test values) reveals increasing efficiency of certain foreign exchange markets. The forecast standard errors of the previous estimates exhibit a significant negative trend in the cases of the mark per dollar rate and of the dollar per Swiss franc rate and no increasing trend in the other currency relations. The results support to a certain degree the presence of foreign exchange speculation in the transition period to the Euro, but rather in the form of stabilising speculation whereas destabilising speculation can largely be denied.

References

Bhandari, J. S., Putnam, B. H. (eds.) (1983): Economic Interdependence and Flexible Exchange Rates. MIT, Cambridge (Mass.) - London.

E. R. Canterbery (1974): The Modern Theory of Speculation and the Net Speculative Residual, Southern Economic Journal,

Doornik, J.A., Hendry, D. F. (1996): PcGive Professional 9.0 for Windows, Thomson, London etc.

Doornik, J.A., Hendry, D. F. (1996): Give win, Thomson, London etc.

Dornbusch, R. (1983): Exchange Rate Economics:Where do we stand? In: Bhandari, J. S., Putnam, B. H. (eds.) (1983): Economic Interdependence and Flexible Exchange Rates. MIT, Cambridge (Mass.) - London, pp. 45-83

Frankel, J. A. 81983):Monetary and Portfolio-Balance Models of Exchange rate Determination. In: Bhandari, J. S., Putnam, B. H. (eds.) (1983): Economic Interdependence and Flexible Exchange Rates. MIT, Cambridge (Mass.) - London, pp. 84-115

Frankel, J. A., Rose, A. K. (1995): Empirical Research on Nominal Exchange Rates. In: Grossman, G. M., Rogoff, K. (eds.): Handbook of International Economics, Vol. III, North-Holland, Amsterdam etc., pp. 1689-1729

Frenkel, J. A.(1981): The collapse of Purchasing Power Parities during the 1970's, European Economic Review 16, 145-165

Gandolfo, G. (1995): International Economics II. International Monetary Theory and Open-Economy Macroeconomics, 2nd revised edition, Springer, Berlin etc.

Giovannini, A. (1991): Money demand and monetary control in an integrated European economy. In: Commission of the European Communities. Directorate-General for Economic and financial Affairs (ed.): The Economics of the EMU. Special edition No 1, 93-106

Jones, R. W., Kenen, P. B. (eds.) (1985):Handbook of International Economics, Vol. II, North-Holland, Amsterdam - New York - Oxford

Kohlhagen S. W. (1979): The Identification of Destabilizing Foreign Exchange Speculation, Journal of International Economics 9, 321-340

Krugman, P. R., Obstfeld, M. (1996): International Economics. Theory and Policy, 4th edition, Addison Wesley, Reading (Mass.) etc.

Levich, R. M. (1985): Empirical Studies of Exchange Rates: Price Behavior, Rate Determination and Market Efficiency. In: Jones, R. W., Kenen, P. B. (Eds.): Handbook of International Economics, Vol. II, North-Holland, Amsterdam etc., 979-1040

Meese, R. A., Rogoff, K. (1988): Was it real? The Exchange Rate-Interest Differential Relation over the Modern Floating Rate Period, Journal of Finance 43, 933-948

Olsen & Associates, Inc., Internet service, exchange rates under Web address: http:www.OANDA.com

Obstfeld, M. (1998): A strategy for launching the Euro, European Economic Review 43, 975-1007

Obstfeld, M./Stockman, A. C. (1985): Exchange Rate Dynamics, in: Jones, R. W., Kenen, P. B. (1985), pp. 917-977

OECD Statistical Compendium ed. 01#1998 (CDRom)

Rogoff, K. (1996): The Purchasing Power Parity Puzzle, Journal of Economic Literature 34, 647-668

Taylor, M. (1995): The Economics of Exchange Rates, Journal of Economic Literature 33, 13-47

Weindl, J. (1994): Europäische Gemeinschaft (EU), 2nd revised edition, Oldenbourg, München, Wien

Resolving the Ellsberg Paradox by Assuming that People Evaluate Repetitive Sampling

Hans Schneeweiss

Universität München

Abstract

Ellsberg (1961) designed a decision experiment where most people violated the axioms of rational choice. He asked people to bet on the outcome of certain random events with known and with unknown probabilities. They usually preferred to bet on events with known probabilities. It is shown that this behavior is reasonable and in accordance with the axioms of rational decision making if it is assumed that people consider bets on events that are repeatedly sampled instead of just sampled once.

Key words: Ellsberg's paradox, rational decision making, Sure Thing Principle, subjective probabilities.

1 Introduction

Ellsberg (1961) designed an experiment, where people had to decide between bets on risky lotteries with known probabilities or on uncertain events, where probabilities were not known. They usually preferred to bet on the lottery thereby blatantly violating the rationality axioms of Bayesian decision theory, sometimes also referred to as Subjective Expected Utility (SEU) theory. This behavior has therefore been called a "paradox". The Ellsberg Paradox has since become the paradigm for a new concept in decision theory: ambiguity. Probability statements can be more or less ambiguous depending on how strong an individual believes in the assertion of these probabilities.

Otherwise rational people seem to express a preference for unambiguous probabilities, i.e., for probabilities that are objective and completely known to them. They shrink from ambiguous probabilities, i.e., probabilities that are only of a subjective kind or that are objective but only vaguely known. A typical example would be an urn (I) with red and black balls of an unknown proportion, out of which one ball is to be drawn. If indeed nothing is known about the proportion of red and black balls in the urn, then one might be indifferent of whether to bet on Red or on Black, just as with an urn (II), where the red and the black balls are in equal number and where this proportion is known. So in both cases the indifference between betting on Red or on Black can be regarded as an expression of assigning equal probabilities to both colors. In the second case (urn II), however, the probability of drawing a red ball, say, is objectively given as $\frac{1}{2}$, whereas in the first case (urn I), the objective probability of the same event is unknown and it is only a subjective probability which can be asserted as being $\frac{1}{2}$. It turns out that, although in both cases most people are indifferent when confronted with a choice of betting on Red or on Black, they typically prefer to have the ball drawn from the urn II with known proportion ($\frac{1}{2}$), regardless of whether they bet on Red or on Black. This behavior is well documented by numerous experiments. It was first made public by Ellsberg (1961) and has since been known as the Ellsberg paradox. It is regarded to be paradoxical because in both urns the subjective probabilities for Black and Red are equal and therefore $\frac{1}{2}$ and yet Black I $\succ$ Black II and at the same time Red I $\succ$ Red II. (Here $\succ$ means "is strictly preferred to"and "Black I" denotes the bet on the event of a black ball being drawn if the ball is drawn from urn I).

Ellsberg also designed another experiment with only one urn but with balls of three different colors, where the nature of the paradox can be studied more closely. We shall analyze this situation in the next section.

The findings of Ellsberg have been verified in a large number of similar betting experiments and many suggestions have been proposed for understanding the apparent paradox. One can, of course, simply ignore the problem and discard the observed behavior as being irrational and not worth any further study. But as the observed behavior in the Ellsberg experiment is rather persistent and therefore can hardly be dismissed on the basis of being irrational, an explanation for it is called for, in particular as this kind of behavior is probably prevalent in many practical decisions, e.g., in economics or in business, see, e.g., Sarin and Weber (1993).

The central trait of the observed behavior seems to be that most people shrink from uncertain events the objective probabilities of which are unknown or only vaguely known. Betting on an event with known objective probability, like Red II, is preferred to betting on an event with the same subjective probability, which however is not substantiated by an objective probability and is therefore ambiguous, like Red I. Ambiguity is a quality attached to probability assertions. A person may assign a probability to some event, but may be more or less certain about the value of this probability. It is questionable whether a measure of ambiguity adequate for all kinds of uncertain circumstances can be found, but as a concept to describe situations as in Ellsberg's experiment it is worth studying.

Attempts have been made to model the behavior of the majority of people in Ellsberg's experiment and to study the conditions under which ambiguity is perceived by individuals in decisions under uncertainty. For a recent survey see Camerer and Weber (1992), see also Keppe and Weber (1995) and Eisenberger and Weber (1995). A famous axiomatic approach that results in a subjective expected utility theory with probabilities replaced by capacities has been proposed by Gilboa (1987), see also Schmeidler (1989). For a recent further development of this approach, where objective probabilities are incorporated in the theory, see Eichberger and Kelsey (1989). For an empirical test see Mangelsdorff and Weber (1994). Recently a different criterion for decision making in the face of uncertainty governed by interval probabilities was proposed by Weichselberger and Augustin (1998). Schneeweiß (1968, 1973) tried to explain Ellsberg's paradox by embedding Ellsberg's experiments in a game theoretic framework.

Here a different approach is chosen. I shall argue that the typical behavior of people in the Ellsberg experiment can be explained by assuming that they consider (subconsciously) the act of drawing a ball from an urn as a repetitive act, despite the fact that they are told the ball will be drawn only once. In evaluating the possible gains and losses from participating in a lottery, people imagine the lottery to be played several times and consider the average amount they might gain or lose. For a lottery (or urn) with known probabilities of gains or losses this average amount is rather certain due to the law of large numbers. But if the probabilities are unknown, the result of repeated lottery draws will also be unknown no matter how many repetitions are considered. When confronted with a choice between urn I with unknown probability and urn II with known probability $\frac{1}{2}$ of drawing a red ball, a person might assign the same subjective probability $\frac{1}{2}$ to Red for both urns as long as one draw is considered. But if that person (perhaps only subconsciously) imagines repeated draws from the urn she chooses and if she is risk averse, then she will choose urn II because it is with this urn only that the average gain of repeated draws will be rather certain, whereas the uncertainty of gains from repeated draws out of urn I will remain uncertain.

The paper will analyze the distribution of gains under repeated draws in Ellsberg's experiment and will show that risk averse people will always prefer the less ambiguous situation, in complete accordance with the axioms of rational choice and thus in accordance with Bayesian decision theory. In the next section the Ellsberg paradox is reviewed in a setting somewhat different from what was described above. Section 3 gives the main argument how to evaluate the result of repeated draws and why less ambiguous events are preferred to more ambiguous ones even if their (subjective) probabilities do not differ. Section 4 contains some concluding remarks.

2 The Ellsberg paradox

The Ellsberg experiment (or rather one of two suggested experiments) consists in bets on the outcome of a single draw from an urn which contains 30 red balls and 60 black or yellow balls in an unknown proportion. A person is given a choice to bet on the outcome of the draw to be Red or to be Black and another choice to bet on whether the outcome will be Red or Yellow or whether it will be Black or Yellow. In each case the person wins 1 Euro if the color he bets upon does indeed show up; otherwise nothing is gained or lost. This decision situation is depicted in the following diagram (Table 1), which shows the payoff function depending on the color of the ball and on the betting act chosen. When asked to choose between bets R or B, most people

Table 1: Payoffs in Ellberg's experiment

Number of balls		30	60	
Bet on	Symbol	Red	Black	Yellow
Red	R	1	0	0
Black	B	0	1	0
Red or Yellow	$R \vee Y$	1	0	1
Black or Yellow	$B \vee Y$	0	1	1

decide for R. When the same people are then asked to choose between $R \vee Y$ or $B \vee Y$, they typically decide for $B \vee Y$. Only few people would choose $R \vee Y$. Some people decide for B in the first decision problem and for $R \vee Y$ in the second problem.

Let us discuss the choice of the first group, the majority of people. (The arguments for the last group are completely analogous.) First one might think that, since nothing is known about the proportion of black and yellow balls, a person should assume, owing to the principle of insufficient reason, that Black and Yellow are equally likely to show up. Not that the person thinks both colors to be in equal proportion in the urn, he only bases his decision on the (implicit) assumption that the proportion is 30:30. Perhaps a better description of this attitude would be to say that the decision is made *as if* the proportion of black and yellow balls were equal, or more technically: the subjective probabilities of Black and Yellow are equal for this person.

For, given that nothing is known about the way the balls were put into the urn, why should there be a higher subjective probability for a black ball to be drawn than for a yellow ball? If someone follows this argument, then he will be indifferent between R and B in the first problem and between $R \vee Y$ and $B \vee Y$ in the second problem. In symbols: $R \sim B$ and $R \vee Y \sim B \vee Y$, because $P(R) = P(B) = \frac{1}{3}$ and $P(R \vee Y) = P(B \vee Y) = \frac{2}{3}$, P being a subjective probability. This, however, is not what is observed as the actual behavior of most people.

One can argue against this reasoning that it assumes at the outset the existence of subjective probabilities. This assumption is indeed what Bayesian decision analysis is based upon. There are strong arguments for making this assumption. For a recent information based argument see Ferschl (1998). Moreover one can prove the existence of subjective probabilities for any "rational" decision maker from certain axioms of consistent (rational) choices between acts with uncertain outcome, Savage (1954). These axioms do not necessarily imply that $P(B) = P(Y)$. This follows only if in addition to the axioms of rational choice the principle of insufficient reason is taken as an extra assumption. But even without this additional principle, the observed behavior of individuals in the Ellsberg experiment stands in contrast to the Bayesian decision rule.

Suppose the decision maker, as a Bayesian, attaches subjective, not necessarily equal, probabilities to the events of drawing a ball with a specific color and suppose he has a Neumann-Morgenstern utility function $u(.)$, where we can take, without loss of generality, $u(1) = 1$ and $u(0) = 0$. Then the expected subjective utilities of the four acts of the Ellsberg experiment are just the subjective probabilities of the events betted upon. Thus if R is preferred to B ($R \succ B$), then $P(R) > P(B)$, which implies $P(R) + P(Y) > P(B) + P(Y)$, and this again implies $R \vee Y \succ B \vee Y$. These preferences, which follow naturally from a Bayesian decision framework are, however, contradicted by the observed behavior of people that instead prefer $B \vee Y$ to $R \vee Y$. (The same contradiction arises for those people — the minority — for which $B \succ R$ and $R \vee Y \succ B \vee Y$; only the very few with $R \succ B$ and $R \vee Y \succ B \vee Y$ have preferences in accordance with Bayesian decision theory.)

The conclusion of the Ellsberg experiment then is that most people, contrary to what Bayesians say, do not base their decision on subjective probabilities. This is seen as a paradox. Against this one may argue that it is a paradox only to Bayesians, that is, only to those that believe in subjective probabilities. But the paradox goes deeper.

The observed conjunction of preferences $R \succ B$ and $B \vee Y \succ R \vee Y$ is paradoxical in that it violates the Sure Thing Principle, Savage (1954). The preference of R to B in the first problem should not change if one gets 1 Euro not only for the color betted upon but also in case yellow turns up regardless of whether one betted on Red or on Black. Note that this 1 Euro is not an additional amount that you might get in addition to the prize of 1 Euro for betting on the right color. You get the extra prize only if you would have lost both of the two bets R and B, whatever your actual bet was; consult Table 1. It is a kind of consolation prize that you get if neither a red nor a black ball is drawn, and this consolation prize should not interfere with your decision whether to bet on Red or on Black. Thus $R \succ B$ should imply $R \vee Y \succ B \vee Y$. The fact that most people, in their behavior, seem to contradict this (almost logical) implication is seen to be paradoxical, at least by those that see the Sure Thing Principle as a self-evident principle of decision making. Note that this argument does not make use of any probability assertions; it does not even use the concept of probability.

3 Repetitive draws

The situation described in Section 2 changes dramatically if instead of having just one draw from the urn several independent draws are considered. After a bet has been made, a ball is drawn from the urn n times with replacements. Each time the color betted upon shows up, the amount of 1 Euro is payed to the decision maker. Let X be the average gain , i.e., the amount gained after n repeated draws divided by n. Then $nX \sim Bin(n, P(C))$, where Bin stands for the binomial distribution and $P(C)$ is the probability of drawing a ball with color C in a single draw. When C is Black or Yellow, this probability depends, in an obvious way, on the proportion p of black balls within the set of black and yellow balls, i.e., the number of black balls divided by 60.

We assume that the betting acts are decided upon by a "rational" person. This means that the decisions of this person are governed by a subjective probability distribution. But now the sample space consists not of the three colors, but rather of the various outcomes of n repeated draws. A convenient way to model probabilities for these outcomes is to assign a subjective probability to the proportion p of black balls and then to compute, in the usual way, conditional objective probabilities for the outcomes of n draws conditional on p. As we are only interested in the average gain X, we may use the conditional probability distribution of X given p: $f(x|p)$. This procedure is based on the obvious assumption that the subjective probability of an event coincides with its objective probability if the latter exists and is known to the decision maker. So the only truly subjective probability distribution is the one for p. Let its distribution function be denoted by $F(p)$. Any "rational" decision maker has a distribution $F(p)$, which is independent of the betting act chosen. The unconditional distribution of X is then given by

$$f(x) = \int f(x|p)dF(p).$$

In particular the distribution of X for the four betting acts is given by the following expressions for $P(X = x)$, $nx = 0, \ldots, n$:

$$\begin{aligned}
R &: \binom{n}{nx}\left(\frac{1}{3}\right)^{nx}\left(\frac{2}{3}\right)^{n(1-x)} \\
B &: \binom{n}{nx}\int_0^1\left(\frac{2}{3}p\right)^{nx}\left(1-\frac{2}{3}p\right)^{n(1-x)} dF(p) \\
R\vee Y &: \binom{n}{nx}\int_0^1\left(1-\frac{2}{3}p\right)^{nx}\left(\frac{2}{3}p\right)^{n(1-x)} dF(p) \\
B\vee Y &: \binom{n}{nx}\left(\frac{2}{3}\right)^{nx}\left(\frac{1}{3}\right)^{n(1-x)}
\end{aligned}$$

A "rational" person following SEU theory bases his decisions on a Neumann-Morgenstern utility function $u(X)$, which in our case should be increasing. That act is preferred for which the expected utility $E\{u(X)\}$ is largest. For a risk averse person the utility function $u(.)$ is concave. We assume, for simplicity, that $u(.)$ is quadratic. The results should, however, hold true also for more general concave utility functions. For a quadratic utility function, $E\{u(X)\}$ is a function of $\mu = E(X)$ and $\sigma^2 = V(X)$. If $u(.)$ is chosen so that $u(0) = 0$ and $u(1) = 1$ and is taken to be increasing for $x \leq 1$, then $u(x) = (a+1)x - ax^2$, $0 < a < 1$, and for any random variable X with range $[0, 1]$, $E\{u(X)\}$ is increasing in μ and decreasing in σ^2. The parameters μ and σ^2 can be easily computed for the four betting acts, see Table 2. We indicate their derivation for the betting act B. We have

$$\begin{aligned}
\mu &= E\{E(X|p)\} = E\left(\frac{2}{3}p\right) = \frac{2}{3}E(p), \\
\sigma^2 &= E\{V(X|p)\} + V\{E(X|p)\} \\
&= E\left\{\frac{2}{3}p\left(1-\frac{2}{3}p\right)\frac{1}{n}\right\} + V\left(\frac{2}{3}p\right) \\
&= \frac{2}{3n}\left\{E(p) - \frac{2}{3}E(p^2)\right\} + \frac{4}{9}V(p).
\end{aligned}$$

Table 2: Mean and variance of average gain X

betting act	μ	σ^2	$\lim_{n\to\infty}\sigma^2$
R	$\frac{1}{3}$	$\frac{2}{9n}$	0
B	$\frac{2}{3}E(p)$	$\frac{2}{3n}M(p)+\frac{4}{9}V(p)$	$\frac{4}{9}V(p)$
$R\vee Y$	$1-\frac{2}{3}E(p)$	$\frac{2}{3n}M(p)+\frac{4}{9}V(p)$	$\frac{4}{9}V(p)$
$B\vee Y$	$\frac{2}{3}$	$\frac{2}{9n}$	0

$$M(p) = E(p) - \tfrac{2}{3}E(p^2)$$

The preferences between bets are determined by the value of

$$E\{u(X)\} = (a+1)\mu - a(\mu^2+\sigma^2),$$

where $0 < a < 1$ and $0 \leq \mu \leq 1$.

For $n = 1$, μ is the probability of the bet to come true, and $E\{u(X)\} = \mu$. This means that of two bets that one is preferred which has the higher probability of coming true. Therefore $R \succ B$ implies $R\vee Y \succ B\vee Y$ as shown in Section 2. This is the betting behavior of a "rational" person if only one draw is considered.

Let us return to repeated draws. If n becomes large then σ^2 will be negligible for the unambiguous bets R and $B\vee Y$, but will be large and will not go to zero for the ambiguous bets B and $R\vee Y$, see the last column of Table 2. Thus one may expect a tendency in each of the two comparisons to prefer the unambiguous bet to the ambiguous one, i.e., $R \succ B$ and $B\vee Y \succ R\vee Y$. Of course, whether this will, in fact, be true depends on the probability distribution of p, in particular, on $E(p)$ and $V(p)$.

To illustrate, let us suppose that the decision maker has a symmetric distribution $F(p)$, so that $E(p) = \frac{1}{2}$. For $n \to \infty$ the expected utilities of the four bets become as in Table 3.

From Table 3 it is obvious that, for any values of a and $V(p)$, $R \succ B$ and at the same time $B\vee Y \succ R\vee Y$. These are exactly the preferences observed for the majority of participants in Ellsberg's experiment. They follow from Bayesian arguments and are therefore the preferences of a "rational" per-

Table 3: Expected utilities

$R:$	$\frac{1}{3}+\frac{2}{9}a$	$B:$	$\frac{1}{3}+\frac{2}{9}a-\frac{4}{9}aV(p)$
$B\vee Y:$	$\frac{2}{3}+\frac{2}{9}a$	$R\vee Y:$	$\frac{2}{3}+\frac{2}{9}a-\frac{4}{9}aV(p)$

son. It is however a person that determines his preferences from viewing the drawing of balls as being repeated an indefinite number of times.

One can generalize this result by allowing the number of red balls to vary. Let r be the ratio of red balls in the urn, which is supposed to be known to the decision maker. In Ellsberg's original experiment $r=\frac{1}{3}$. A simple computation, analogous to the previous one, leads to the expected utilities (for $n\to\infty$) of Table 4, where we assumed a symmetric distribution for p, as before. Noting that $0\le V(p)\le\frac{1}{4}$, it is easy to see, by letting r

Table 4: Expected utilities with general r

$R:$	$r+ar(1-r)$	$B:$	$\frac{1}{2}(1-r)(1+\frac{a}{2}+\frac{a}{2}r)$
			$-a(1-r)^2V(p)$
$B\vee Y:$	$(1-r)(1+ar)$	$R\vee Y:$	$\frac{1}{2}(1+r)(1+\frac{a}{2}-\frac{a}{2}r)$
			$-a(1-r)^2V(p)$

go to zero, that $B\succ R$ and $B\vee Y\succ R\vee Y$ for sufficiently small r, where the point of switching from $R\succ B$ to $B\succ R$ depends on the subjectively perceived amount of risk, $V(p)$, and on the measure of aversion of risk, a. Such a switching strategy has actually been postulated by Ellsberg himself. Note that under a minimax criterion no switching of the kind described is allowed to take place.

Similar arguments lead to analogous conclusions for Ellsberg's first experiment described in the Introduction. Let p be the proportion of black balls in urn I and let, as before, X be the average gain of n repeated independent draws from the urn chosen and for the color betted upon. Then mean and variance of X are determined as in Table 5, corresponding to Table 2. For $n=1$, $E\{u(X)\}=\mu$, which is just the probability of winning the bet. It follows , for a "rational" person, that $R\,II\succ R\,I$ implies $B\,I\succ B\,II$, which, however, typically is not observed. On the other hand, for n large

Table 5: Mean and variance of X in Ellsberg's first experiment

betting act	μ	σ^2	$\lim_{n\to\infty}\sigma^2$
$R\ II$	$\frac{1}{2}$	$\frac{1}{4n}$	0
$R\ I$	$1 - E(p)$	$\frac{1}{n}E\{p(1-p)\} + V(p)$	$V(p)$
$B\ I$	$E(p)$	$\frac{1}{n}E\{p(1-p)\} + V(p)$	$V(p)$
$B\ II$	$\frac{1}{2}$	$\frac{1}{4n}$	0

$(n \to \infty)$ and assuming $E(p) = \frac{1}{2}$, the expected utilities for $R\ II$ and $B\ II$ are both $\frac{1}{2} - \frac{a}{4}$ and for $R\ I$ and $B\ I$ they are $\frac{1}{2} - \frac{a}{4} - aV(p)$. It follows that a "rational" person will have preferences $R\ II \succ R\ I$ and at the same time $B\ II \succ B\ I$, which corresponds to the behavior of the majority of people in Ellsberg's experiment.

4 Conclusion

We can explain Ellsberg's paradox by assuming that people, subconsciously and erroneously, evaluate the possible outcomes of the experiment as if the draws from the urn were repeated an indifferent number of times. They are assumed to have a concave (possibly quadratic) utility function and a subjective probability distribution over the unknown "states of the world", which in this case are the unknown values of the proportion of balls in the urn. They then "compute" the subjective expected utility of the average gain from a bet on a particular color and choose the bet with the biggest expected utility. In doing so, they are in accordance with Bayesian SEU as well as with the actual behavior observed in Ellsberg's experiment. It turns out that ambiguity aversion is nothing but risk aversion in a SEU framework.

I must admit, though, that this explanation replaces one contradiction of rational decision theory with another one. In the original interpretation, where people are supposed to fully understand the experimental set up, which is that indeed just one ball is to be drawn, their behavior is in conflict with the Sure Thing Principle and so they are seen to behave irrationally. In the interpretation proposed in this paper, their behavior is irrational in that they misconceive the important, albeit a bit artificial, trait of the experiment that only one draw is to be executed. In the first interpretation people show ambiguity aversion in the second they show risk aversion.

Is there a "rational" explanation why people in a situation like Ellsberg's experiment intuitively think of repeated draws even though they are told that only one draw will be executed? I should like to argue that in practical decision situations under uncertainty the repetitive element is prevalent.

Consider an entrepreneur who wants to invest in an enterprise with uncertain profits. Suppose the entrepreneur can buy shares of a firm that for a long time in the past showed varying yearly profits with constant mean and variance and that will supposedly continue with that performance in the future. To be more specific, yearly profits of that firm are *i.i.d.* $N(\mu_1, \sigma_1^2)$ with known μ_1 and σ_1^2. Now suppose there is another possibility for investment. The entrepreneur can invest in a newly founded firm, which will have a rather constant, hardly varying stream of yearly profits π, the amount of which however is unknown. Let us, for the sake of simplicity, assume that π is constant (but unknown). Depending on the future development of the market the firm has business in, π can turn out to be high or low, but whatever value it will have in the future, this value will stay constant.

If the entrepreneur is a "rational" decision maker in the Bayesian sense , he will assign a probability distribution to π. Suppose $\pi \sim N(\mu_2, \sigma_2^2)$, where it so happens that the mean of this subjective distribution is the same as the mean of the objective distribution in the first case: $\mu_2 = \mu_1$, but where $\sigma_2^2 < \sigma_1^2$. If variances were also equal the two investments would only differ in their ambiguity, the first one being unambiguous, the second one being very ambiguous. Now if the entrepreneur invested his money just to receive a profit after one year and then went out of business, he would prefer the uncertain second alternative to the first one because the second alternative has the lower variance and both have equal means for the profit of this one year. However such a situation is rather unrealistic. An entrepreneur cannot so easily quit his engagement, especially not in the second case. If profits π turn out to be low, he will, of course, come to know this very soon, in fact after one year, but so will everybody else. So he will be able to disengage from his investment only with a loss of money. Therefore the entrepreneur has to consider not just the profit of one year but rather the whole stream of profits over the years. He might wish to evaluate an average profit (or rather an average of discounted profits, a case, where we could argue in a similar, but more complicated, way and that we shall not follow up here). In doing so he will most probably prefer the first investment even though it has the higher variance (the means being equal). The reason is that for the average profit the variance in the first investment goes to zero if the number of years increases but remains positive and constant for the second investment no matter how many years the investor takes into account. What looks as a case of ambiguity aversion actually is risk aversion.

As this kind of situation seems to arise quite often in practice, we should not be surprised to discover that people behave in Ellsberg's experiment as if they considered not just one draw but several draws and thus come to a conclusion which seems to contradict the axioms of rationality but is in fact in accordance with these axioms if seen from the perspective of a long term investment.

Acknowledgement

I thank Thomas Augustin for some helpful comments on an earlier draft of the paper.

References

[1] Camerer, Colin and Martin Weber (1992). Recent developments in modelling preferences: Uncertainty and ambiguity. *Journal of Risk and Uncertainty* 5, 325 – 370.

[2] Eichberger, Jürgen and David Kelsey (1999). E-Capacities and the Ellsberg paradox. Forthcoming in *Theory and Decision*.

[3] Eisenberger, Roselies and Martin Weber (1995). Willingness-to-pay and willingness-to-accept for risky and ambiguous lotteries. *Journal of Risk and Uncertainty* 10, 223 – 233.

[4] Ellsberg, D. (1961). Risk, ambiguity, and the Savage axioms. *Quarterly Journal of Economics* 75, 643 – 669.

[5] Ferschl, Franz (1998). Information value as a metacriterion for decision rules under strict uncertainty. In Küchenhoff, H., Galata R., editors, *Econometrics in Theory and Practice (Festschrift for Hans Schneeweiß)*. Physica, Heidelberg, 279 – 289.

[6] Gilboa, I. (1987). Expected utility theory with purely subjective non-additive probabilities. *Journal of Mathematical Economics* 16, 65 – 88.

[7] Keppe, Hans -Jürgen and Martin Weber (1995). Judged knowledge and ambiguity aversion. *Theory and Decision* 39, 51 – 77.

[8] Mangelsdorff, Lucas and Martin Weber (1994). Testing Choquet expected utility. *Journal of Econometric Behavior and Organization* 25, 437 – 457.

[9] Sarin, Rakesh K. and Martin Weber (1993). Effects of ambiguity in market experiments. *Management Science* 39, 602 – 615.

[10] Savage, L. J. (1954). *The Foundations of Statistics.* Wiley, New York.

[11] Schmeidler, D. (1989). Subjective probability and expected utility without additivity. *Econometrica* 57, 571 – 587.

[12] Schneeweiß, Hans (1968). Spieltheoretische Analyse des Ellsberg-Paradoxons. *Zeitschrift für die gesamte Staatswissenschaft* 124, 249 – 255.

[13] Schneeweiss, Hans (1973). The Ellsberg paradox from the point of view of game theory. *Inference and Decision* 1, 65 – 78.

[14] Weichselberger, Kurt and Thomas Augustin (1998). Analysing Ellsberg's paradox by means of interval-probability. In Küchenhoff, H., Galata, R., editors, *Econometrics in Theory and Practice (Festschrift for Hans Schneeweiß).* Physica, Heidelberg, 291 – 304.

Part 2:

Statistics and Econometrics

Maximum Likelihood Estimation for the VAR-VARCH Model: A New Approach

Shuangzhe Liu and Wolfgang Polasek

Institute of Statistics and Econometrics
University of Basel

Abstract

We consider a general multivariate conditional heteroskedastic time series model and derive the information matrix of the maximum likelihood estimator by using the matrix differential calculus techniques of Magnus and Neudecker (1991). We discuss the VAR-VARCH model as a special case, and demonstrate the maximum likelihood estimation of the information matrix in an example with simulated data.

Key words: VAR-VARCH model; volatile time series; maximum likelihood; information matrix; matrix differential calculus.

Introduction

Since Engle (1982) and Bollerslev (1986) the literature on ARCH (autoregressive conditional heteroskedastic) and GARCH (generalized ARCH) models has been growing rapidly. Applications in economics and finance for volatile time series can be found in, e.g. Bollerslev, Chou and Kroner (1992), Mills (1993), Bera and Higgins (1995) and Palm (1996). We refer to Engle and Kroner (1995) for alternative multivariate generalized ARCH models, Geweke (1989) for Bayesian studies on ARCH and generalized ARCH models, Polasek and Kozumi (1996) for a Bayesian approach treating a VAR-VARCH model (vector autoregressive model with ARCH errors) in the random coefficient framework.

Wong and Li (1997) generalizes the so-called CHARMA (conditional heteroskedastic autoregressive moving-average) model in the univariate case of Tsay (1987). For the multivariate CHARMA model, Wong and Li (1997) uses the so-called star product, see, e.g. MacRae (1974) and Roger (1980), to derive the information matrix for maximum likelihood estimation. The star product is introduced and used for the chain rule in matrix differential calculus. But its application to deriving and presenting results can be complicated in some situations. We notice that when using the standard concept and techniques of *matrix differential* in, e.g. Magnus (1988) or Magnus and Neudecker (1991) it is advantageous to implement the chain rule in good notations and to make calculations shorter and more efficient. See also e.g. Liu (1995) for recent results and applications in econometrics. In the present paper, we will use the standard techniques to study a general multivariate time series model, which is parameterized by only conditional mean and conditional variance and which contains the CHARMA model and the VAR-VARCH model as special cases. As we will see, the analysis of the model is not only shorter and more general, but it will also reveal that the information matrix of the CHARMA model in Wong and Li (1997) misses some terms and therefore is not correct.

The plan of this paper is as follows: In Section 2, we outline the normal log-likelihood function and the maximum likelihood estimation procedure and present the information matrix. In Section 3, we analyze the VAR-VARCH model in a special case and give the associated version of the information matrix. In Section 4, we discuss a numerical example with simulated data. In Section 5, we summarize the paper with some final remarks. In the appendix, the derivation of the information matrix can be found.

Maximum likelihood estimation for heteroskedastic time series

Consider a general multivariate conditional heteroskedastic time series model of the following form

$$y_t = \mu_t + u_t, \quad t = 1, ..., T, \tag{1}$$

where u_t is an $M \times 1$ disturbance vector, y_t is a vector of time series of dimension M, i.e., a realization of an independently and identically normally distributed stochastic process which is characterized by both the $M \times 1$ conditional mean vector $E(y_t \mid \psi_{t-1}) = \mu_t$ and $M \times M$ conditional variance matrix $Var(y_t \mid \psi_{t-1}) = H_t$, where ψ_{t-1} indicates the realized values of the conditional information set, μ_t is an $M \times 1$ vector and H_t is an $M \times M$ positive definite matrix.

In model (1), we assume that u_t has a normal distribution with conditional mean vector $E(u_t \mid \psi_{t-1}) = 0$ and conditional variance matrix $E(u_t u_t' \mid \psi_{t-1}) = H_t$. Furthermore, let θ be a $p \times 1$ vector of parameters of interest and assume that $\mu_t = \mu_t(\theta)$ and $H_t = H_t(\theta)$ are functions of θ, $t = 1, ..., T$. The relevant part (kernel) of the log-likelihood function is

$$\begin{aligned} L(y, \theta) &= \sum_{t=1}^{T} L_t(y_t, \theta) \\ &= -\frac{1}{2}\sum_{t=1}^{T} \log \mid H_t \mid -\frac{1}{2}\sum_{t=1}^{T}(y_t - \mu_t)' H_t^{-1}(y_t - \mu_t). \end{aligned} \tag{2}$$

In order to understand the new approach presented in this paper to deriving the representation of the information matrix $I(\theta)$ in terms of μ_t and H_t, $t = 1, ..., T$, we first review the four step approach of Wong and Li (1997) as follows:

Step 1: Derive the derivative of the log-likelihood function $L(y, \theta)$ with respect to θ defined as

$$f(y, \theta) = \frac{\partial L(y, \theta)}{\partial \theta'},$$

where θ is a $p \times 1$ vector and $f(y, \theta)$ is a $1 \times p$ vector.

Step 2: Derive the expectation of $f(y, \theta)$ with respect to y and evaluate it at the point $\theta = \tilde{\theta}$ to get

$$g(\tilde{\theta}, \theta) = Ef(y, \theta \mid \tilde{\theta}),$$

where E denotes the expectation taken with respect to the normal distribution, $\tilde{\theta}$ is an auxiliary parameter vector of order $p \times 1$ and $g(\tilde{\theta}, \theta)$ is a scalar function of both $\tilde{\theta}$ and θ.

Step 3: Calculate the derivative of $g(\tilde{\theta}, \theta)$ with respect to $\tilde{\theta}$

$$s(\tilde{\theta}, \theta) = \frac{\partial g(\tilde{\theta}, \theta)}{\partial \tilde{\theta}'},$$

which is a $p \times p$ matrix with each element being a scalar function of both $\tilde{\theta}$ and θ.

Step 4: Evaluate $s(\tilde{\theta}, \theta)$ at the point $\tilde{\theta} = \theta$ to establish the information matrix

$$I(\theta) = s(\tilde{\theta}, \theta)|_{\tilde{\theta} = \theta}, \tag{3}$$

which is of order $p \times p$ and a matrix function of the parameter θ.

This approach depends on derivative evaluation. In contrast, we propose a second order differential approach based on the standard matrix differential calculus techniques in Magnus and Neudecker (1991) to derive the information matrix $I(\theta)$ in the following way:

Step 1: Consider the first order differential of $L_t = L_t(y_t, \theta)$, $t = 1, ..., T$, with respect to θ as

$$F_t(y_t, \theta) = d_\theta L_t,$$

where θ is a $p \times 1$ vector.

Step 2: Calculate the expectation of $F_t(y_t, \theta)$ with respect to y and evaluate it at $\theta = \tilde{\theta}$ to get

$$G_t(\tilde{\theta}, \theta) = E[F_t(y_t, \theta|\tilde{\theta})],$$

where $\tilde{\theta}$ is a $p \times 1$ auxiliary parameter vector and $G_t(\tilde{\theta}, \theta)$ is a scalar function of both $\tilde{\theta}$ and θ.

Step 3: Derive the differential as $G_t(\tilde{\theta}, \theta)$ with respect to $\tilde{\theta}$ by

$$S_t(\tilde{\theta}, \theta) = d_{\tilde{\theta}} G_t(\tilde{\theta}, \theta).$$

Step 4: Evaluate $S_t(\tilde{\theta}, \theta)$ at $\tilde{\theta} = \theta$ and use the equation

$$\sum_{t=1}^{T} S_t(\tilde{\theta}, \theta)|_{\tilde{\theta}=\theta} = (d\theta)' I(\theta) d\theta \tag{4}$$

which corresponds to the second order differential of $L(y, \theta)$, to obtain finally the representation of the $p \times p$ information matrix $I(\theta)$.

Now we present the main result for the information matrix of the maximum likelihood estimator for model (1) as follows:

Theorem 1: The information matrix of the maximum likelihood estimator is given by

$$\begin{aligned} I(\theta) &= \frac{1}{2}\sum_{t=1}^{T}\left(\frac{\partial \mathrm{vech} H_t}{\partial \theta'}\right)' D'(H_t^{-1} \otimes H_t^{-1}) D \frac{\partial \mathrm{vech} H_t}{\partial \theta'} \\ &\quad + \sum_{t=1}^{T} (d\theta)' \left(\frac{\partial \mu_t}{\partial \theta'}\right)' H_t^{-1} \frac{\partial \mu_t}{\partial \theta'} d\theta, \end{aligned} \tag{5}$$

where vech denotes the vectorization operator which eliminates all supradiagonal elements of the matrix and $\text{vech}H_t$ is an $M(M+1)/2\times 1$ vector, D is the $M^2\times M(M+1)/2$ duplication matrix and $\otimes$ indicates the Kronecker product.

Proof: See Appendix.

More properties of vech and D can be found in, e.g. Magnus (1988) or Magnus and Neudecker (1991). Furthermore, the four submatrices of $I(\theta)$ for $\theta=(\theta_1',\theta_2')'$ are

$$\begin{aligned} I_{11} &= \frac{1}{2}\sum_{t=1}^{T}\left(\frac{\partial \text{vech}H_t}{\partial\theta_1'}\right)' D'(H_t^{-1}\otimes H_t^{-1})D\frac{\partial \text{vech}H_t}{\partial\theta_1'} \\ &\quad +\sum_{t=1}^{T}\left(\frac{\partial\mu_t}{\partial\theta_1'}\right)' H_t^{-1}\frac{\partial\mu_t}{\partial\theta_1'}, \qquad (6)\\ I_{12} &= \frac{1}{2}\sum_{t=1}^{T}\left(\frac{\partial \text{vech}H_t}{\partial\theta_1'}\right)' D'(H_t^{-1}\otimes H_t^{-1})D\frac{\partial \text{vech}H_t}{\partial\theta_2'} \\ &\quad +\sum_{t=1}^{T}\left(\frac{\partial\mu_t}{\partial\theta_1'}\right)' H_t^{-1}\frac{\partial\mu_t}{\partial\theta_2'}, \qquad (7)\\ I_{21} &= I_{12}' \qquad (8) \end{aligned}$$

and

$$\begin{aligned} I_{22} &= \frac{1}{2}\sum_{t=1}^{T}\left(\frac{\partial \text{vech}H_t}{\partial\theta_2'}\right)' D'(H_t^{-1}\otimes H_t^{-1})D\frac{\partial \text{vech}H_t}{\partial\theta_2'} \\ &\quad +\sum_{t=1}^{T}\left(\frac{\partial\mu_t}{\partial\theta_2'}\right)' H_t^{-1}\frac{\partial\mu_t}{\partial\theta_2'}. \qquad (9) \end{aligned}$$

Note that there is an error in Wong and Li's (1997) representation for the information matrix (in the case of the multivariate CHARMA model): the second part of the right-hand side of equation (5) is missing. As shown below, I_{12} of Wong and Li (1997), given by

$$I_{12}=-\frac{1}{2}\sum_{t=1}^{T}\frac{\partial \text{vec}'H_t^{-1}}{\partial\theta_1}\cdot\frac{\partial \text{vec}H_t}{\partial\theta_2'}, \qquad (10)$$

can be re-expressed as the first part of equation (7).

From the matrix differential result

$$dH_t^{-1} = -H_t^{-1}(dH_t)H_t^{-1},$$

we obtain by vectorization

$$\begin{aligned} d\text{vec}H_t^{-1} &= -(H_t^{-1} \otimes H_t^{-1}) d\text{vec}H_t \\ &= -(H_t^{-1} \otimes H_t^{-1}) D d\text{vech}H_t \\ &= -(H_t^{-1} \otimes H_t^{-1}) D \frac{\partial \text{vech}H_t}{\partial \theta_1'} d\theta_1. \end{aligned} \tag{11}$$

Then, we can insert (11) in (10) to prove

$$\begin{aligned} &-\frac{1}{2}\sum_{t=1}^{T} \frac{\partial \text{vec}' H_t^{-1}}{\partial \theta_1} \cdot \frac{\partial \text{vec}H_t}{\partial \theta_2'} \\ &= \frac{1}{2}\sum_{t=1}^{T} \left(\frac{\partial \text{vech}H_t}{\partial \theta_1'}\right)' D'(H_t^{-1} \otimes H_t^{-1}) D \frac{\partial \text{vech}H_t}{\partial \theta_2'}, \end{aligned}$$

which is the same as the first part of (7).

Maximum likelihood estimation for the VAR-VARCH model

As an example of model (1), we consider the following M dimensional VAR(k)-VARCH(q) model in a special case based on, e.g. MathSoft (1996):

$$y_t = \mu_t + \varepsilon_t, \quad t = 1, ..., T, \tag{12}$$

where $y_t = (y_{1t}, y_{2t}, ..., y_{Mt})'$ is an $M \times 1$ vector of time series, μ_t is the $M \times 1$ mean vector assumed to be

$$\mu_t = B_0 + B_1 y_{t-1} + ... + B_k y_{t-k} \tag{13}$$

where B_0 is a $M \times 1$ vector and B_i, $i = 1, ..., k$, is an $M \times M$ diagonal matrix of unknown AR parameters. ε_t is an $M \times 1$ vector of error terms, its mean is $E(\varepsilon_t) = 0$ and its conditional variance is H_t specified as

$$\text{vech}H_t = A_0 + A_1 \text{vech}\varepsilon_{t-1}\varepsilon_{t-1}' + ... + A_q \text{vech}\varepsilon_{t-q}\varepsilon_{t-q}', \tag{14}$$

where $\text{vech}\varepsilon_{t-j}\varepsilon_{t-j}' = (\varepsilon_{1t-j}^2, \varepsilon_{1t-j}\varepsilon_{2t-j}, ..., \varepsilon_{Mt-j}^2)'$, $j = 1, ..., q$, A_0 is an $N \times 1$ vector and A_j, $j = 1, ..., q$, is an $N \times N$ diagonal matrix of unknown ARCH parameters ($N = M(M+1)/2$).

For model (12), we partition $\theta = (\theta_1', \theta_2')'$, where $\theta_1 = (B_0', \text{dg}'(B_1), \ldots, \text{dg}'(B_k))'$ is a $M(k+1) \times 1$ vector of AR parameters in the mean equation and

$\theta_2 = (A_0', \mathrm{dg}'(A_1), ..., \mathrm{dg}'(A_q))'$ is an $N(q+1) \times 1$ vector of ARCH parameters of the variance equation, where dg(.) indicates a vector containing only the diagonal elements of the matrix. Based on such notation and the notion that the associated information matrix $I(\theta)$ is block diagonal, as in the univariate case discussed by e.g. Mills (1993), the four submatrices (6) through (9) of $I(\theta)$ are calculated to be

$$I_{11} = \sum_{t=1}^{T} X_t' H_t^{-1} X_t, \tag{15}$$

$$I_{12} = 0, \tag{16}$$

$$I_{21} = I_{12}' = 0 \tag{17}$$

and

$$I_{22} = \frac{1}{2} \sum_{t=1}^{T} Z_t' D' (H_t^{-1} \otimes H_t^{-1}) D Z_t. \tag{18}$$

Notice that

$$\frac{\partial \mu_t}{\partial \theta_1'} = X_t = (I_M, X_{t-1}, ..., X_{t-k}) \tag{19}$$

and

$$\frac{\partial \mathrm{vech} H_t}{\partial \theta_2'} = Z_t = (I_N, Z_{t-1}, ..., Z_{t-q}) \tag{20}$$

are used. Here,

$$X_{t-i} = \mathrm{diag}(y_{1t-i}, y_{2t-i}, ..., y_{Mt-i})', \quad i = 1, ..., k$$

is an $M \times M$ diagonal matrix, I_M is an $M \times M$ identity matrix,

$$Z_{t-j} = \mathrm{diag}(\varepsilon_{1t-j}^2, \varepsilon_{1t-j}\varepsilon_{2t-j}, ..., \varepsilon_{Mt-j}^2), \quad j = 1, ..., q$$

is an $N \times N$ diagonal matrix and I_N is an $N \times N$ identity matrix. I_{11} is of order $M(k+1) \times M(k+1)$, I_{12} is $M(k+1) \times N(q+1)$, I_{21} is $N(q+1) \times M(k+1)$ and I_{22} is $N(q+1) \times N(q+1)$, with $N = M(M+1)/2$.

Example

First we introduce the model and the representation of the information matrix; we then present an estimate of the information matrix for our simulated data.

The model and information matrix

Consider the following bivariate VAR(1)-VARCH(1) model ($M = 2$):

$$\begin{pmatrix} y_{1t} \\ y_{2t} \end{pmatrix} = \begin{pmatrix} \mu_{1t} \\ \mu_{2t} \end{pmatrix} + \begin{pmatrix} \varepsilon_{1t} \\ \varepsilon_{2t} \end{pmatrix}, \quad t = 1, ..., T, \tag{21}$$

where $y_t = (y_{1t}, y_{2t})'$ is the t-th 2×1 observable vector, the mean $\mu_t = (\mu_{1t}, \mu_{2t})'$ is

$$\begin{pmatrix} \mu_{1t} \\ \mu_{2t} \end{pmatrix} = \begin{pmatrix} \beta_{10} \\ \beta_{20} \end{pmatrix} + \begin{pmatrix} \beta_{11} & 0 \\ 0 & \beta_{22} \end{pmatrix} \begin{pmatrix} y_{1t-1} \\ y_{2t-1} \end{pmatrix}, \tag{22}$$

with $\beta_{10}, \beta_{20}, \beta_{11}$ and β_{22} being scalar parameters, $\varepsilon_t = (\varepsilon_{1t}, \varepsilon_{2t})'$ is the t-th 2×1 error vector with mean

$$E\begin{pmatrix} \varepsilon_{1t} \\ \varepsilon_{2t} \end{pmatrix} = 0 \tag{23}$$

and conditional variance matrix

$$H_t = \begin{pmatrix} h_{11t} & h_{12t} \\ h_{12t} & h_{22t} \end{pmatrix}, \tag{24}$$

which is a 2×2 diagonal positive definite matrix. Also, the conditional variance equation can be written for $h_t = (h_{11t}, h_{12t}, h_{22t})'$ containing the diagonal elements of H_t as

$$\begin{pmatrix} h_{11t} \\ h_{12t} \\ h_{22t} \end{pmatrix} = \begin{pmatrix} \alpha_{10} \\ \alpha_{20} \\ \alpha_{30} \end{pmatrix} + \begin{pmatrix} \alpha_{11} & 0 & 0 \\ 0 & \alpha_{22} & 0 \\ 0 & 0 & \alpha_{33} \end{pmatrix} \begin{pmatrix} \varepsilon^2_{1t-1} \\ \varepsilon_{1t-1}\varepsilon_{2t-1} \\ \varepsilon^2_{2t-1} \end{pmatrix}, \tag{25}$$

with $\alpha_{10} > 0$, $\alpha_{20} > 0$, $\alpha_{30} > 0$, $\alpha_{11} \geq 0$, $\alpha_{22} \geq 0$ and $\alpha_{33} \geq 0$ such that $H_t > 0$ exists.

Partion $\theta = (\theta'_1, \theta'_2)'$, where $\theta_1 = (\beta_{10}, \beta_{20}, \beta_{11}, \beta_{22})'$ is specific for only the mean equation and $\theta_2 = (\alpha_{10}, \alpha_{20}, \alpha_{30}, \alpha_{11}, \alpha_{22}, \alpha_{33})'$ only for the variance equation. Based on (15) through (18) we get the four submatrices of the information matrix $I(\theta)$ for this model as follows:

$$I_{11} = \sum_{t=1}^{T} X'_t H_t^{-1} X_t, \tag{26}$$

where I_{11} is of order 4×4, H_t is given as in (24) and

$$X_t = \begin{pmatrix} 1 & 0 & y_{1t-1} & 0 \\ 0 & 1 & 0 & y_{2t-1} \end{pmatrix}.$$

$$I_{12} = 0, \tag{27}$$

which is of order 4×6.

$$I_{21} = I'_{12} = 0, \tag{28}$$

which is of order 6×4.

Finally,

$$I_{22} = \frac{1}{2}\sum_{t=1}^{T} Z'_t D'(H_t^{-1} \otimes H_t^{-1}) D Z_t, \tag{29}$$

where I_{22} is of order 6×6, H_t is as in (24),

$$D = \begin{pmatrix} 1 & 0 & 0 \\ 0 & 1 & 0 \\ 0 & 1 & 0 \\ 0 & 0 & 1 \end{pmatrix}$$

and

$$Z_t = \begin{pmatrix} 1 & 0 & 0 & \varepsilon_{1t-1}^2 & 0 & 0 \\ 0 & 1 & 0 & 0 & \varepsilon_{1t-1}\varepsilon_{2t-1} & 0 \\ 0 & 0 & 1 & 0 & 0 & \varepsilon_{2t-1}^2 \end{pmatrix}.$$

Numerical analysis

Having presented the information matrix, we estimate it by using S-PLUS. We generate data of T=500 observations for the model introduced in Section 4.1 with the following parameters:

$$\begin{aligned} \beta_{10} &= 0.1, \\ \beta_{20} &= 0.3, \\ \beta_{11} &= -0.7, \\ \beta_{22} &= 0.2 \end{aligned}$$

for the mean equation (21) and

$$\begin{aligned} \alpha_{10} &= 0.1, \\ \alpha_{20} &= 0.2, \\ \alpha_{30} &= 0.5, \\ \alpha_{11} &= 0.2, \\ \alpha_{22} &= 0.01, \\ \alpha_{33} &= 0.1 \end{aligned}$$

for the variance equation (24).

The elements of the maximum likelihood estimate $\hat{\theta}$ estimated via the S+GARCH module (see MathSoft (1996)) are

$$\begin{aligned}
\hat{\beta}_{10} &= 0.11522, \\
& \quad (0.00190714) \\
\hat{\beta}_{20} &= 0.33394, \\
& \quad (0.00479464) \\
\hat{\beta}_{11} &= -0.69968, \\
& \quad (0.00073739) \\
\hat{\beta}_{22} &= 0.20206 \\
& \quad (0.00147598)
\end{aligned}$$

for the mean equation (21) and

$$\begin{aligned}
\hat{\alpha}_{10} &= 0.01168, \\
& \quad (0.00001457) \\
\hat{\alpha}_{20} &= 0.02650, \\
& \quad (0.00000451) \\
\hat{\alpha}_{30} &= 0.06015, \\
& \quad (0.00007936) \\
\hat{\alpha}_{11} &= 0.12359 \\
& \quad (0.00042226) \\
\hat{\alpha}_{22} &= 0.10913 \\
& \quad (0.00009292) \\
\hat{\alpha}_{33} &= 0.09621 \\
& \quad (0.00046628)
\end{aligned}$$

for the variance equation (24).

Our maximum likelihood estimates of the two blocks $I_{11}(\theta)$ and $I_{22}(\theta)$ of the information matrix based on the maximum likelihood estimate $\hat{\theta}$ are

$$\hat{I}_{11} = \begin{pmatrix} 13474819.19 & -6032053.48 & 742244.12 & -2436914.71 \\ (0.00496006) & & & \\ -6032053.48 & 2708442.57 & -334577.75 & 1094430.79 \\ & (0.01108182) & & \\ 742244.12 & -334577.75 & 1533695.19 & -417551.44 \\ & & (0.00087323) & \\ -2436914.71 & 1094430.79 & -417551.44 & 883242.10 \\ & & & (0.00160627) \end{pmatrix}$$

and

$$\hat{I}_{22} = \begin{pmatrix} 237870044.33 & -214568221.88 & 48414361.10 & 6227689.76 & -12706580.38 & 6488303.49 \\ (0.02848742) & & & & & \\ -214568221.88 & 193945982.60 & -43853316.24 & -5795100.37 & 11861693.37 & -6076253.14 \\ & (0.06333079) & & & & \\ 48414361.10 & -43853316.24 & 9937203.13 & 1349228.63 & -2770539.05 & 1423816.62 \\ & & (0.14101185) & & & \\ 6227689.76 & -5795100.37 & 1349228.63 & 460475.27 & -956900.32 & 497268.93 \\ & & & (0.37703603) & & \\ -12706580.38 & 11861693.37 & -2770539.05 & -956900.32 & 1994598.11 & -1039686.58 \\ & & & & (0.37014664) & \\ 6488303.49 & -6076253.14 & 1423816.62 & 497268.93 & -1039686.58 & 543592.23 \\ & & & & & (0.36481706) \end{pmatrix}$$

Remarks

We now comment on the main findings of this paper, in order.

1. In the first three steps of the matrix differential based approach to obtaining the information matrix $I(\theta)$ in section 3, we need only L_t, the log-likelihood at the t-th observation, $t = 1, ..., T$, of the time series. In the last step, we obtain the information matrix $I(\theta)$ from the log-likelihood function over all T observations. This new approach makes the mathematical computation of $I(\theta)$ simpler.

2. By obtaining the information matrix $I(\theta)$ from (4) instead of (3), we use the elegance and the advantage of the matrix differential calculus techniques developed in Magnus and Neudecker (1991). The derivation is shorter than the one in Appendix 1 of Wong and Li (1997) for the case of the multivariate CHARMA model, and gives the correct representation of $I(\theta)$.

3. The new approach is very general and can be used to derive the information matrix for the log-likelihood function of several other (time series) models as well. One such case is a special CHARMA model considered in

Ling and Deng (1993). Also, using the matrix differential calculus in Magnus and Neudecker (1991), it is possible to derive an equation to show that Wong and Li's (1997) algorithm is equivalent to an iteratively weighted least squares approach.

Appendix

Proof of Theorem 1: Due to (2), the log-likelihood function can be written as

$$\begin{aligned} L(y,\theta) &= \sum_{t=1}^{T} L_t \\ &= -\frac{1}{2}\sum_{t=1}^{T}\log \mid H_t \mid -\frac{1}{2}\sum_{t=1}^{T}(y_t-\mu_t)'H_t^{-1}(y_t-\mu_t) \\ &= -\frac{1}{2}\sum_{t=1}^{T}\log \mid H_t \mid -\frac{1}{2}\sum_{t=1}^{T}\mathrm{tr}H_t^{-1}(y_t-\mu_t)(y_t-\mu_t)'. \end{aligned} \tag{30}$$

Now we proceed in the way introduced in Section 2.

Step 1: We take differentials $d_\theta L_t$ of L_t with respect to θ (via μ_t and H_t):

$$\begin{aligned} F_t(y_t,\theta) &= d_\theta L_t \\ &= -\frac{1}{2}d\log \mid H_t \mid -\frac{1}{2}\mathrm{tr}(dH_t^{-1})(y_t-\mu_t)(y_t-\mu_t)' \\ &\quad -\frac{1}{2}\mathrm{tr}H_t^{-1}d[(y_t-\mu_t)(y_t-\mu_t)'] \\ &= -\frac{1}{2}\mathrm{tr}H_t^{-1}dH_t+\frac{1}{2}\mathrm{tr}H_t^{-1}(dH_t)H_t^{-1}(y_t-\mu_t)(y_t-\mu_t)' \\ &\quad +\frac{1}{2}\mathrm{tr}H_t^{-1}[d\mu_t(y_t-\mu_t)'+(y_t-\mu_t)d\mu_t'] \\ &= \frac{1}{2}\mathrm{tr}H_t^{-1}[(y_t-\mu_t)(y_t-\mu_t)'-H_t]H_t^{-1}dH_t \\ &\quad +(y_t-\mu_t)'H_t^{-1}d\mu_t. \end{aligned} \tag{31}$$

Step 2: We take the expectation of (31) with respect to y and evaluate it at $\theta=\tilde{\theta}$ to get

$$\begin{aligned} G_t(\tilde{\theta},\theta) &= E[F_t(y_t,\theta|\tilde{\theta})] \\ &= \frac{1}{2}\mathrm{tr}H_t^{-1}[\tilde{H}_t+(\tilde{\mu}_t-\mu_t)(\tilde{\mu}_t-\mu_t)'-H_t]H_t^{-1}dH_t \\ &\quad +(\tilde{\mu}_t-\mu_t)'H_t^{-1}d\mu_t. \end{aligned} \tag{32}$$

Step 3: We obtain from (32)

$$\begin{aligned} S_t(\tilde{\theta},\theta) &= d_{\tilde{\theta}}G_t(\tilde{\theta},\theta) \\ &= \frac{1}{2}\mathrm{tr}H_t^{-1}[d\tilde{H}_t + d\tilde{\mu}_t(\tilde{\mu}_t-\mu_t)' + (\tilde{\mu}_t-\mu_t)d\tilde{\mu}_t{}']H_t^{-1}dH_t \\ &\quad + d\tilde{\mu}_t' H_t^{-1} d\mu_t \\ &= \frac{1}{2}\mathrm{tr}H_t^{-1}d\tilde{H}_t H_t^{-1}dH_t + \mathrm{tr}H_t^{-1}d\tilde{\mu}_t(\tilde{\mu}_t-\mu_t)'H_t^{-1}dH_t \\ &\quad + d\tilde{\mu}_t' H_t^{-1} d\mu_t. \end{aligned} \tag{33}$$

Step 4: We evaluate (33) at $\tilde{\theta}=\theta$:

$$\begin{aligned} \sum_{t=1}^{T} S_t(\tilde{\theta},\theta)|_{\tilde{\theta}=\theta} &= \frac{1}{2}\sum_{t=1}^{T}\mathrm{tr}H_t^{-1}(dH_t)H_t^{-1}dH_t \\ &\quad + \sum_{t=1}^{T} d\mu_t' H_t^{-1} d\mu_t. \end{aligned} \tag{34}$$

Because H_t is symmetric, we rewrite (34) as

$$\begin{aligned} \sum_{t=1}^{T} S_t(\tilde{\theta},\theta)|_{\tilde{\theta}=\theta} &= \frac{1}{2}\sum_{t=1}^{T}(d\theta)'\left(\frac{\partial \mathrm{vech} H_t}{\partial\theta'}\right)' D'(H_t^{-1}\otimes H_t^{-1})D\frac{\partial \mathrm{vech} H_t}{\partial\theta'}d\theta \\ &\quad + \sum_{t=1}^{T}(d\theta)'\left(\frac{\partial\mu_t}{\partial\theta'}\right)' H_t^{-1}\frac{\partial\mu_t}{\partial\theta'}d\theta, \end{aligned} \tag{35}$$

where vech denotes the vectorization operator which eliminates all supradiagonal elements of the matrix and $\mathrm{vech}H_t$ is an $M(M+1)/2\times 1$ vector, D is the $M^2\times M(M+1)/2$ duplication matrix and $\otimes$ indicates the Kronecker product.

Based on (4), we establish the information matrix by (35).

References

Bera A.K., Higgins M.L. (1995) On ARCH Models: Properties, Estimation and Testing. In Oxley L., George D.A.R., Roberts C.J., Sayer S. (Eds.) Surveys in Econometrics. Blackwell, Oxford, 215-272

Bollerslev T. (1986) Generalized Autoregressive Conditional Heteroskedasticity. Journal of Econometrics 31: 307-327

Bollerslev T., Chou R.Y., Kroner K.F. (1992) ARCH Modelling in Finance. Journal of Econometrics 52: 5-59

Engle R.F. (1982) Autoregressive Conditional Heteroskedasticity with Estimates of Variance of United Kingdom Inflations. Econometrica 50: 987-1007

Engle R.F., Kroner K.F. (1995) Multivariate Simultaneous Generalised ARCH. Econometric Theory 11: 122-150

Geweke J. (1989) Exact Predictive Densities in Linear Models with ARCH Disturbances. Journal of Econometrics 44: 307-325

Ling S., Deng W.C. (1993) Parametric Estimate of Multivariate Autoregressive Models with Conditional Heterocovariance Matrix Errors. Acta Mathematicae Applicatae Sinica 16: 517-533

Liu S. (1995) Contributions to Matrix Calculus and Applications in Econometrics. Thesis Publishers, Amsterdam

MacRae E.C. (1974) Matrix Derivatives with an Application to an Adaptive Linear Decision Problem. Annals of Statistics 2: 337-346

Magnus J.R. (1988) Linear Structures. Oxford University Press, Oxford

Magnus J.R., Neudecker H. (1991) Matrix Differential Calculus with Applications in Statistics and Econometrics, revised edition. John Wiley, Chichester

MathSoft (1996) S+GARCH User's Manual, Version 1.0, Data Analysis Products Division, MathSoft, Seattle

Mills T.C. (1993) The Econometric Modelling of Financial Time Series. Cambridge University Press, Cambridge

Palm F.C. (1996) GARCH Models of Volatility. In: Maddala G.S., Rao C.R. (Eds.) Statistical Methods in Finance. Elsevier Science B.V., Amsterdam, 209-240

Polasek W., Kozumi H. (1996) The VAR-VARCH Model: A Bayesian Approach. In: Lee J.C., Johnson W.O., Zellner A. Modelling and Prediction Honoring Seymour Geisser. Springer, New York, 402-422

Rogers G.S. (1980) Matrix Derivatives. Marcel Dekker, New York

Tsay R.S. (1987) Conditional Heteroscedastic Time Series Models. Journal of the American Statistical Association 82: 590-604

Wong H., Li W.K. (1997) On a Multivariate Conditional Heteroscedastic Model. Biometrika 84: 111-123

A Note on the Herfindahl Index of Concentration

Gerhart Bruckmann

Department of Statistics
University of Vienna

Over the last decades, Descriptive Statistics has increasingly slipped into a cinderella role, overshadowed by her much more glamorous younger sister Inductive Statistics. Franz Ferschl is one of the few who have had a heart also for cinderella[1]. In a volume in his honour, therefore, it seems appropriate also to pay some attention to this badly neglected girl.

Amongst all feasible indices of (absolute) concentration, the well-known Herfindahl index

$$\mathbf{H} = \sum_{i=1}^{N} \mathbf{p}_i^2$$

satisfies a number of theoretical requirements; furthermore, within a broad class of indices which fulfil these requirements, it is the index which is easiest to calculate[2]. p_i is the share which the i-th unit (firm) holds of the total turnover (or employment) of a particular branch, with

$$\sum_{i=1}^{N} \mathbf{p}_i = 1$$

(Example: $p_1 = .4$, $p_2 = .3$, $p_3 = .2$, $p_4 = .1$; $H = .16 + .09 + .04 + .01 = .30$)

---

[1] Ferschl, Franz, Deskriptive Statistik (3rd ed.), Heidelberg 1985.

[2] Bruckmann, Gerhart, Einige Bemerkungen zur statistischen Messung der Konzentration., Metrika 14, 1969, p.183-213.
Bruckmann Gerhart, "Konzentrationsmessung", in: Bleymüller, Gehlert, Gülicher, Statistik für Wirtschaftswissenschaftler (11th ed.), Vahlen, München, 1998.

In the case of maximum concentration $(p_1 = 1, p_2 = \ldots = p_N = 0)$, $H = 1$; in the case of minimum concentration $\left(p_1 = \cdots = p_N = \frac{1}{N}\right)$, $H = N \cdot \frac{1}{N^2} = \frac{1}{N}$.

In practical applications, however, often only the shares of the n largest units are known, whereas the (single) shares of the remaining N-n smaller units are unknown; often, even the number of smaller units (N-n) is unknown. In this note, there will be shown that the Herfindahl index is robust in respect to this fact.

Let us, hence, denote with p_n the share of the n-th largest unit (ordered by size). Any one of the remaining N-n units, therefore, must have a share smaller than (or equal to) p_n. Let us denote by P the total share of these remaining units:

$$P = \sum_{i=n+1}^{N} p_i$$

The contribution of these N-n units to the H index is

$$\sum_{i=n+1}^{N} P_i^2 = C$$

C reaches its maximum value in the case of the most unequal distribution within the N-n units, i.e. if $\frac{P}{p_n}$ firms have each a share of p_n, the others a share of 0:

$$C_{max} = \frac{P}{p_n} \cdot p_n^2 = P.p_n$$

C reaches ist minimum value in case $p_i = \frac{P}{N-n}$, i = n+1, …, N :

$$C_{min} = (N-n)\left(\frac{P}{N-n}\right)^2 = \frac{P^2}{N-n}$$

Hence,

$$\frac{P^2}{N-n} \leq C \leq P.p_n$$

Note that the upper bound is independent from any knowledge concerning the number of smaller firms, and that the lower bound approaches 0 if N is large.

Example: $p_n = .05$, $P = .20$, $N\text{-}n = 10$:

$$.004 \leq C \leq .01$$

Even in this - rather unlikely - example that no information is available on firms below a share of $p_n = .05$, and that their cumulative share is as high as 20 %, the contribution of the unknown smaller firms to the H index remains below .01. The H index, therefore, can safely be regarded a robust measure of concentration, in the sense that it is practically unaffected by lack of information concerning smaller units.

A Generalization and Optimization of a Measure of Diversity

Helmut Beran

Institute of Systems Sciences, University of Linz

Abstract

Some properties of a previously defined index of diversity (Beran, 1994) are derived. Based on a bivariate generalization of this index, a measure of association, the codiversity, is developed, and a geometrical representation is given. If two variables A and B are viewed as input and output variables, respectively, an algorithm for optimizing the codiversity of the system is outlined and applied to an example demonstrating its usefulness in the design of experiments.

1 Introduction

Diversity is a concept which has played a major role in ecology and other related disciplines for a long time. In ecology, the diversity of an ecosystem is directly related to the number of species present. However, given a fixed number of, say k, species, the relative abundance of these species is also considered a main criterion for assessing diversity. Thus, a system is considered more diverse if the number of species is increased, but in case of fixed k, the more evenly all individuals are distributed among the species.

For a long time, quantitative measures of diversity have been sought for by ecologists. In the ecological literature of the past decades, a great number of articles deal with this problem in a more or less professional way without coming to a satisfactory end.

The main problem – which diversity shares with other quantitative descriptive measures – lies in the fact that an intuitive concept usually allows many different ways to be transformed into a formal instruction for calculation. Measures of central tendency or of dispersion can also be defined in various ways without any single one of them being clearly conceptually superior to all others. However, it was usually some favorable characteristics and, even more, the mathematical tractability or the suitability for advanced statistical inference that led to the dominance of one or a few of the many feasible realizations.

One reason why an intuitve notion of a certain aspect of a (statistical) distribution cannot be transformed uniquely into a “statistic”, i.e. a single number, is that this procedure requires a massive compression of information. Usually all the data at

hand are condensed into a single value, and this can of course be performed in many ways.
Are there any guidelines at all that can help with a proper choice of a statistic? Ferschl (1985) postulates three properties a "good" statistic should fulfill in order to characterize a certain aspect of a distribution:

- adequacy
- conveyance of information
- precision.

Adequacy concerns the degree of correspondence between the statistic and the intuitive measurement concept of the user. The conveyance of information is judged by the extent to which the raw data enter the calculation. The precision is connected with questions of how strongly the statistic is influenced by chance mechanisms in the data, i.e. with the problem of robustness of the statistic, and the like.
It is not surprising that ecologists have paid little attention to these requirements. Diversity indices were chosen mainly due to personal favors or disfavors or according to some superficial advantage or to an analogy in formally related fields. This eventually led to a plethora of different, mostly incommensurable measures, a situation, which culminated in the resigned formulation of a "non-concept" of diversity by Hurlbert (1971).
At first, relatively little assistance came from professional statisticians. One reason might be that the posed problem formally corresponds to a question which has not been in any major focus of statistical interest, namely the development of descriptive statistical measures characterizing the distribution of nominal variables. When dealing with nominal variables, questions of assessing the interdependence of two or more such variables determined the prevailing trend in research, resulting in the development of measures of association rather than characterizations of the distribution of a single nominal variable.
A diversity index is supposed to depict the variety of species of an ecosystem in an ecological context; in a statistical sense it can be viewed as a measure of dispersion of a nominal variable. The only quantities that can be used for the calculation of this measure are therefore k, the number of classes or categories the variable can assume, and f_i, $i = 1,\ldots,k$, the number of individuals in the i-th class.
Yet in the seventies and eighties, along with the emerging field of statistical ecology, fruitful attempts towards a systematic treatment and clarification of the problem were accomplished, among others, by Hill (1973), Patil and Taillie (1982), and Rao (1982). Starting from different models and (occasionally not too plausible) assumptions they individually arrived at one-parametric "families" of diversity indices. Although these papers established formal frames and contributed substantially towards a unified approach to the hitherto unstructured multitude of different indices (most of the previously implemented diversity statistics can be subsumed under one or the other of these families), the concepts still lacked a stringent guidance as to how the parameters of the family are to be selected in order to adapt to specific situations.
The author showed (Beran, 1994) that a set of plausible assumptions leads to a unique choice among the possible candidates for a diversity statistic. This set of assumptions does not represent an ex-post-characterization of a given index (as

can frequently be seen in literature, when a pseudo-justification of a specific choice is to be given), but is an attempt to successively reduce the number of feasible measures until a single diversity index remains, which fulfills all the imposed criteria.

Due to the objectives of this method the resulting statistic is not only an adequate representation of the intuitive concept of the user but will reflect the structure of the system to be described as closely as possible.

2 The Derivation of a System–conforming Measure of Diversity

A detailed description of the assumptions and formal derivation of this statistic was given by Beran (1994). However, to make the following extensions of the concept and the involved terminology intelligible, a short review of the procedure seems necessary.

A finite set of elements is partitioned into k classes by a nominal variable $A = \{A_1, A_2, ..., A_k\}$. Let's assume that the i-th class contains f_i elements, $\sum f_i = n$. Denote by $p(A_i) \equiv p_i = f_i / n$ the relative frequency of the i-th class.

We are looking for a statistic $d(A) = d(p_1, p_2, ..., p_k)$ of this distribution fulfilling the following properties:

(I) $d(A) \geq 0$

(II) $d(A)$ is symmetric in its arguments p_i

(III) $d(A)$ is continuous in the p_i

(IV) $d(p_1, ..., p_k, 0, ..., 0) = d(p_1, ..., p_k)$

(V) $d(1,0,0,...,0) \leq d(p_1, ..., p_k) \leq d(1/k, 1/k, ..., 1/k)$

(VI) $k_1 > k_2 \Rightarrow d(1/k_1, 1/k_1, ..., 1/k_1) > d(1/k_2, 1/k_2, ..., 1/k_2)$

(VII) $1 \leq d(p_1, p_2, ..., p_k) \leq k$

Most of the widely-used diversity indices comply with requirements (I) through (VI), as these reflect rather trivial properties, which suggest themselves by the intuitive notion of diversity. However, (VII) goes a step further towards the previously mentioned systems conformity. If it is combined with the additional condition that the measure actually assumes its upper limit, if the elements are uniformly distributed over all classes, and its lower limit, if all elements lie in one class, the value of the statistic can be directly interpreted as the *number of classes* a uniformly distributed population with the same value of $d(A)$ would have.

It was shown in the article cited above (Beran, 1994) that these prerequisites are met by a large class of solutions,

$$d(A)=1/\varphi^{-1}\left[\sum_{i=1}^{k} p_i\varphi(p_i)\right], \tag{1}$$

$\varphi(p)$ strictly monotone and continuous. This expression represents the reciprocal of a generalized mean value of the relative class frequencies p_i.
Further steps towards the intended systems conformity require the extension to more than one nominal variable, i.e. a simultaneous partitioning of the population by two or more characteristics.
If we consider two such variables $A=\{A_1,\dots,A_k\}$ and $B=\{B_1,\dots,B_m\}$ the combined classification of the population results in relative frequencies

$$p(A_iB_j),\quad i=1,\dots,k;\quad j=1,\dots,m,\quad \sum_{i=1}^{k}\sum_{j=1}^{m} p(A_iB_j)=1.$$

If we define the conditional distribution in the usual way:

$$p(A_i|B_j)=p(A_iB_j)/p(B_j)$$

we are capable of introducing the concept of independence into our calculus of diversity.
We are led to denoting the expression

$$d(AB)=1/p(AB)=\left\langle\varphi^{-1}\left\{\sum_{i=1}^{k}\sum_{j=1}^{m} p(A_iB_j)\varphi\left[p(A_iB_j)\right]\right\}\right\rangle^{-1} \tag{2}$$

as *bivariate* or *compound* diversity of the variables A and B, and

$$d(A|B)=1/p(A|B)=\left\langle\varphi^{-1}\left\{\sum_{j=1}^{m} p(B_j)\varphi\left[p(A|B_j)\right]\right\}\right\rangle^{-1}=$$

$$=\left\langle\varphi^{-1}\left\{\sum_{j=1}^{m} p(B_j)\sum_{i=1}^{k} p(A_i|B_j)\varphi\left[p(A_i|B_j)\right]\right\}\right\rangle^{-1} \tag{3}$$

as *conditional* diversity of A, given B.
These definitions permit the introduction of the remaining requirements for a unique statistic:

(VIII) $d(A|B)\le d(A)$

(IX) $d(AB)=d(A)d(B)$, if A and B are independent from each other (in the ordinary sense)

(X) $d(AB)=d(A)d(B|A)=d(B)d(A|B)$, if A, B are possibly dependent.

The application of these requirements reduces the class of admissible functions in (1) to $\varphi(p) = \ln p$ rendering the unique diversity measure

$$v(A) = \exp\left[-\sum_{i=1}^{k} p(A_i)\ln p(A_i)\right] = \prod_{i=1}^{k}\left[\frac{1}{p(A_i)}\right]^{p(A_i)} \tag{4}$$

For details, the reader is again referred to Beran (1994).
We shall now derive some properties of this measure $v(A)$.[1]
As $v(A)$ fulfills assumptions (I) through (X) it follows from (VII) that $v(A)$ is bounded between 1 and k:

$$1 \le v(A) \le k\,, \tag{5}$$

in which $v(A) = k$ for the uniform distribution: $p_i = 1/k,\ i = 1,\ldots,k$; $v(A) = 1$ for extreme inequality: one $p_i = 1$, all the other $p_i = 0$.
Due to (VIII) we have:

$$v(A|B) \le v(A), \tag{6}$$

the equal sign valid only in the case of independence of A and B.
Postulate (X) together with (5) and (6) renders the important chain of inequalities

$$1 \le v(A|B) \le v(A) \le v(AB) \le v(A)v(B) \le km \tag{7}$$

where $k = n(A)$ and $m = n(B)$ are the number of different categories of A and B, respectively. In addition, we can derive from (X) that

$v(A|B) = 1$ is equivalent to $v(AB) = v(B)$.

What is the meaning of this latter relation?
From previous reasoning it follows that this can only be fulfilled if for all j=1,2,...m we have:

$$p(A_i|B_j) = \begin{cases} 1 & \text{for one and only one } i \\ 0 & \text{for all others} \end{cases}$$

i.e. the outcome of B determines completely the outcome of A (but not necessarily vice versa, as the complete dependence of one variable on the other is – contrary to independence – not symmetrical).

---

[1] This notation refers to the proposal by Adam (1984) to name this unique specialization of a diversity measure as „variety" to distinguish between the concept and the statistic. In this paper, however, we retain the term „diversity" for the specific statistic, as well.

3 The Concept of Codiversity

In the preceding consideration the concept of the compound diversity $d(AB)$ of two nominal variables and the conditional diversity $d(A|B)$ were introduced in order to formulate conditions which eventually led to the unique statistic $v(A)$.
We will outline that the concept of multivariate diversity is not only a prerequisite to solve the problem of establishing a unique choice out of a great variety of diversity indices. As the assumptions (VIII) through (X) are very much based on intuitive notions of systems conformity, they lend themselves to further investigations into adapting our specific diversity measure to analyzing matters of independence or association of nominal variables. We will even see that beyond that, diversity can serve as a control device in specific statistical systems.
Using previously defined quantities, let us introduce the statistic

$$v(A,B) := v(AB)/\left[v(A|B)v(B|A)\right] . \tag{8}$$

It follows immediately that

$$v(A,B) = v(A)v(B) / v(AB). \tag{9}$$

An operative representation of this expression can be deduced easily:

$$v(A,B) = \prod_i \prod_j \left\{p(A_i B_j)/\left[p(A_i)p(B_j)\right]\right\}^{p(A_i B_j)} . \tag{10}$$

As $v(A,B)$ by definition is symmetric in the variables A and B, we coin the name "codiversity" for it.
In concrete situations, one variable can, of course, be regarded as independent, the other as dependent on the former. We will follow this idea in more detail later.
At first we state a few properties of $v(A,B)$.
From (9) it follows that $v(A,B) \geq 1$, in which the equal sign holds iff A and B are independent .
An upper bound can be estimated in the following way:
We write

$$v(A,B) = v(A)/v(A|B) = v(B)/v(B|A). \tag{11}$$

As stated before, we call A totally dependent on B, if the outcome of B uniquely determines the outcome of A. In this case

$$v(AB) = v(B), \quad v(A|B) = 1, \text{ and therefore}$$

$$v(A,B) = v(A) \leq v(B). \tag{12}$$

In analogy, if B is totally dependent on A, we have

$$v(A,B) = v(B) \leq v(A) . \tag{13}$$

If A and B are mutually totally dependent on each other, it follows that

$$\nu(A,B) = \nu(A) = \nu(B) = \nu(AB). \tag{14}$$

In all other cases, $\nu(A,B)$ must be smaller than $\nu(A)$ and $\nu(B)$, because

$$\nu(A|B) > 1, \quad \nu(B|A) > 1.$$

We therefore get the relation

$$1 \leq \nu(A,B) \leq \min[\nu(A), \nu(B)]. \tag{15}$$

The border values are assumed in case of independence and total dependence, respectively.
Including previous results we can expand this sequence of inequalities:

$$\begin{aligned} 1 \leq \nu(A,B) \leq \min[\nu(A), \nu(B)] &\leq \max[\nu(A), \nu(B)] \\ &\leq \nu(AB) \leq \nu(A)\nu(B) \leq n(A)n(B). \end{aligned} \tag{16}$$

Another ordered chain, involving conditional diversities, can be written:

$$1 \begin{matrix} \nearrow \leq \nu(A|B) \leq \nu(A) \leq \searrow \\ \searrow \leq \nu(A|B) \leq \nu(A) \leq \nearrow \end{matrix} \nu(AB) \leq \nu(A)\nu(B) \leq n(A)n(B)\,. \tag{17}$$

An order relation between the ("directional") conditional diversities and the ("nondirectional", symmetrical) codiversities cannot be established, as these statistics show opposite behavior with respect to the association between A and B: The conditional diversities $\nu(A|B)$, $\nu(B|A)$ vary from 1 to $\nu(A)$ or $\nu(B)$ with increasing degree of independence, whereas the codiversity $\nu(A,B)$ in this case has a decreasing tendency in its range of values.

4 A Geometrical Interpretation of Codiversity

A special advantage of the interpretation of our diversity statistic is based on the requirement of systems conformity which was the force behind our derivation. Thus, as stated before, the value of the diversity $\nu(A)$ can directly be interpreted as the number of classes a uniformly distributed population must have in order to render the same numerical value of the diversity index („principle of the equivalent uniform distribution").
This notion lends itself to the interpretation of codiversity, as well. In Figure 1 we depict this situation for the case of complete mutual dependence of the variables A and B. The necessary conditions

$$n(A) = n(B), \; \nu(A) = \nu(B)$$

are taken into account.

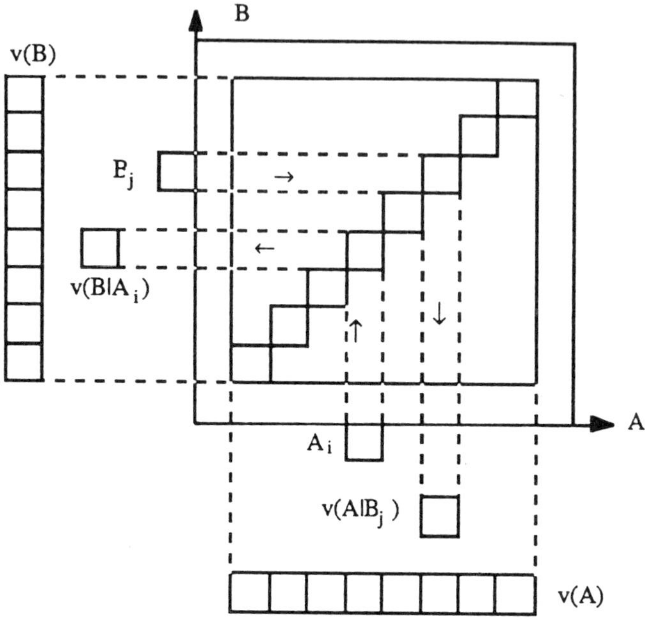

Figure 1: Geometrical representation of diversities in the case of total mutual dependence of the variables A and B.

The unit value of diversity is represented by a square with unit length. The value of the diversity is consequently represented by the number of the assigned squares. For increased comprehension we can view the inner (large) square as representation of an autonomous bivariate *uniform* distribution with $\nu(A) = \nu(B)$ classes. The classes A_i, B_j could then be regarded as the "effective" classes of the uniform distribution. In our example we assume $\nu(A) = \nu(B) = 8$ effective classes. Performing an appropriate permutation of the categories A_i, the bivariate diversity $\nu(A,B)$ can be represented by the diagonal row of squares, and its numerical value is given by the number of these squares. It is apparent that the total mutual dependence results in a minimum configuration of $\nu(AB)$. In case of independence this figure would fill out the total inner square rendering the numerical value $\nu(A)\cdot\nu(B)$. We recognize that the ratio $\nu(AB)/[\nu(A)\nu(B)]$ is an (inverse) measure of the degree of association between A and B. A direct measure can be devised by the reciprocal of $\nu(A,B)$,

$$\kappa(A,B) = \frac{\nu(AB)}{\nu(A)\nu(B)} \; . \tag{18}$$

Acccording to a proposal by Adam (1984) we call $\kappa(A,B)$ the *coefficient of constriction* of the bivariate distribution of A and B, as it measures the reduction of the maximum possible bivariate diversity due to the „constraints“ which the associative structure of the system imposes on the variables A and B.

In our example $\kappa(A,B)=8/64=1/8$ and $\nu(A,B)=8$.
Of course, assumed that A and B are independent, a value of $\kappa(A,B)=1$ or $\nu(A,B)=1$ would result.
The general case with a medium degree of association is shown in Figure 2. Again, in order to allow a comparison with the other examples, we assume that the transformed uniform distribution has univariate diversities $\nu(A)=\nu(B)=8$. From the figure we see that $\kappa(A,B)=21/64=.33$ and $\nu(A,B)=3.2$. Both values lie between the extremes, which were dealt with in the preceding examples.

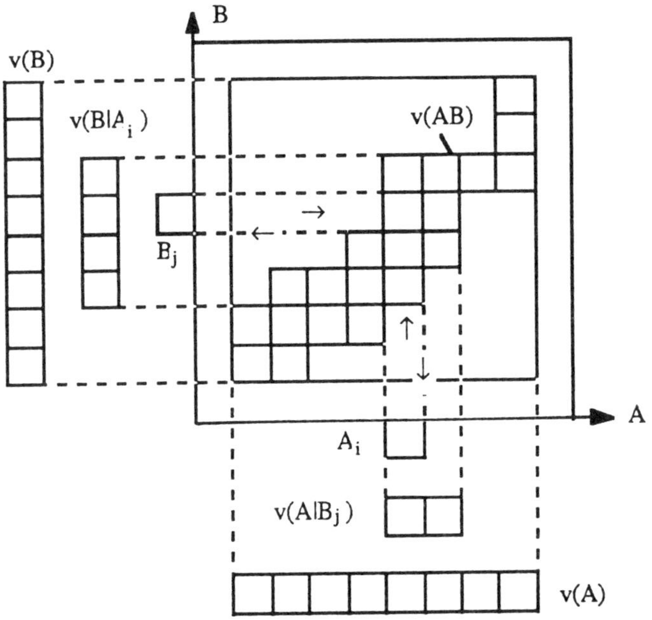

Figure 2: Geometrical representation of the diversities of two dependent variables A and B.

5 The Optimization of Codiversity

The codiversity $\nu(A,B)$, as defined in (8) is symmetric in A and B and can be viewed as a measure of association between the two variables, as was justified in the preceding chapter. However, in many practical cases, A and B need not necessarily be equivalent in an interpretative sense. As in the study of multivariate quantitative variables, measured on an interval scale, one variable may often be thought of as the independent variable, the other as the dependent (response) variable(s). We do not intend to develop a regression calculus based on diversity measures in an analogous way, as linear regression can be viewed as the

directional counterpart of undirected correlation. However, the concept of codiversity is apt to analyze and even optimize directional problems.
Take again Figure 2. If A is considered the independent and B the dependent variable the transformation to a uniform distribution suggests the following interpretation:
One "step" of variable A, say A_i, enables us to "control" a number of (4 in our example) steps of variable B. (In the case of total mutual dependence, each step of A can intrinsically control only one step of B). If we recall the geometrical interpretation, codiversity $v(A,B)$ may therefore be considered a measure of the controllability of the system. As we may exchange the role of variables A and B, controllability as measured by $v(A,B)$ is still a symmetric property of the system.
A directional aspect, however, can be introduced by a problem, which expresses an unsymmetric treatment of the two variables:
Given the transition probabilities (or relative conditional frequencies) $p(B_j|A_i)$, how should the distribution of the input variable A be chosen in order to maximize the codiversity $v(A,B)$? [2]
In order to arrive at a procedure for maximizing the codiversity $v(A,B)$, we state that our univariate diversity measure $v(A)$ corresponds closely to Shannon's entropy measure [3]

$$H(A) = -\sum_{i=1}^{k} p(A_i) \ln p(A_i) \tag{19}$$

The connection between the two quantities is easily recognized as

$$v(A) = e^{H(A)} . \tag{20}$$

For the purpose outlined in Chapter 1, Shannon's entropy – although highly favored by some ecologists as a diversity index – is no suitable solution of our problem, since it lacks some of the properties established as prerequisites for our looked-for diversity statistic. One major drawback of $H(A)$ is that its numerical value as a logarithmic transformation of $v(A)$ cannot be directly interpreted as the number of categories of an equivalent uniform distribution and thus violates the required systems conformity.
Nevertheless, relation (20) offers a great benefit. It allows to make use of formal results that have been obtained in information theory in the course of investigating properties of the entropy measure and that can be applied to $v(A)$ by appropriate transformations.
The relevant quantity for our optimizing problem, namely the codiversity $v(A,B)$, also corresponds to a well-known quantity in information theory, the so-called transinformation (or synentropy) T:

---

[2] In this context, the name *control diversity* could be used instead of codiversity.
[3] Shannon uses the dyadic logarithm for reasons that lie in its application in information theory. For our general-purpose considerations, the natural logarithm proves more suitable.

$$T = \ln v(A,B) = \ln(AB) - \ln v(A|B) - \ln v(B|A) = \\ = H(AB) - H(A|B) - H(B|A). \tag{21}$$

It is not necessary here to enlarge on the role of the transinformation in information theory, but as T and $v(A,B)$ are order-preserving quantities, the problem of maximizing the codiversity can be mapped to the problem of maximizing the transinformation. The latter problem was solved, at least in principle, in information theory (see e.g. Peters, 1967; Kämmerer, 1974), the solution yet bearing major flaws, which demands a modification, as we shall see later.
First, it is necessary to define a new quantity:

$$c(A_i,B) := \prod_{j=1}^{n(B)} \left[\frac{p(A_i B_j)}{p(A_i)p(B_j)} \right]^{p(B_j|A_i)}, \qquad i = 1,\dots,n(A). \tag{22}$$

There is a close relation between this expression and the codiversity, as we can deduce from (10):

$$v(A,B) = \prod_{i=1}^{n(A)} c(A_i,B)^{p(A_i)} = \prod_{i=1}^{n(A)} \prod_{j=1}^{n(B)} \left[\frac{p(A_i B_j)}{p(A_i)p(B_j)} \right]^{p(A_i B_j)}. \tag{23}$$

Thus it can be recognized that $v(A,B)$ is a (geometric) mean of the $c(A_i,B)$. From $p(A_i B_j) = p(A_i)p(B_j|A_i)$ it is conceivable that the codiversity $v(A,B)$ can be written solely in terms of the transition probabilities $p(B_j|A_i)$ and the distribution $p(A_i)$ of the input variable. As we assume that the transition probabilities are known, the optimizing problem reduces to the proper choice of the $p(A_i)$.
By introducing the dummy quantities $c(A_i,B)$ it is possible to formulate the optimizing condition by reverting to the analogous problem in information theory (cf. Peters, 1967 or Kämmerer, 1974).
A necessary condition for $v(A,B)$ taking on a maximum is that the following conditions hold:

$$c(A_i,B) = \text{const.} \equiv c \quad \text{for all} \quad i = 1,\dots,n(A). \tag{24}$$

As a mean value of the $c(A_i,B)$, $v(A,B)$ also must equal this value:

$$c(A_i,B) = v(A,B) = c\,, \qquad i = 1,\dots,n(A). \tag{25}$$

For further calculations, we pass to logarithms. From (22) and putting $n(A) \equiv k$, $n(B) \equiv m$ we get:

$$\ln c(A_i,B) = \sum_{j=1}^{m} p(B_j|A_i) \ln p(B_j|A_i) - \sum_{j=1}^{m} p(B_j|A_i) \ln p(B_j), \quad i = 1,\dots,k. \tag{26}$$

In order to write the condition for the maximum

$$\ln c(A_i, B) = \ln v(A, B)\,, \qquad i = 1, \ldots, k \tag{27}$$

in a more compact way, we introduce the following quantities:
P is the known matrix of the transition probabilities:

$$\mathbf{P} \equiv \mathbf{P}(B|A) = \begin{bmatrix} p(B_1|A_1) & \cdots & p(B_1|A_k) \\ \vdots & & \vdots \\ p(B_m|A_1) & \cdots & p(B_m|A_k) \end{bmatrix}.$$

Let $\mathbf{p}_1$ denote the required vector of the distribution of the input variable

$$\mathbf{p}_1 \equiv \mathbf{p}(A) = \begin{bmatrix} p(A_1) \\ \vdots \\ p(A_k) \end{bmatrix}, \qquad p(A_i) \geq 0\,, \quad \sum_{i=1}^{k} p(A_i) = 1\,,$$

which is to be constructed in such a way as to maximize the codiversity.
Let $\mathbf{e}_1'$ be a vector with k dimensions and $\mathbf{e}_2'$ a vector with m dimensions, consisting only of ones:

$$\mathbf{e}_1' \equiv \mathbf{e}'(A) = \underbrace{(1, 1, \ldots, 1)}_{k}, \qquad \mathbf{e}_2' \equiv \mathbf{e}'(B) = \underbrace{(1, 1, \ldots, 1)}_{m}.$$

Let $\mathbf{p}_2'$ denote the resulting output vector in the case of optimization:

$$\mathbf{p}_2' \equiv \mathbf{p}'(B) = (p(B_1), p(B_2), \ldots, p(B_m))\,, \quad p(B_j) \geq 0\,, \quad \sum_{j=1}^{m} p(B_j) = 1\,.$$

Finally, we introduce the following auxiliary quantities:

$$\mathbf{q}_2' \equiv \mathbf{q}'(B) = (\ln p(B_1), \ln p(B_2), \ldots, \ln p(B_m))\,,$$

$$\mathbf{Q} \equiv \mathbf{Q}(B|A) = \begin{bmatrix} p(B_1|A_1) \ln p(B_1|A_1) & \cdots & p(B_1|A_k) \ln p(B_1|A_k) \\ \vdots & & \vdots \\ p(B_m|A_1) \ln p(B_m|A_1) & \cdots & p(B_m|A_k) \ln p(B_m|A_k) \end{bmatrix}.$$

Due to

$$\mathbf{e}_2'\mathbf{P} = \left(\sum_{j=1}^{m} p(B_j|A_1), \ldots, \sum_{j=1}^{m} p(B_j|A_k) \right) = \underbrace{(1, 1, \ldots, 1)}_{k} = \mathbf{e}_1' \tag{28}$$

and using (26), the logarithmized form (27) of the condition for the maximum can be written:

$$\mathbf{e}_2'\mathbf{Q} - \mathbf{q}_2'\mathbf{P} = [\ln v(A, B)]\,\mathbf{e}_2'\mathbf{P}\,. \tag{29}$$

Setting

$$\ln v(A,B) \equiv T\,, \quad \ln c(A_i,B) \equiv T_i$$

equation (29) is equivalent to

$$(T_1, T_2, \dots, T_k) = (T, T, \dots, T)\,. \tag{30}$$

The unknowns in (29) are $v(A,B)$ and the quantities $\ln p(B_j)$.
From (29) we get immediately

$$(\mathbf{q}_2' + T\mathbf{e}_2')\mathbf{P} = \mathbf{e}_2'\mathbf{Q}\,. \tag{31}$$

By transposing we have the usual form

$$\mathbf{P}'(\mathbf{q}_2 + T\mathbf{e}_2) = \mathbf{Q}'\mathbf{e}_2\,. \tag{32}$$

This is a system with k equations and the m unknowns

$$\ln[v(A,B)p(B_j)]\,, \qquad j = 1,\dots,m\,. \tag{33}$$

The i-th row of the set of equations can be written in an explicit form:

$$\sum_{j=1}^{m} p(B_j|A_i)\ln[v(A,B)p(B_j)] = \sum_{j=1}^{m} p(B_j|A_i)\ln p(B_j|A_i)\,, \qquad i = 1,\dots,k\,. \tag{34}$$

If we denote with $\mathbf{r}$ a column vector with the m components (33), we can alternatively write (32) as

$$\mathbf{P}'\mathbf{r} = \mathbf{Q}'\mathbf{e}_2\,. \tag{35}$$

Provided we had found a solution $\mathbf{r}$ of this system. It would then suffice to delogarithmize the components of $\mathbf{r}$ in order to get the optimal codiversity:

$$\sum_{j=1}^{m} v(A,B)p(B_j) = v(A,B)\,, \tag{36}$$

since the requirement $\sum_{j=1}^{m} p(B_j) = 1$ was an essential part of the optimizing condition (25).

Then the exact form of the vector $\mathbf{p}_2 = \mathbf{p}(B)$ of the output distribution can be deduced.

By using

$$p(B_j) = \sum_{i=1}^{k} p(A_iB_j) = \sum_{i=1}^{k} p(A_i)p(B_j|A_i),$$

the required vector of the input distribution $\mathbf{p}_1 = \mathbf{p}(A)$ can be found from

$$\mathbf{P}\mathbf{p}_1 = \mathbf{p}_2\,. \tag{37}$$

We now state an apparent flaw in the derivation of the solution, which obviously remained undetected. By viewing the argumentation in e.g. Peters (1967) or Kämmerer (1974), which leads to the optimality condition (24), it can be noticed that the premise

$$\sum_{i=1}^{k} p(A_i) = 1 \tag{38}$$

is used, however the self-evident presupposition of non-negativity of the basic probabilities

$$p(A_i) \geq 0\,, \qquad i = 1,\ldots,k \tag{39}$$

is neither stated nor used.
This omission has the consequence that the outlined straight-forward algorithm may lead to a solution with one or more probability components being negative. How can we deal with such a seemingly unreasonable result?
If we interpret each possible vector of real numbers $\{p(A_i),\, i = 1,\ldots,k\}$ as a point in k-dimensional (Euclidean) space, condition (38) defines a hyperplane of dimension $k-1$; the k conditions (39) can be realized by cutting this hyperplane (38) with the k hyperplanes $p(A_i) = 0,\ i = 1,\ldots,k$.
The resulting region of the hyperplane (38) contains the points which represent *permissible* probability distributions of the input variable. The value of the codiversity can be plotted on a "normal" to this hyperplane in each point representing such a permissible distribution, yielding as closure a hypersurface of dimension $k-1$. It is feasible that the maximum of this function may lie outside that part of the hyperplanes (38), bounded by the conditions (39), which gives an explanation for the possible surprising result, indicated above.
For the further procedure one has to follow in such a case, we take advantage of a result of Fano (1966). He could show that $\ln v(A,B)$ (i.e. the transinformation in information theory) is a convex function of the distribution of the input vector. It follows that $\ln v(A,B)$ has neither relative minima nor saddle points. If $\ln v(A,B)$ had several relative maxima, the function value would be identical for all these points and for all linear combinations of them.
If $\ln v(A,B)$ assumes its maximum outside the admissible region, the *allowed* maximum must therefore lie at the border of the admissible region, i.e. on the intersection with a hyperplane $p(A_i) = 0$.
We can thus proceed as follows:
If at least one of the components is negative, the components of the input vector must be set to zero, one by one, in order to realize the intersections with the coordinate-hyperplanes, and the algorithm repeated. As it is not known in advance for which component this procedure will result in admissible solutions, it is necessary to successively set $p(A_i) = 0$ for all i's. Accompanying, the i-th column of matrix $\mathbf{P}$ with the elements $p(A_i) = 0$, $i = 1,\ldots,k$, must also be eliminated.
In the set of solutions rendered by this procedure we discard those which still contain negative components, and out of the remaining we take the solution with

the highest value of $v(A,B)$ as the optimal choice. If this maximum value $v(A,B)=c$, for this solution $c(A_i,B)=v(A,B)=c$ must hold for all i's except the one for which $p(A_i)$ was set equal to zero.
If at this step we get no solution with only non-negative components, two components have to be set to zero, again trying out all possible selections, and so on.
If at the very beginning, the condition $k=m$ is not fulfilled or if in case $k=m$ the rank of matrix $\mathbf{P}$ is less than k, we can perform the algorithm using a Moore-Penrose general inverse $\mathbf{P}^+$ to enter into systems (35) and (37). In general, this will lead to suitable results.
If $k>m$, and the rank of $\mathbf{P}$ is m, we must set $k-m$ components of the distribution of the input variable to zero and then start the above algorithm. Again, all such possible choices of components have to be tried out in succession.

6 Applications and Example

The optimization of the input-output-structure as performed in the previous chapter enhances our knowledge of the functionality of the system adding to the information rendered by the transition probabilities.
Beyond, we can anticipate some practical implications. Possible applications could be in the optimal control of technical systems or in the analysis of biological or ecological systems. Developped for nominal variables, the previous considerations can of course be applied to other levels of measurement, as ordinal or interval (with a proper categorization of the measurement scale) as well. A mixture of types of variables can also be taken into account. Concrete applications are still to be worked out.
We shall put our emphasis to a problem which plays a major role in applied statistics, namely experimental design. Its main aim is to devise an existing association between variables in a most efficient way through deliberate planning. Usually, the behavior of a response variable is studied under varying values of one or more independent variables. One aspect that is not taken into account in classical experimental design, is how to choose the frequencies of the various conceived classes of the input variable to translate in an optimal way into the possible categories of the output variables. Our concept of codiversity measures this transformation in a way which was outlined in Chapter 5. The higher the value of codiversity the better can the behavior of the output variable be controlled by the input variable.
Thus, codiversity can be viewed as a quantitative measure of the intuitive concept of the degree to which the information contained within the system can be „exploited".
Optimization of codiversity is based on a known structure of the system, expressed by transition probabilities. In practice the latter will not always be known, especially in the case of the design of experiments. For the solution of our problem we therefore need to perform a preliminary investigation with arbitrarily (e.g. uniformly) distributed input vector, which in general will not be optimal in the

above sense. It serves for the estimation of the transition probabilities, which in turn can be used to optimize codiversity in the next step. This method is justified if we assume the transition probabilities to be invariant system properties independent of the distribution of the input variable.
The following example is based on a real field experiment assessing the influence of the amount of a fertilizer, applied to experimental plots, on the crop yield of these plots. The example was stated by Adam (1963) and reports the result of 193 experimental plots. The range of fertilizer intensity (variable A) was divided into $k = 6$ classes (of ascending magnitude), the range of crop yield (variable B) into $m = 6$ classes, as well. The frequency distribution is shown in Table 1.

Table 1: Absolute frequencies for fertilizer experiment. (A_i: classes of fertilizer intensity, B_j: classes of yield)

	A_1	A_2	A_3	A_4	A_5	A_6	
B_1	21	13	0	0	0	0	34
B_2	0	12	0	0	0	0	12
B_3	0	0	13	0	0	0	13
B_4	0	0	16	19	0	0	35
B_5	0	0	1	20	21	13	55
B_6	0	0	0	5	16	23	44
	21	25	30	44	37	36	193

The original experiment was analyzed by using classical statistical methods. For our purpose, neither the fact that the variables were measured on an interval scale, nor the numerical values of their class centers or even their order is relevant.
From Table 1 we can calculate the original input and output distribution:

$$\mathbf{p_0}(A) = (0.109 \;\; 0.129 \;\; 0.155 \;\; 0.229 \;\; 0.192 \;\; 0.186)$$

$$\mathbf{p_0}(B) = (0.176 \;\; 0.062 \;\; 0.067 \;\; 0.182 \;\; 0.285 \;\; 0.228)\,.$$

Table 2 shows the resulting transition probabilities. It can now be used as the starting point of our algorithm to maximize the codiversity.

Table 2: Transition probabilities $p(B_j|A_i)$ for fertilizer experiment.

	A_1	A_2	A_3	A_4	A_5	A_6
B_1	1.000	0.519	0	0	0	0
B_2	0	0.481	0	0	0	0
B_3	0	0	0.432	0	0	0
B_4	0	0	0.536	0.432	0	0
B_5	0	0	0.032	0.454	0.568	0.360
B_6	0	0	0	0.114	0.432	0.640

Applying the procedure outlined in Chapter 5 we get the following results:

maximum codiversity: $v(A,B) = 3.336$,
corresponding distribution of the output variable B:

$$\mathbf{p}_2' = \mathbf{p}'(B) = (0.300 \ \ 0.071 \ \ 0.241 \ \ 0.082 \ \ 0.142 \ \ 0.164) \ ,$$

corresponding distribution of the input variable A:

$$\mathbf{p}_1' = \mathbf{p}'(A) = (0.223 \ \ 0.148 \ \ 0.557 \ \ -0.498 \ \ 0.696 \ \ -0.126) \ .$$

We recognize that the „solution" for $\mathbf{p}_1'$ fulfills the condition that the sum of the components is 1, however two components are negative contradicting their essence as being probabilities (or relative frequencies). Thus, a case that has been theoretically anticipated, actually has occurred, and we must resort to the procedure previously outlined in chapter 5.
Setting $p(A_i) = 0$ successively for all components and repeating the optimizing algorithm, results in solutions which all but one still have at least one negative component. The single admissible solution is reached by setting $p(A_4) = 0$.This solution renders the maximum (admissible) codiversity

$$\hat{v}(A,B) = 3.156$$

with the corresponding distribution vectors

$$\hat{\mathbf{p}}_2' = \hat{\mathbf{p}}'(B) = (0.317 \ \ 0.075 \ \ 0.130 \ \ 0.154 \ \ 0.150 \ \ 0.174)$$

$$\hat{\mathbf{p}}_1' = \hat{\mathbf{p}}'(A) = (0.237 \ \ 0.157 \ \ 0.290 \ \ 0 \qquad 0.132 \ \ 0.184)$$

For a check we calculate the values of the quantities $c(A_i, B)$ defined earlier in (22).
We get the result

$$v(A_i, B) = \begin{cases} 3.156 & i = 1,2,3,5,6 \\ 2.646 & i = 4 \end{cases}$$

which is fully in accordance with theory.
Finally, some characteristic quantities are being compared for the original and the optimum design from Table 3.

Table 3: Characteristic quantities in the original and the optimum design

	experimental design	
	original	control-optimized
# of classes of fertilizer intensity	6	5
# of classes of crop yield	6	6
diversity of fertilizer classes $v(A)$	5,82	4,81
diversity of yield classes $v(B)$	5,00	5,47
bivariate diversity $v(AB)$	11,60	8,33
codiversity $v(A,B)$	2,51	3,16
„blind“ diversity $v(A\|B)v(B\|A)$	4,62	2,64

We notice, that the codiversity has increased, as was to be expected from optimizing the structure.
Recalling the definition (8) of codiversity we call the denominator $v(A|B)v(B|A)$ the *blind diversity*: It can be interpreted as a reduction factor of the full bivariate diversity. According to previous considerations, the bivariate diversity can be preserved at its original value in case of total mutual dependence and reduced to 1 in case of independence, signalling the lack of any influence that can be exerted on variable B by variable A. Values between these extremes express a varying degree of association. If we employ the notion of the „equivalent uniform distribution“ once more, the value of the blind diversity denotes how many „steps“ of the overall bivariate diversity are condensed into one step of the codiversity (or control diversity) and are therefore indistinguishable with respect to the controllability of the system. The more independent the variables A and B, as (inversely) measured by the codiversity, the less influence can be exerted on the system by external manipulation, which conforms to reasoning and experience.
In our example the value of the blind diversity as compared between the two situations reveals that a much greater proportion of the original diversity remains at disposal for controlling purposes in the optimum case than in the case of the original, arbitrary choice of the input variable.
The concept outlined above still needs further consideration as to its practical implications. Also, the connection to classical methods of associaton analysis has to be investigated more thoroughly.
However, we could show that the quantity $v(A)$ is not only a very well-based diversity measure in its original sense, but lends itself to generalizations and applications to problems of association and control, suggesting - although it was originally worked out for nominal-scaled variables - the inclusion of variables measured on any scale.

References

- Adam, A. (1963): Systematische Datenverarbeitung bei der Auswertung von Versuchs- und Beobachtungsergebnissen. Physica, Würzburg.
- Adam, A. (1984): Grundriß einer statistischen Systemtheorie. In: Festschrift für Wilhelm Winkler (Hrsg.: A. Adam). Schriftenreihe der Österreichischen Statistischen Gesellschaft, Bd. 1., Orac, Wien.
- Beran, H. (1994): Eine systemkonforme Maßzahlbildung für klassifikatorische Merkmale. OR Spektrum 16, 81 - 88.
- Fano, R.M. (1966): Informationsübertragung. R. Oldenbourg, München - Wien.
- Ferschl, F. (1985). Deskriptive Statistik, 3.A., Physica, Würzburg -Wien.
- Hill, M.O. (1973): Diversity and Evenness: A Unifying Notation and its Consequences. Ecology 54, 427 - 432.
- Hurlbert, S.H. (1971): The Nonconcept of Species Diversity: A Critique and Alternative Parameters. Ecology 52, 577 - 586.
- Kämmerer, W. (1974): Einführung in mathematische Methoden der Kybernetik. Akademie-Verlag, Berlin.
- Patil, G.P.; Taillie, C. (1982): Diversity as a Concept and its Measurement. J. Am. Stat. Assoc., 77: 548 - 567.
- Peters, J. (1967): Einführung in die allgemeine Informationstheorie. Kommunikation und Kybernetik in Einzeldarstellungen, Bd. 6, Springer, Berlin - Heidelberg - New York.
- Rao, C.R. (1982): Analysis of Diversity: A Unified Approach. In: Statistical Decision Theory and Related Topics III, Vol. 2. Academic Press, London - New York - Toronto, 233 - 250.

A Subjective Bayes Approach to the Queueing System $M/E_k/c$

Harald Schmidbauer and Angi Rösch

University of Munich

Abstract

What do we really know about the values of the parameters, e.g. traffic intensity, of a queueing system in a specific application? No matter how long we observe the system, our knowledge will always be uncertain. There is a variety of reasons why this aspect should not be neglected, for example, it may be important to detect discrepancies between desirable and real parameter values. We adopt the subjective Bayesian concept of statistics in order to take this uncertainty explicitly into account. In this framework we discuss how learning about the parameters from observations, departing from a state of no information, proceeds in the system $M/E_k/c$, and some advantages of the subjective approach. A real-life example is used for illustration.

1 Introduction

Research in queueing systems and networks proceeds usually along one of the following lines: (i) Given certain parameters of the system (e.g., arrival and service rates), find performance measures (e.g., average queue length), or find an optimal control policy; (ii) find conditions on the parameters which ensure that a certain property of the queue or network (e.g., equilibrium exists) be fulfilled. In the first case, it is implicitly assumed that the relevant parameters are known, whereas the second case imposes restrictions on the parameters, no matter what we know about the values of the parameters in specific applications. In either case, statistical issues are neglected.

A justification of this approach may be found in the overall paradigm of operations research, namely *to set the parameters* of a system such that operations may be conducted in a desirable way. However, setting the parameters of a system is often only the second step, which is preceded by carefully observing the system and gathering all relevant data. In other queueing situations, the description, and not the management, of the queueing process may be more important, for example when an existing service system is to be evaluated. The detection of discrepancies between desired and real parameters ("real" in the sense that their consequences are observed) may also be important.

No matter how long we observe a queueing system, our knowledge of the system parameters will always remain uncertain. A statistical approach can help us to take the uncertain nature of our knowledge explicitly into consideration and define a framework for inference about the parameters.

There are two broad classes of concepts for statistical inference, depending on the philosophical point of view that we adopt. In the *objectivist* concept the system parameters are regarded as fixed in the sense of a physical parameter that exists independently of observers and observations. It is then meaningful to estimate the parameters in question such that the error (difference of true value and estimate) or a function of the error (such as the squared error) is small. The performance of an estimate is then evaluated by taking into account all possible observations. In this context, using the mean square error implies a frequentist criterion.

On the other hand, the *subjectivist* concept is based on the idea that an observer should express his or her knowledge of a system parameter in terms of a probability distribution for that parameter. In this sense the system parameter is a random variable. Repeated observations of the system lead us from a prior distribution of the parameters (prior to observations) to a posterior distribution. The tool for the passage from prior to posterior distribution is Bayes' theorem. In this concept, all inference about the parameters is based on the posterior distribution, and hence only on the observations which have really been made. It should be emphasized that the mere use of Bayes's theorem does not imply that a subjective approach is adopted, as we will see below.

Whereas there are thousands of articles dealing with the analysis of queueing systems and networks, the number of articles concerned with statistical inference in the queueing context does not seem to exceed a few dozen. An account of estimates of arrival and service rates in single-server queueing systems within the framework of objective statistics is given by Basawa and Prabhu [1]. They analyze the long-run properties of maximum likelihood and moment estimates under different sampling schemes. A similar approach is used by Bhat and Rao [3], who extend classical asymptotic theory to hypothesis testing in queueing systems.

A comprehensive exposition of a subjective Bayesian framework for statistical inference is given, and exemplified on the $M/M/1$ queueing system, by McGrath, Gross and Singpurwalla [6] and McGrath and Singpurwalla [7]. The subjective Bayesian approach rests on the assumption that an observer's beliefs, expressed in his or her prior distribution of the system parameters, provide the basis for learning through observations. This is different from the empirical Bayes approach, which assumes that there is a parametric family of prior distributions whose parameters (the super-parameters) are themselves regarded as realizations of a random variable. In this approach the prior distribution is estimated via estimating the super-parameters, and in this sense it is meaningful to speak of a "true" prior, whereas this is not meaningful in the subjective Bayesian approach. Thiruvaiyaru and Basawa [12] apply the empirical Bayesian approach to queueing systems, the sampling scheme in which they discuss properties of their estimates, however, has raised a poignant criticism, see Singpurwalla [9]. In an empirical Bayesian setting, Sohn [10], [11] models influences of covariates on the arrival and service intensity and investigates the effect of misspecification, which means that the "true" prior is different from the model.

The present paper deals with learning about the parameters of the system $M/E_k/c$ within the framework of subjective Bayesian analysis. We do therefore not resort to a further level which involves super-parameters, but regard the prior distribution as reflecting the observer's beliefs. We do not assume a particular parametric form of a prior distribution. This is different from McGrath et al. [6], who use the Erlang model as prior distribution because it is "flexible enough to capture many subjective feelings about λ and μ that the analyst has," and who also apply a bivariate lognormal distribution to model dependent parameters λ and μ. The point of view taken in the present paper is that it is reasonable to begin inference with a noninformative prior, which should be selected on convincing grounds.

This paper is organized as follows. Chapter 2 gives a very brief review of the queueing system $M/E_k/c$. The theory of learning about the arrival rate, service rate, and traffic intensity, and how to find noninformative priors, is developed in chapter 3. The theory is applied to a copy-shop which is modeled as an $M/E_2/2$ queueing system in chapter 4.

2 The Queueing System $M/E_k/c$

2.1 Definition

The queueing system $M/E_k/c$ is defined by the following assumptions: There are c identical service stations ("identical" with respect to service time distribution). Incoming customers are served in FIFO discipline. A customer is served as soon as there is a free service station. Waiting customers form a queue, and there is just one queue in front of all c service stations. Queueing space is supposed to be unlimited. Customers arrive according to a Poisson stream, i.e. interarrival times are iid exponential random variables A_i with density $p(a|\lambda) = \lambda\exp(-\lambda a)$ with a parameter $\lambda > 0$. Service times S_i are assumed to be iid Erlang-k random variables; their density is

$$p(s|\mu) = \frac{(k\mu)^k}{(k-1)!} s^{k-1} \exp\{-k\mu s\} \tag{1}$$

with a parameter $\mu > 0$ and k a natural number (see Müller [8]). In the case $k = 1$ this is the exponential density with parameter μ. It holds that

$$\mathrm{E}(A) = \frac{1}{\lambda}, \quad \mathrm{var}(A) = \frac{1}{\lambda^2}, \quad \mathrm{E}(S) = \frac{1}{\mu}, \quad \mathrm{var}(S) = \frac{1}{k\mu^2},$$

that is, if $k > 1$ an Erlang-k random variable has less variation than an exponential random variable with the same expectation (its coefficient of variation is $1/\sqrt{k}$, compared to 1 in the case of an exponential random variable). The class of Erlang distributions provides thus more flexibility than the exponential distribution. Due to its characteristic property of being forgetful, the exponential distribution is often a suitable model for interarrival times, whereas service times may often be modeled by an Erlang distribution. This will also be seen in the example below. The Erlang distribution is easily handled mathematically since the Erlang-k distribution is the k-fold convolution of an exponential distribution. We may therefore also think of a customer's service time as being the sum of k iid exponential random variables. (The Erlang-k distribution is an example of a phase model. — The Erlang distribution is also a special case of the Gamma distribution.)

2.2 System Characteristics

Under the assumptions stated above, the average number of arrivals per time unit is λ, while the average number of customers served per time unit is at most $c \cdot \mu$. The relation of λ and $c\mu$, which is usually expressed in terms of the traffic intensity

$$\rho = \frac{\lambda}{c \cdot \mu},$$

provides therefore a criterion for the quality of the long-run development of the system. An equilibrium distribution exists if and only if $\rho < 1$. In this case, the system will, after sufficient time, reach a steady-state condition which means that the distribution of the number of customers in the system will remain constant and is independent of the system state at time $t = 0$. If $\rho < 1$, the traffic intensity is also the percentage of time that at least one of the servers is busy, so that $1 - \rho$ is the share of time that the system is idle. Another important performance parameter is the steady-state expected number of customers in the system. Bounds and tables of numerical values are given by Hillier and Yu [5]. Steady-state distributions of the number of customers are also not available in general.

2.3 Learning About the Parameters λ, μ, ρ

In what follows it is assumed that all three parameters λ, μ, and ρ are unknown. The Erlang parameter k is supposed to be known. The task is then to use observations from the service process in $M/E_k/c$ to gain inference about the parameters λ, μ and ρ. It is important to specify the form of observations. Following McGrath and Singpurwalla [7] (their cases 1 to 3), we assume that we are given sequences $(a_1, \ldots, a_n)$ and $(s_1, \ldots, s_m)$ of interarrival times and service times, respectively. As will be seen in the next subsection, learning about the parameters λ and μ, and hence ρ, is then possible via Bayes' theorem without assuming that equilibrium exists.

Depending on the model assumptions and the availability of distributions of the system state, it may also be possible to use observations of another kind for learning about the parameters. For example, observing the number of customers who are present in the system at epochs $t_1 < t_2 < \ldots < t_n$ (as in [7], case 4) allows, via Bayes' theorem, learning about ρ provided that either time-dependent (transient) state probabilities or steady-state probabilities are available, if these probabilities may be written in terms of ρ alone. Steady-state probabilities are sufficient for inference if $t_i << t_{i+1}$, that is there is sufficient time for the system to reach equilibrium after having been observed. We will not pursue this approach because equilibrium probabilities are not available in our intended model.

2.4 Learning on the Basis of Noninformative Priors

2.4.1 The Problem of Noninformative Priors

The Bayesian machinery requires prior distributions for the (random) parameters about which we want to learn from system observations.

The first question arising here is: For which of the priors λ, μ, and ρ should priors be given? Priors for the three parameters should be designed in a consistent manner. With assumed independence of λ and μ, the design of priors for λ and μ will result in one for the parameter ρ, the latter being the quotient of λ and $c \cdot \mu$. On the other hand, the priors of λ and μ are not identifiable from a prior for ρ when we assume pairwise independence. Also, as we stated above, it is not possible, in our model, to start with a prior distribution for ρ and apply Bayes' theorem directly, without refering to λ and μ, since the necessary likelihoods are not available.

Next, the question of information: Is there an argument or reliable prior information that supports any specific prior distributions, a parametric family of prior distributions at its best? Proceeding on the assumption that the traffic intensity in the system is below the critical value (i.e. $\rho < 1$), don't we have to admit that further prior information is not available, about neither of the three parameters? Even certain knowledge about the traffic intensity will not give any hint, not even any restrictions on the range of λ and μ. Hence, what is needed here is a prior that does not favor some parameter values over others, that does not pinpoint anything, apart from a parameter space restriction for ρ at most; in other words: *noninformative prior*.

If for a parameter of interest, say θ, a noninformative density is desired, it seems reasonable to give equal weight, that is equal density, to all possible values of θ. Using this (naive) argument, we arrive at the *uniform noninformative prior* $\pi(\theta) \propto d$ for some $d > 0$, where d may be chosen such that π is a proper density if the range (the support) of θ is restricted.

Starting now with a uniform noninformative prior for ρ, e.g.

$$\pi(\rho) \propto 1, \quad \rho \in (0, \infty),$$

or immediately with the proper uniform prior given steady state conditions,

$$\pi(\rho) = 1, \quad \rho \in (0, 1),$$

for reasons of pairwise independence we do not arrive at definite consistent priors for either λ or μ. Vice versa, if we start with uniform noninformative priors for both λ and μ,

$$\pi(\lambda) \propto 1, \quad \pi(\mu) \propto 1, \quad \lambda, \mu \in (0, \infty),$$

we would not be led to a uniform prior for ρ, not even to any one: Since λ and μ are independent, the joint prior density being

$$\pi(\lambda, \mu) \propto 1, \quad \lambda, \mu \in (0, \infty),$$

the density of $\rho = \lambda/(c\mu)$ should read

$$\pi(\rho) = \int_0^\infty \pi(\rho \cdot c\mu, \mu) \cdot c\mu \, \mathrm{d}\mu \quad \propto \quad \int_0^\infty c\mu \, \mathrm{d}\mu.$$

Analoguous relations prevent us from finding a prior for $\lambda = \rho \cdot c\mu$ given uniform priors for ρ and μ, or for $\mu = \lambda/(c\rho)$ given uniform priors for ρ and λ. We have to conclude, that uniform noninformative priors can not be assigned to all *three* parameters, and strictly speaking not even to *two* out of them, without risk of inconsistent results.

2.5 System-Suited Priors for λ and μ

In order to find priors that are system-suited, i.e. that are based on the system structure, we consider the following "invariance under reformulation argument" (see Berger [2]). It takes into account that the parameter λ is a *Poisson* parameter; and a similar argument can then be applied to the Erlang parameter μ. The number $N(T)$ of customer arrivals to the system in a time interval of length T is a Poisson variable. The parameter λ is the average number of arrivals for $T = 1$, and it holds that $\mathrm{E}(N(T)) = T \cdot \mathrm{E}(N(1)) = T \cdot \lambda$. However, our situation of non-information is reflected in that the specification of the time unit is arbitrary, and hence the time interval to which the parameter λ is related. We consider now the experiment which would result if our time unit were T. The distribution of the random variable $\Lambda = \mathrm{E}(N(1))$ should then be independent of T, in order to reflect our situation of non-information. Then the probability that the average number of arrivals in the considered time interval is less than some value λ equals the probability that the variable Λ is less than λ/T, formally:

$$P\{\mathrm{E}(N(T)) \leq \lambda\} = P\{T \cdot \mathrm{E}(N(1)) \leq \lambda\} = P\{\Lambda \leq \lambda/T\}.$$

Differentiation leads to

$$\frac{\mathrm{d}}{\mathrm{d}\lambda} P\{\Lambda \leq \lambda/T\} = h(\lambda/T)/T,$$

where h is the density of Λ. How can we choose h such that the required independence of T be fulfilled? — Choose $h(\lambda) \propto 1/\lambda$.

The same prior would have been suggested by the method of Jeffreys (1961) (see Berger [2]), which is to choose

$$\pi(\lambda) = [I(\lambda)]^{1/2}$$

as a noninformative prior, where

$$I(\lambda) = -\mathrm{E}_\lambda\left[\frac{\partial^2 f(X|\lambda)}{\partial \lambda^2}\right]$$

is the expected Fisher information, in our case refering to the distribution of a Poisson variable X.

However we reason, we are led to the following noninformative priors for λ and μ (though improper priors):

$$\pi(\lambda) \propto 1/\lambda, \quad \pi(\mu) \propto 1/\mu, \qquad \lambda, \mu \in (0, \infty).$$

2.6 Priors for ρ

The question now is: Do we get a noninformative prior for ρ that can be adjusted to these assumptions? The answer is not straightforward, as we shall see in a moment. Taking into account the product nature of the joint prior (due to the assumed independence)

$$\pi(\lambda, \mu) = \pi(\lambda) \cdot \pi(\mu),$$

we get the expression

$$\pi(\rho) = \int_0^\infty \pi(\rho \cdot c\mu, \mu) \cdot c\mu \, \mathrm{d}\mu \quad \propto \quad \frac{1}{\rho} \int_0^\infty \pi(\mu) \, \mathrm{d}\mu, \tag{2}$$

on the one hand,

$$\pi(\rho) = \int_0^\infty \pi(\lambda, \lambda/(c\rho)) \cdot \frac{\lambda}{c\rho^2} \, \mathrm{d}\lambda \quad \propto \quad \frac{1}{\rho} \int_0^\infty \pi(\lambda) \, \mathrm{d}\lambda \tag{3}$$

on the other hand, where $\rho \in (0, \infty)$. Here the proportionality property holds whenever the integrals converge, i.e. when μ (or λ) has a proper density — which is not the case for the system-suited priors that were derived above. We encounter here a lack of argument in deriving a prior for ρ. However, we also realize that, in order to get a prior for ρ of the type $\pi(\rho) \propto 1/\rho$, it suffices to assume that *one* of λ or μ has the system-suited prior and the other *any proper* prior.

Let us now consider a combination of noninformative system-suited and uniform priors, namely

$$\pi(\lambda) \propto 1/\lambda, \quad \pi(\rho) = 1, \quad \lambda \in (0, \infty), \ \rho \in (0, 1),$$

reflecting the assumption that equilibrium exists. Then, the joint density of λ and ρ is, due to pairwise conditional independence,

$$\pi(\lambda, \rho) \propto \frac{1}{\lambda}.$$

Therefore

$$\pi(\mu) = \int_0^1 \pi(\rho \cdot c\mu, \rho) \cdot c\rho \, \mathrm{d}\rho \quad \propto \quad \frac{1}{\mu} \int_0^1 \mathrm{d}\rho = \frac{1}{\mu},$$

which is the system-suited prior for μ! The same result is found by integrating with respect to λ:

$$\pi(\mu) = \int_0^\infty \pi(\lambda, \lambda/(c\mu)) \cdot \frac{\lambda}{c\mu^2} \, \mathrm{d}\lambda \quad \propto \quad \int_0^{c\mu} \frac{1}{c\mu^2} \, \mathrm{d}\lambda = \frac{1}{\mu}.$$

Thus, we have found a consistent combination of two system-suited priors and a uniform prior.

The above discussion may be summarized in the following

Result: If, for the arrival rate λ, we assume the noninformative, system-suited, improper prior density

$$\pi(\lambda) = 1/\lambda, \quad \lambda \in (0, \infty),$$

then

- without further assumption, the corresponding prior of ρ will be

$$\pi(\rho) = 1/\rho, \quad \rho \in (0, \infty),$$

  whatever (proper) prior we choose for μ;

- assuming that equilibrium exists, the corresponding prior of ρ will be

$$\pi(\rho) = 1, \quad \rho \in (0, 1),$$

  and the corresponding prior of μ will also be

$$\pi(\mu) = 1/\mu, \quad \mu \in (0, \infty).$$

These implications hold also when λ and μ are interchanged.

2.7 Learning About λ, μ and ρ

Probabilities on the parameter space conditional on a given sample of system observations serve as the frame of reference for Bayes procedures. Hence, our goal is now to derive the posterior distributions by adopting the Bayesian viewpoint of learning from observations.

Let

$$z_1 = (a_1, \ldots, a_n), \quad \text{and} \quad z_2 = (s_1, \ldots, s_m)$$

be the (random) sample of interarrival times a_i, and of service times s_i respectively, in the system $M/E_k/c$, i.e. a_i are independent realizations of an exponential and s_i of an Erlang-k random variable.

Then, applying Bayes' theorem, it holds for any of the three parameters of interest, say θ vicariously, that

$$p(\theta|z_1, z_2) = \frac{p(z_1, z_2|\theta) \cdot \pi(\theta)}{\int_0^\infty p(z_1, z_2|\theta) \cdot \pi(\theta)\, d\theta},$$

where $\pi(\theta)$ is the corresponding noninformative prior. — In the following we will choose priors of the system-suited type

$$\pi(\theta) \propto 1/\theta, \quad \theta \in (0, \infty),$$

θ standing for either λ or μ. To begin with, without assuming equilibrium, we will choose this type of density also for ρ.

Before proceeding to find the likelihoods of observations needed in this formula, we notice that the parameter λ is independent of the observations z_2, and reversely, that the parameter μ is independent of the observations z_1, whereas the parameter ρ depends on both groups of observations, z_1 and z_2.

Starting with λ and μ, the corresponding formula components are then

$$p(z_1|\lambda) = \lambda^n \exp\{-\lambda \sum_{i=1}^{n} a_i\},$$

and

$$p(z_2|\mu) = \frac{(k\mu)^{km}}{(k-1)!^m} \prod_{i=1}^{m} s_i^{k-1} \exp\{-k\mu \sum_{i=1}^{m} s_i\}$$

(see (1)). Therewith, the Bayes formula gives the posteriors

$$p(\lambda|z_1) = \frac{\left(\sum_{i=1}^{n} a_i\right)^n}{\Gamma(n)} \lambda^{n-1} \exp\{-\lambda \sum_{i=1}^{n} a_i\},$$

and

$$p(\mu|z_2) = \frac{\left(k\sum_{i=1}^{m} s_i\right)^{km}}{\Gamma(km)} \mu^{km-1} \exp\{-k\mu \sum_{i=1}^{m} s_i\},$$

respectively. These are Gamma densities, and thus we have the distribution models

$$\lambda|z_1 \overset{L}{=} (n, \sum_{i=1}^{n} a_i), \quad \mu|z_2 \overset{L}{=} \text{Gamma}(km, k\sum_{i=1}^{m} s_i),$$

where the symbol $\overset{L}{=}$ means equivalence in distribution, and Gamma(p, b) denotes a Gamma distributed random variable with mean p/b and variance p/b^2. (The Gamma distributions are the conjugate class to the Erlang distributions.) Since λ and μ are independent, the joint posterior is simply the product of the individual posteriors.

Concerning ρ we are faced with two alternatives. The first alternative is to derive the posterior as the distribution of the quotient of λ and $c\mu$, applying the two posteriors found above, and without reapplying Bayes' formula, and especially without prior for ρ. Using a property of the quotient of two Gamma variables (see Müller [8]) it can be shown that

$$\frac{km}{n} \cdot \frac{\sum_{i=1}^{n} a_i}{k \sum_{i=1}^{m} s_i} \cdot c\rho | z_1, z_2 \stackrel{L}{=} F(2n, 2km), \tag{4}$$

where $F(2n, 2km)$ denotes an F-distributed random variable with $2n$ and $2km$ degrees of freedom, which has the mean $n/(n-1)$ and the variance $n^2(n + km - 1)/(km(n-1)^2(n-2))$.

The second alternative is to apply the Bayesian approach directly. However, we will see that in any case the reference of ρ to λ and μ is indispensible since the observations z_1, z_2 cannot be explained by the traffic intensity alone. Therefore, the likelihood given ρ can not be found without a method of additional conditioning on either λ or μ, applying the corresponding prior. Taking λ, we find

$$\begin{aligned} p(z_1, z_2 | \rho) &= \int_0^\infty p(z_1, z_2 | \rho, \lambda) \cdot \pi(\lambda) \, \mathrm{d}\lambda \\ &= \int_0^\infty p(z_1 | \lambda) \cdot p(z_2 | \mu = \lambda/(c\rho)) \cdot \pi(\lambda) \, \mathrm{d}\lambda \\ &\propto \frac{(\frac{k}{c\rho})^{km}}{(k-1)!^m} \prod s_i^{k-1} \int_0^\infty \lambda^{n+km-1} \exp\{-\lambda(\sum_{i=1}^{n} a_i + \frac{k}{c\rho} \sum_{i=1}^{m} s_i)\} \, \mathrm{d}\lambda \\ &= \frac{\Gamma(n+km)}{(k-1)!} \cdot \frac{(\frac{k}{c\rho})^{km}}{(\sum a_i + \frac{k}{c\rho} \sum s_i)^{n+km}} \cdot \prod s_i^{k-1}, \end{aligned}$$

Γ denoting the Gamma function. Then, from Bayes' formula we get, after some reorganization,

$$p(\rho | z_1, z_2) \propto \frac{(\frac{k}{c\rho})^{km+1}}{(\sum a_i + \frac{k}{c\rho} \sum s_i)^{n+km}} \propto (c\rho)^{n-1} \cdot \left(c\rho \cdot \frac{\sum a_i}{k \sum s_i} + 1\right)^{-(n+km)},$$

where we recognize again the posterior in (4).

Although the second method works with the non-adjusted prior $\pi(\rho) \propto 1/\rho$, and even more, although the two methods actually use different sets of prior information, they coincide in one posterior density for ρ! Whereas in the first method no prior information for ρ is considered, the second method works without any prior for μ, provided that it is proper for the reasons discussed above. Obviously, the posteriors have compensated for the lack of argument which was mentioned above.

2.8 The Case $\rho < 1$

We shall now examine the effect of the prior information that the traffic intensity ρ is below the critical value, i.e. $\rho < 1$. Actually, if $\rho \geq 1$, a steady state of the system does not exist since too many costumers would then arrive for the c service channels to be able to serve them. The assumption that an equilibrium exists may be supported by the mere observation of short queues. Hence, on the one hand we must find the joint posterior distribution of λ and μ given the constraint $\rho < 1$ — the marginal posteriors are not touched by that information, since separately, the spaces of parameter values are not touched. On the other hand our interest will focus on the posterior distribution of ρ given $\rho < 1$.

The posterior distribution of ρ, given that steady state exists, can be expressed in the form

$$p(\rho|z_1, z_2, \rho < 1) = \frac{p(\rho|z_1, z_2)}{P\{\rho < 1|z_1, z_2\}}, \quad \rho < 1, \tag{5}$$

whose components can be obtained from the F-distribution in (4). The denominator gives the posterior probability that a steady state exists for the system, i.e.

$$P\{\rho < 1|z_1, z_2\} = \int_0^{c^\star} f(u)\, du$$

with

$$c^\star = c \cdot \frac{km}{n} \cdot \frac{\sum_{i=1}^n a_i}{k\sum_{i=1}^m s_i},$$

and f being the density of an F-distribution with $2n$ and $2km$ degrees of freedom.

The joint posterior of λ and μ given $\rho < 1$ is

$$p(\lambda, \mu|z_1, z_2, \rho < 1) = \frac{p(\lambda, \mu|z_1, z_2)}{P\{\rho < 1|z_1, z_2\}}, \quad \lambda < c\mu,$$

with the joint posterior of λ and μ in the numerator. As expected, the marginal posterior distributions reduce to $p(\lambda|z_1)$ and $p(\mu|z_2)$ respectively, $\lambda, \mu \in (0, \infty)$. Of course, in case either λ or μ is additionally given, these posteriors are as follows:

$$p(\lambda|z_1, z_2, \mu, \rho < 1) = \frac{p(\lambda\,|z_1)}{P\{\lambda < c\mu\,|z_1, \mu\}}, \quad \lambda \in (0, c\mu)$$

$$p(\mu|z_1, z_2, \lambda, \rho < 1) = \frac{p(\mu\,|z_2)}{P\{\mu > \lambda/c\,|z_2, \lambda\}}, \quad \mu \in (\lambda/c, \infty),$$

where the corresponding posteriors remain to be inserted, and that is a Gamma density, respectively.

Finally, one may think about a noninformative prior for ρ *designed under the assumption* of an existing equilibrium, $\rho < 1$. We remarked earlier that the uniform prior $\pi(\rho) = 1$, $\rho \in (0,1)$, to some extent is consistent with the system-suited priors for λ and μ. We are stopped right at the beginning, however, since in our model, unlike the queueing model M/M/1, there is a lack of formulae for the likelihood $p(z_1, z_2|\rho, \rho < 1)$. Thus, we will not get along without any additional assumption concerning prior distributions of λ, or μ respectively. That method will coincide with our second one leading to the posterior (4) for ρ, but with the result

$$p(\rho|z_1, z_2, \rho < 1) \;\propto\; \frac{(\frac{k}{c\rho})^{km}}{(\sum a_i + \frac{k}{c\rho}\sum s_i)^{n+km}} \;\propto\; (c\rho)^n \cdot \left(c\rho \cdot \frac{\sum a_i}{k\sum s_i} + 1\right)^{-(n+km)},$$

with $\rho < 1$, where the F-distribution in (4) cannot be identified. But we notice the following relation to a posterior $\tilde{p}(\rho|z_1, z_2, \rho < 1)$ which is derived from the F-distribution in (4) (see (5)):

$$p(\rho|z_1, z_2, \rho < 1) = \frac{\rho \cdot \tilde{p}(\rho|z_1, z_2, \rho < 1)}{\mathrm{E}_{\tilde{p}}(\rho|z_1, z_2, \rho < 1)}.$$

Obviously, applying a uniform prior of ρ leads to a posterior that is pushed to the right under increase of skewness compared to the posterior in (5).

If we apply the (improper) prior $\pi(\rho) \propto 1/\rho$, $\rho \in (0,1)$, on the other hand, we are finally led to the posterior stated in (5), and there will just be a restriction of the parameter space from the very beginning.

3 Example

The arrival times of customers and their service times in a copy-shop with two copying machines were recorded during a whole day. "Service" means that either the customer tells the clerk his wishes which are then carried out by the clerk, or self-service. Owing to the very unequal intensity of the incoming customer stream before and after 2 p.m., it was found useful to treat both cases separately. The upper stemplots in Figure 1 show the interarrival times (the time that elapsed between two subsequent arrivals) and the lower stemplot shows the service times. Each value is in minutes, with the seconds cut off. There are more arrivals than services because some customers didn't wait for being served but left their orders.

Interarrival times...

...before 2 p.m.:

0⋆	00001122334
0•	678889
1⋆	033344
1•	57
2⋆	44
2•	7
3⋆	3
3•	
4⋆	
4•	5
5⋆	2
5•	

...after 2 p.m.:

0⋆	000011111112222223334444
0•	566667778899
1⋆	0113
1•	8
2⋆	002
2•	
3⋆	
3•	5
4⋆	
4•	
5⋆	
5•	

Service times:

0⋆	1122333444
0•	555567888889999
1⋆	000011223444
1•	5555555556666778
2⋆	0002234
2•	557
3⋆	14
3•	789
4⋆	0
4•	
5⋆	2
5•	6

Figure 1: Stemplots of interarrival and service times in a copy-shop

The stemplots of the interarrival times, as well as that of the service times, have characteristic shapes. The hypotheses that interarrival times are exponentially distributed and service times are E_2 distributed are not rejected ($\alpha = 0.05$). It is therefore assumed that $M/E_2/2$ is an appropriate model for descibing this copy-shop. We may apply the observed data to formula (4) (with $k = 2$ and $c = 2$)) in order to learn about the parameters λ, μ, and ρ. The posterior density of ρ, for both before and after 2 p.m., is displayed in Figure 2. With this distribution, the probability that $\rho > 1$ is approximately 0.134 (before 2 p.m.) and 0.418 (after 2 p.m.). Keeping in mind that $1/\lambda$ and $1/\mu$ are the average interarrival time and average service time, respectively, the event $\rho > 1$ has the appealing interpretation that there are more customers than can be served, or, in other words: that there is a potential of customers which cannot be served with the present capacity. The probability $P\{\rho > 1\}$ is the subjective probability, after one day's observations, that this is the case. This probability can help to decide whether the copy-shop's capacity should be increased, and how long to continue the observations.

A final remark about the prior density of ρ is in order. Starting without any knowledge of the system, our prior probability that equilibrium exists in our system may well be 50%. Formally, this is not reflected in a *constant* prior density for ρ, since this assumption leads to $P\{\rho < 1\} = 1/\infty = 0$. However, if we define the prior density of ρ as $1/\rho$, the corresponding probability becomes ∞/∞, which reflects our intuition much better than the "naive" guess that the prior density of ρ is constant.

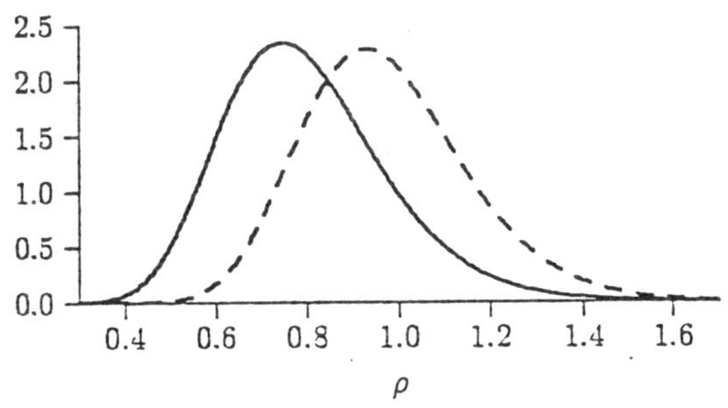

Figure 2: Posterior density of ρ before (thick line) and after 2 p.m. (dashed line)

4 Conclusions

The uncertain nature of our knowledge about parameters is the starting point for statistical approaches. In the subjectivist concept the parameters are regarded as random variables. Evaluating observations means learning about the parameters then, that is stepping from prior distributions to posterior distributions by means of Bayes' theorem.

We discussed how learning about parameters from observations, departing from a state of no information, proceeds in the system $M/E_k/c$. The state of no information is reflected in our choice of prior distributions: They are noninformative in the sense that they do not favor any parameter values over others, that are suited to the system structure. The idea that equilibrium exists may be incorporated.

The parameters with which we were concerned are the system parameters λ and μ in the distribution models, but we focus our interest on a parameter derived from these: the traffic intensity $\rho = \lambda/(c\mu)$. The task of finding a posterior for ρ, based on likelihoods expressed only in terms of ρ, finds its limits in the nonavailability of steady-state distributions of the system.

An economic interpretation of the posterior probability $P\{\rho > 1\}$ is found in a real-world example. This probability has no analogue in classical statistical inference.

Questions concerning sampling schemes were neglected. Keeping in mind economic applications of the present approach, an important question in this respect is how long the system should be observed in order to gain information which is reliable enough for making a decision. Finally, it would also be desirable to develop a model that allows for nonhomogeneous customer input. These may be topics of future research.

References

[1] Basawa I.V., Prabhu N.U. (1981): Estimation in single server queues. *Naval Research Logistics Quarterly* 28, 475 – 487

[2] Berger J.O. (1985): *Statistical Decision Theory and Bayesian Analysis.* (2nd edn.) Springer, New York.

[3] Bhat U.N., Rao S. Subba (1987): Statistical analysis of queueing systems. *Queueing Systems* 1, 217 – 247

[4] Ferschl Franz (1964): *Zufallsabhängige Wirtschaftsprozesse.* Physica-Verlag, Wien und Würzburg

[5] Hillier F.S., Yu O.S. (1981): *Queueing Tables and Graphs.* North Holland, New York

[6] McGrath Michael F., Gross Donald, Singpurwalla Nozer D. (1987): A subjective Bayesian approach to the theory of queues I — modeling. *Queueing Systems* 1, 317 – 333

[7] McGrath Michael F., Singpurwalla Nozer D. (1987): A subjective Bayesian approach to the theory of queues II — inference and information in $M/M/1$ queues. *Queueing Systems* 1, 335 – 353

[8] Müller P.H. (1991): *Lexikon der Stochastik.* (5. Auflage) Akademie Verlag, Berlin

[9] Singpurwalla, Nozer D. (1992): Discussion of Thiruvaiyaru and Basawa's "Empirical Bayes estimation for queueing systems and networks." *Queueing Systems* 11, 203 – 206

[10] Sohn So Young (1996a): Influence of a prior distribution on traffic intensity estimation with covariates. J. Statist. Comput. Simul. 55, 169 – 180

[11] Sohn So Young (1996b): Empirical Bayesian analysis for traffic intensity: $M/M/1$ queues with covariates. *Queueing Systems* 22, 383 – 401

[12] Thiruvaiyaru Dharma, Basawa Ishwar V. (1992): Empirical Bayes estimation for queueing systems and networks. *Queueing Systems* 11, 179 – 202

Cooperation as the Stimulating Power for the Austrian Automobile Industry - Results of an Empirical Study

Carola Kratzer and Ulrike Leopold-Wildburger[1]

Department of Statistics and Operations Research,
Karl-Franzens-University Graz, Austria

Abstract
The following report focuses on the automobile industry, being one of the most important branches of employment and growth world-wide. Since the automobile industry is highly globalised and competitive many western companies are engaged in Asia. Part of this paper is the statistical analysis of an empirical study including a questionnaire carried out in India combined with ideas on trust and commitment formation.

Keywords: Asia, Automobile Industry, Cooperation, Economic Development, India, Questionnaire, Trust.

Vertrauen ist für alle Unternehmen das größte Kapital
(Albert Schweitzer)

1. Introduction

In view of the massive consolidations within the automobile industry during the last few months and also the rapid growth of the Austrian automobile sector it is important to keep abreast of further information within this area.

---

[1] Corresponding author

Although being a rather small economy within the European Union, Austria attracts a number of important automobile companies of the world. For example, the biggest independent automobile supplier of the world MAGNA has increased its engagement by signing a trade contract with the Austrian company Steyr-Daimler-Puch AG recently. A few years ago Chrysler set up its only European production base in Austria.

No industrial sector in the world employs more people and adds more to the GDP of different countries than the automobile sector. This fact makes it interesting to investigate the phenomenon of its strength, and also the fact that the automobile companies face stiff competition worldwide.

This study tries to bring some light into this complex industry and to show how decisions about cooperations are realised. In this context the study shall also highlight the connection between trust and prosperous commitments between partners.

An especially significant kind of economic processes are the new developments of international cooperation. The biggest steps are taken by the big automobile producers through takeovers or through mergers. This is the reason for considering and investigating them in more detail. These mergers have put pressure on the automobile industry to find global partners in order not to be pushed out by larger companies. We want to find out how the merger partners are chosen and selected and whether trust and calculativeness respectively, play a role in the decision process.

Within the large U.S. and German firms economic growth is going ahead and the representatives of these companies are thinking in terms of expansion and the creation of new development paths. Austrian companies are also obliged to follow this strategy to survive the international competition. However, we should take into account the way in which a study on calculativeness and trust could increase our understanding for foreign culture circles.

Even though the economic situation in Asia is in its worst state since the beginning of the nineties, the situation offers many opportunities for European companies seeking an investment for the future. Low interests rates and low valuation of an enterprise open expanding companies certain opportunities in the Asian region which they did not have just a few years before.

In the following chapter we want to figure out how the decision for such a project arose and further, why India has been chosen for this study.

2. The Current Situation of the Automobile Sector - Globalisation and the Movement Towards Asia

"This merger between Daimler Benz and Chrysler will kick over all the dominoes, have all the smaller auto companies assessing who they are and what they are. Automobiles are a commodity, and the big guys with the low costs are going to be the survivors . . .".
(Gerald C. Meyers, University of Michigan and former CEO of American Motor, which Chrylser bought in 1987).

This statement highlights that competition in the automobile sector is getting tougher and tougher.

Due to high labour costs Europe has become less and less attractive for investors. Moreover, general stagnation in the European market has led to globalisation of the work force and capital.

Besides the big conglomeration the automobile producers are outsourcing as much as they can and decreasing the number of suppliers to reduce costs. In this manner the automobile suppliers industry is undergoing an upgrading especially the first-tier suppliers, that is, the suppliers who provide the components directly to the car producers. Computer-assisted production is being used more and more in the automobile sector.

The automobile production is becoming centered in the newly industrialized countries (NIC) including Argentina, Brazil, China, India, Mexico and the Republic of Korea as shown in the following Table 1:

Year	World total production in million of vehicles	NIC's percentage
1970	29.44	3 %
1975	33.0	8.5 %
1980	38.5	9.5%
1985	44.8	9 %
1990	48.3	12%
1995	51.8	17 %

Table 1: The Automobile production 1970 – 1995 (UNIDO, Survey of Selected World Industries)

Therefore the industry - not only the global players but also medium and small sized companies as well as the service sector - have opened up new markets. The low labour costs, but increasingly also other cost factors, are seen as the main reason for opening Asian markets. Other important goals are to gain resources and to secure the general strategic position of the enterprise within the global market.

Many companies choose Asia for their foreign investments mainly because of the

- **low labour costs**
- **most highly qualified work force**
- **liberal economic policy**
- **strategic geographical position**
- **favourable economic situation (low interest rates, devalued currency)**
- **growing middle class and**
- **growing demand.**

In short, these markets still have very good potential on the supply-side as well as on the demand-side. But it should be noted that only products which are labor-intensive, but of low-level technology can be produced cheaper in developing or newly industrialised countries. Despite the current problems, investments in Asian countries can be expected to increase independently of EU support.

One might assume that the countless disadvantages of a foreign investment would prevent companies to take the first step towards Asia. A foreign engagement is of course connected with high risk and cost. Following points hinder an investment:

sluggish bureaucracy	disastrous infrastructure
corruption	legal problems
political risks	cultural differences
technology drain	expectations are too high

Table 2: Disadvantages at an investment in the Asian region
(Deutsche Außenhandels- und Verkehrsakademie Bremen, Indien, ein Markt der Zukunft?)

Furthermore one must decide on the kind of engagement. If one favours a commitment formation and a definitive cooperation, a suitable partner must be found. Because of their low-risk preference European entrepreneurs in general - and the Austrians in particular - have problems in engaging in foreign regions.

In this connection we should recall Coase who argued already in 1960 that subject matter is decisive in the long run: „What economists study is the working of the social institutions which bind together the economic system: firms, markets for goods and for services, labor markets, capital markets, the banking system, international trade, and so on. It is the common interest in these social institutions that distinguishes the economics profession. Economists study the economic system as a unified whole, ... that they are more likely to uncover the basic interrelationships within a social system than is someone less accustomed to looking at the working of a system as a whole ... Also the study of economics makes it difficult to ignore factors which are clearly important and which play a part in all social systems."

These remarks are analysed by Williamson (1993) and he points out that the economic approach, rather than the subject matter, is what has to be stressed in situations of engagements. He associates calculativeness of one´s partner and trust in general with the economic approach and with the progressive extension of economics into the related social sciences.

3. Asian Investment Exemplified of an Austrian Automobile Company

The following study shall focus on an Austrian automobile company, which has engaged in Asia due to the international competition in the automobile sector. This company wanted to use its competitive advantages abroad, open new markets and profit from the existing locational advantage.

- Market profiles were created for the following countries:

- **Malaysia**
- **South Korea**
- **Vietnam**
- **Indonesia**
- **India and**
- **Thailand.**

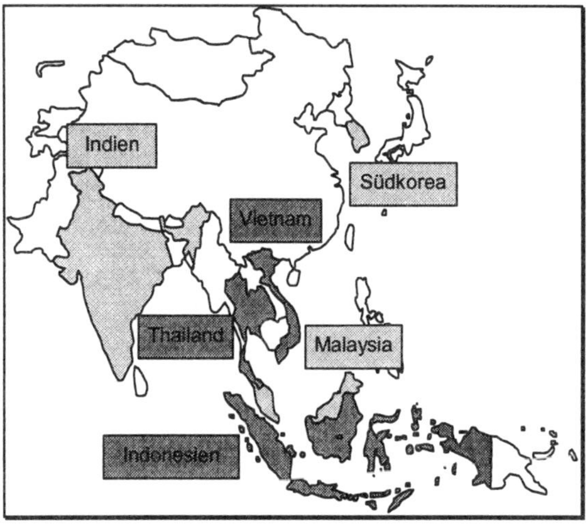

Figure 1: South East Asia

China, being one of the most emerging and discussed markets has not been chosen because of the many restrictions in the country and because of the low income of the population leading to insufficient demand.

After the completion of market profiles only Malaysia, South Korea and India were taken into consideration, because they are exactly those countries where a local and, in a certain sense, independent automobile industry already exists.

More detailed market profiles focus on the general economic situation, the stage of development of the automobile and component sector (contribution of own engineering versus simple imitation), including company profiles, the costs, the demand as well as the investment possibilities, investment incentives and subsidies by the state. When all the advantages and disadvantages were weighted, India emerged as the most potential partner country. A summary in Table 3 shows the weighting of the different aspects.

Weighting:

1. National automobile producers
2. Generating Information
3. Costs
4. Demand-Potential
5. Government

	South Korea	India	Malaysia
Producers	6	around 15	3
Stage of development	own development	identical imitation	adaptation
Full Range Producers*	6	1	0
Investments in R&D	0.4% of turnover	0.7% of turnover	cooperation with Lotus and Kia
Generating Information	easy	hard	quite easy
Costs	increasing strongly	low	quite high
Demand-Potential	saturation	boom is expected	small national market
Opening of the market	1979	1991	1985

** Full Range Producers produce all kind of automobile types, from cars to heavy trucks.*

Table 3: Decision process and weighting

The decision for the Indian market and the following detailed studies have resolved in a first investment in India with 25 engineers, which shall serve the Asian market. More investments are to come, if the engagement shall prove profitable.

4. India - An Overview with Regard to the Automobile Industry

The developed and the newly industrialised Asian countries need foreign investments in order to receive technology transfers. Local companies with their outdated technology shall be restructured and modernised with capital from foreign investments.These countries are going to grant various kinds of investment support, like tax-free-areas or tax incentives to attract foreign capital; usually on the condition that foreign companies should set up business in the country instead of only exporting to India. For this reason high import taxes are charged for many products.

Share-holding limits to prevent foreign investors from draining out the labour market and resources are set up by the state; the government also wants to keep control over the companies in this way. Foreign companies are generally in favour of such an arrangement because they save development costs and obtain the important contacts to the state officials and others, for example free taxes or duties. But due to many problems with the different cultures and attitudes of people, many companies nowadays tend to set up a 100%-owned subsidiary and hire local consultants.

The strong interest in the automobile industry is based on the fact that the automobile sector is one of the most important and largest industries in the world. Experts estimate that one car consists of about 20,000 single parts (Association of Indian Automobile Manufacturers). This technology needs a fast and complex component industry and a huge labour force. It is further said that for every job in an automobile plant, several jobs are needed elsewhere; for instance, in Germany every seventh job depends on the automobile industry (survey of the University of Cologne in VDA). Therefore an automobile plant is vital for a strong economy.

India itself is an open market only since 1991. About 15 automobile producers and countless automobile suppliers have taken the bulk of the market today. Before 1991 the Indian population was forced to choose between only two different car-models and had to put up with extensive waiting times for delivery, the potential for an engagement is still very high (India Today).

The wage costs per hour (about one tenth of the equivalent European wage costs) are the lowest in all of the examined markets and the demand potential the highest. In the year 2000 the population of India will even exceed the Chinese population and the growing middle class and the purchasing power of its population will continue to grow rapidly (see Table 3). Even the current disturbances on the Asian market did not harm this expansion.

During the late nineties, nearly all important European automobile companies have entered the Indian market. But companies such as Mercedes Benz or BMW with expensive models had to realise that the time for expensive and high quality cars has not come yet. Nevertheless, the battle on the market sections has begun; this fact has also been documented in a recent issue of *India Today*.

The new Indian government is determined to keep on pushing the automobile sector and to pay more attention to the poor infrastructure, which still hinders much development.

5. Empirical Study

5a. Trust as the Basis of an Efficient Cooperation

In analyzing the formation of commitments and cooperations one should inquire into these theoretical fundaments in a certain methodological way. Generally we can state that intensive family ties prevent trust from developing beyond the confines of the family. This central thesis of Fukuyama´s book (1995) on trust implies that societies characterised by a prevalence of strong social ties (such as the Indian society) produce less trust among their members than societies, in which social and interpersonal ties are weaker, do.

Part of the questionnaire directed at India´s most important automobile-companies were questions on their planned strategies for the next five years. Figure 2 shows the most frequently mentioned strategies. All the strategies could be quantified, except entering into cooperation. This answer will be discussed with the topic *trust* in this and the following chapter.

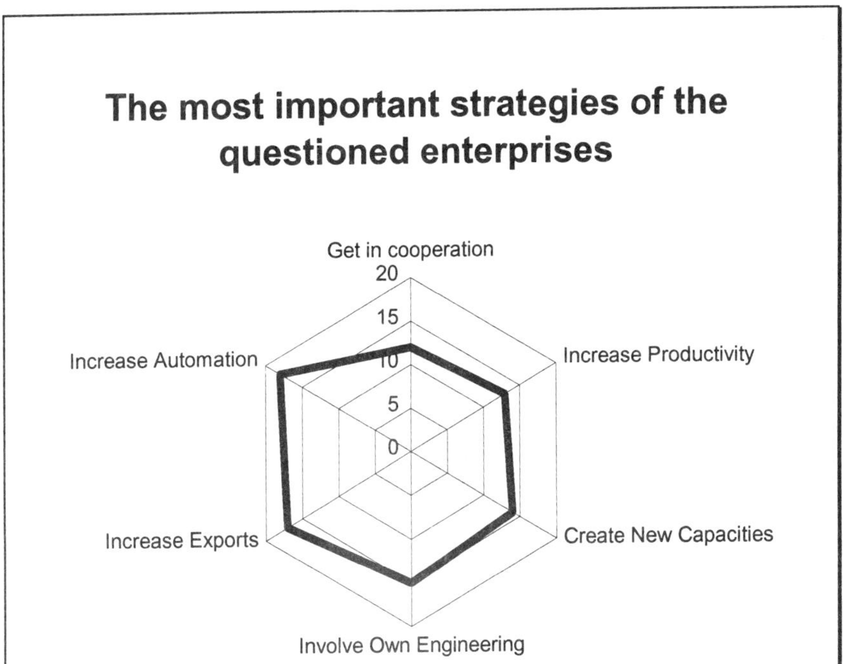

Figure 2: The most important strategies of the questioned enterprises

Trust can be said to be the sure expectancy that you can rely on someone. *Collins* describes trust as *a reliance on and confidence in the truthfulness,or the reliability of a person or thing.* This means that trust is always connected with something positive. In business terms, trust is a fair relationship, openness, and good sensibility in order to raise the working atmosphere. It seems obvious that a good company atmosphere can raise the productivity of an enterprise.

In various critical articles it is maintained that you cannot treat theoretically these so-called "soft" facts like trust. One also notes that trust-aspects have lead to failures, but no one yet has discovered any model to measure the rate of trust in a company.

A direct survey would definitely lead to a bias. Parameters for an analysis could be the productivity, e.g. the output per person. Here a cross check evaluation of the same company with two different managers would be interesting. But one could also measure comparable companies in the same field of business and the same rate of automation and same products.

Trust shall generally exist between all contract partners; be they the consumer and companies, the consumer and the product itself (goodwill), companies and suppliers, the employees and their superiors, the employees in relation to one another (teamwork). The same holds true of companies and their business- and cooperation-partners (Helm/Mehlhorn/Strohmayer), as described below. Often efficient transactions are based on trust. In short, trust plays a vital role in all important areas of the economy, such as trust, human resource management, marketing, leadership, organisation etc.

One important basis of all efficient trust-relationships should be between the superior and his employee. Leadership is mainly based on trust and example. Lack of trust can lead to high fluctuation and early retirements among the personnel and therefore high costs through training and insufficient performance.

Obviously trust alone is not enough; further factors are also essential for a good organisational atmosphere (Thomas) such as social infrastructure and wages, information and responsibility. Changes in the process of a company often fail because of the character of the attempted transformation. In general a principle can be stated: stop changing people - take them as they are. In this connection Malik (1994) formulates his guideline as how to build up trust between managers and their employees.

The foregoing brings up the question whether trust leads to higher efficiency or whether it can in some cases lead to a lower efficiency. An organisation climate which is too comfortable might discourage innovations.

5b. Evaluation of the Empirical Study

The questions of the empirical study on trust, carried out for the above mentioned Austrian company, are as follows:

- Is the management of your company satisfied with this cooperation?
- Yes ▒ No ▒

- Why is the management of your company satisfied and what does it especially appreciate in this cooperation?
  ▒ Teamwork
  ▒ Reliability
  ▒ Quality
  ▒ Trust in general

- Why is management dissatisfied? Problems with the
  ▒ Teamwork
  ▒ Reliability
  ▒ Quality
  ▒ Trust in general

  occurred.

In an interview the topic of trust was asked as an open question. The answers received did therefore not correspond exactly to the three questions above.

In the context of the empirical study **20 local Indian companies** - mainly the trend-setters in the automobile sectors - were interviewed. The data received were not extensive enough for a further detailed statistical evaluation and interpretation, respectively.

Of the 20 companies interviewed 16 are in strategic alliances with foreign companies. The main reason for this is the technology transfer without which they could not survive in the competition.

Ten of the 16 companies are in favour of their cooperation partners. They trust them totally. Two further companies gave positive replies concerning their cooperation partners.

A further interesting result of the study is that the Indian companies prefer a cooperation with Western countries, especially countries in middle Europe, rather than cooperate with Japan (unsatisfied companies). Europeans are perceived as honouring their commitments.

There are two groups of answers given. One is the group who finds the existing cooperation satisfying or even extremly good, the other is the group with exactly the opposite position (see Figure 3).

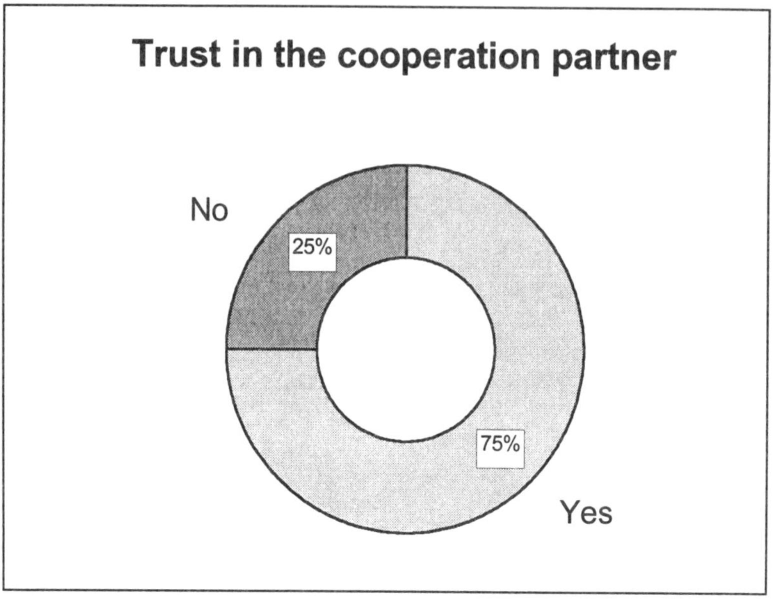

Figure 3: Trust in the cooperation partner

The detailed answers to the question lead to the following results:
Some companies are of the opinion that they have found the most suitable cooperation partner. They trust the partner entirely and exhaust the existing potential of cooperation jointly. The Europeans are appreciated for their fair way of doing business and their respect showed towards their partners. They try to understand the problems, whereas the Japanese partners do not care for the needs of the Indian partners. In many cases the reason for satisfactory partnership is based on the fact that the Indians sought their cooperation partners thoughtfully.

The experiences of Indian companies made with Japanese cooperation partners are rather unpleasant. The Japanese force export prohibitions upon their Indian partners and are sometimes unpredictable. Nevertheless, three Indian companies interviewed are still pleased in a certain way with their Japanese partners.

The main result of the interviews is that the Indians base their decision on trust, when setting up cooperations. Lack of trust was the reason for the breaking up many cooperation-negotiations in recent times. The fear of a buy-out by the foreign partner is always present.

6. Evaluation

The study described above can be expected to show the tremendous role of the automobile industry in the world economy. This industry sector here dealt with, is as representative of the ways in which business cooperations are set up.

In the last few years especially the automobile sector has moved more and more of its production to newly industrialised or developing Asian countries. Meanwhile this region is the home of more than 50% of the world´s population and produces one third of its gross national product. This globalisation of products and of knowledge changes the competition situation and the countries in a way that only the industrialisation in the beginning of this century did. The automobile industry is on the brink of adjusting its structures to this new situation. There is no way to avoid the booming regions of this world, if you want to be successful globally.

An important Austrian automobile enterprise has met these challenges by its engagement in India.

Part of the investment process of this enterprise was a questionnaire survey in which the question of trust towards a potential cooperation partner was dealt with. The most important result of this survey was the fact that the Indians - like their Europeans competitors - base their business connections and commitment formations on trust.

Acknowledgements

The authors want to thank SFT for enable the extension of the questionnaire with the questions concerning the topic on *trust.*
Further the authors want to thank Lutz Beinsen and Gustav Feichtinger and Jaakko Hintikka for several valuable suggestions which have improved the presentation of the paper.

REFERENCES

Association of Indian Automobile Manufacturers, (1997), *The Indian Automobile Industry & The Indian Auto Ancillary & Auto Component Industry*, New Delhi.

Coase Ronald H., (1960), The Problem of Social Cost, *The Journal of Law and Economics 3*, 202- 230.

Deutsche Außenhandels- und Verkehrsakademie Bremen, *Indien, ein Markt der Zukunft?*, Bremen 1995.

Fukuyama F., (1995), *Trust: The Social Virtues and the Creation of Prosperity*, New York, Free Press.

Gheczy, (1993), Führung durch Vertrauen, *Management-Zeitschrift IO, 9*, 30-33.

Helm/Mehlhorn/Strohmayer, (1996), Die Vertrauensproblematik bei zwischenbetrieblichen Kooperationen in der mittelständischen Industrie, *Zeitschrift für Planung 1*, 73-90.

India Today, The plan of action, April 1998.

Kratzer Carola, (1998), *Analytische Betrachtung des Automobilmarktes in ausgewählten asiatischen Staaten*, Dissertation, Graz.

Malik Fredmund, (1994), *Malik on Management. 8*/94.

Sprenger Reinhard, (1996), Psycho Klamauk, Die Mitbestimmung, *Magazin der Hans-Boeckler-Stiftung 2*, , 20-23.

Thomas, (1995), Gegen die Gleichgültigkeit, *Der Arbeitgeber 19*, 680-682.

UNIDO, (1996), *Survey of Selected World Industries*, Vienna.

Verband der deutschen Automobilindustrie (VDA), (1996), *AUTO 1996*, Annual Report, Frankfurt.

Williamson Oliver E., (1993), Calculativeness, Trust, and Economic Organization, *Journal of Law&Economics, XXXVI,* 453-486.

Yamagishi Toshio, Cook Karen S., Watabe Motoki, (1998), *Uncertainty, Trust and Commitment Formation in the United States and Japan*, WP; Hokkaido University.

Part 3:

Operations Research

Lot Sizing and Queueing Models

Some Remarks on KARMARKAR'S Model

Klaus-Peter Kistner

University of Bielefeld, Faculty of Economics

Abstract

KARMARKAR'S model is well recognized in production management and inventory theory: Using the (M/M/1) queueing model, the relation between lot-sizes and mean time in the system is derived for a stochastic inventory model.

In this paper, a short description of KARMARKAR'S model is given and fundamental inconsistancies between implicit assumptions of this and the (M/M/1) queueing model are demonstrated. Using well known results of queueing theory, these inconsistencies can be removed. It turns out, however, that - due to the law of large numbers - the model tends to a deterministic one for sufficiently large lot-sizes. Hence, KARMARKAR'S approach cannot be used to describe the behaviour of stochastic production systems.

1. Introduction

In the last years, a change of emphasis may be observed in the theory of mass production: Traditional approaches mainly rely on lot sizing models balancing set-up cost and holding cost; during the last decades interest has changed to the application of queueing models in production management. Specifically, the models of SOLBERG [1977], TEMPELMEIER [1986] and KISTNER/STEVEN [1990], describing the flow of orders through a production network, and the queueing theoretic model of KISTNER [1994] to evaluate the zero-inventory concept may be quoted.

In particular, KARMARKAR [1987] presented a broadly accepted approach to determine optimal lot-sizes by queueing theoretic arguments. At the first glance, this model seems to be quite an ingenious application of the (M/M/1) queueing model considering set-up times in determining optimal batches. However, implicit assumptions, necessitated by the application of the (M/M/1) queueing model, turn out to be contradictory.

This paper is organized as follows:

(1) Inconsistencies between implicit assumptions of KARMARKAR'S approach and the (M/M/1) queueing model are shown.

(2) Although the critic is – due to LESSINGS [1768] verdict – not obliged to improve what he criticizes, it will be demonstrated that inconsistencies in KARMARKAR'S model can be removed using well known results of queueing theory.

(3) The conclusion for this approach is, however, quite astonishing: Queueing theoretic problems resulting from the stochastics of the process considered vanish more or less due to the law of great numbers.

2. A Short Presentation of KARMARKAR'S Model

In order to give a short presentation of KARMARKAR'S model, the following symbols are introduced (cf. KARMARKAR [1987, p. 412]):

d	-	Total demand rate: mean number of items arriving in one unit of time
p	-	Processing rate of the production unit: Mean number of items being processed in one unit of time
λ	-	Average arrival rate of batches
τ	-	Mean setup time per batch
$\bar{x}$	-	Mean processing time per batch
μ	-	Processing rate of a batch
ρ	-	Capacity utilization
q	-	Batch size: number items in a batch

Between these parameters, the following tautologies are valid:

$$\lambda = \frac{d}{q} \tag{1}$$

$$\bar{x} = \tau + \frac{q}{p} \tag{2}$$

$$\mu = \frac{1}{\bar{x}} = \frac{p}{p \cdot \tau + q} \tag{3}$$

$$\rho = \frac{\lambda}{\mu} = \lambda \cdot \bar{x} = \frac{d}{p} + \frac{d \cdot \tau}{q} \tag{4}$$

Assuming the (M/M/1) model of queueing theory, the mean number of batches in the system is given by:

$$\bar{n} = \frac{\rho}{1-\rho} = \frac{\frac{d}{p} + \frac{d \cdot \tau}{q}}{1 - \frac{d}{p} - \frac{d \cdot \tau}{q}} \tag{5}$$

From the formula of Little [1961] one can get the mean time a batch spends in the system:

$$\bar{T} = \frac{\bar{n}}{\lambda} = \frac{\tau + \frac{q}{p}}{1 - \frac{d}{p} - \frac{d \cdot \tau}{q}} \tag{6}$$

To derive general properties of the relation between the batch size q and its mean time spent in the system, one observes:

(1) In order to reach stochastic equilibrium, the capacity utilisation ρ has to be strictly less than one; hence it follows from (4) that the minimum lot sizes is given by

$$q < \frac{d \cdot \tau}{1 - \frac{d}{p}} \tag{7}$$

For

$$q \to \frac{d \cdot \tau}{1 - \frac{d}{p}}$$

q as well as $\bar{T}$ tend to infinity.

(2) For large q, $\bar{T}$ approaches from above a linear bound

$$\bar{T} > \frac{\tau + \frac{q}{p}}{1 - \frac{d}{p}}$$

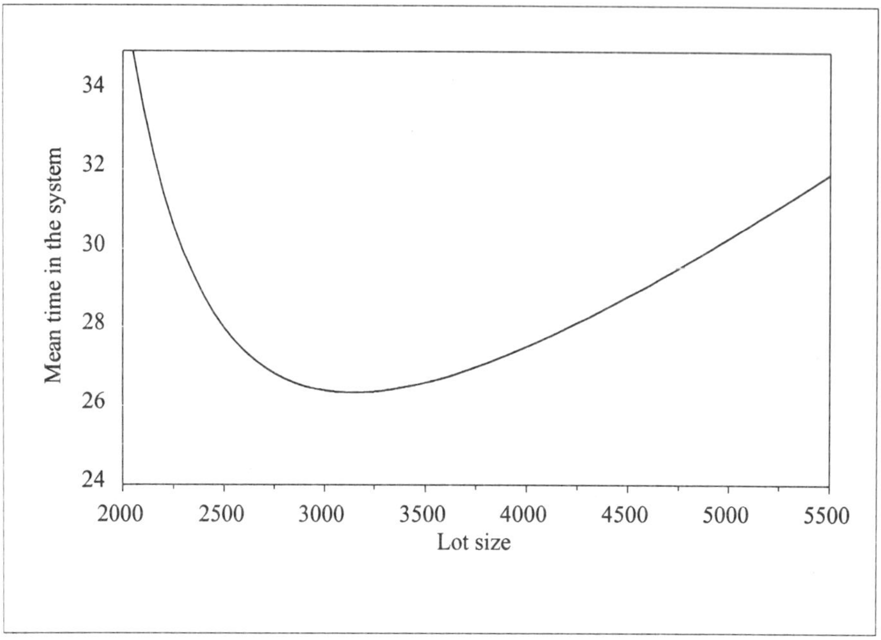

Fig. 1: Mean time in the system as a function of the lot size

(3) The first derivative of (6) yields the batch size minimizing the mean time spent in the system (cf. Rother [1998, S. 154])

$$q^o = \frac{\tau\left[\bar{x}\cdot p+\sqrt{\bar{x}\cdot p^3}\right.}{p-\bar{x}} \tag{8}$$

The relation between the mean time spent in the system $\bar{T}$ and the lot-size q is visualized in Fig. 1 for the following parameter values:

$d = 1250 \quad p = 1500 \quad \tau = 0{,}2$

3. A Critique of KARMARKAR'S Model

The application of the queueing model (M/M/1) to determine the relation between lot-sizes and the mean time spent in the system relies upon two crucial assumptions:

(1) The arrival of batches can be described by a POISSON-stream with rate

$$\lambda = \frac{d}{q}$$

(2) Completion times of lots, that is the sum of set-up times and processing times, are exponentially distributed random values with parameter

$$\mu = \frac{1}{\bar{x}} = \frac{p}{p \cdot \tau + q}$$

We now claim that

(1) these assumptions are not consistent with other implicit requirements of the model; consequently, the (M/M/1) model of queueing theory cannot be applied

(2) the model can, however, be analysed with well-known general results of queueing theory

(3) these results demonstrate that KARMARKAR'S model cannot be an appropriate representation of stochastics in a production unit.

In order to prove these claims, we introduce the following random variables and their moments defined in Tab. 1.

Completion times are equal to the sum of set-up R and processing times of batches B:

$$V = R + B$$

If both random variables are independent, the density of completion times is given by

$$\varphi_V(t) = \int_0^\infty \varphi_R(u)\varphi_B(t-u)\mathrm{d}u \tag{9}$$

Table 1: Random variables of interest and their moments

Random variable	Distribution	Density	Mean value	Variance	Coefficient of variation
Interarrival times of batches A	$\Phi_A(t)$	$\varphi_A(t)$	E(A)	Var(A)	$C(A)$
Set-up times R	$\Phi_R(t)$	$\varphi_R(t)$	E(R)	Var(B)	$C(R)$
Processing times B	$\Phi_B(t)$	$\varphi_B(t)$	E(B)	Var(C)	$C(B)$
Completion times V	$\Phi_V(t)$	$\varphi_V(t)$	E(V)	Var(V)	$C(V)$

The LAPLACE-transform of this convolution integral is equal to

$$\Phi_V^*(s) = \int_0^\infty e^{-st} \varphi_V(t) \mathrm{d}t = \Phi_R^*(s) \cdot \Phi_B^*(s) \tag{10}$$

Dividing both sides of (10) by $\Phi_R^*(s)$, we conclude that the LAPLACE-transform of processing times has to satisfy the condition

$$\Phi_B^*(s) = \frac{\Phi_V^*(s)}{\Phi_R^*(s)} \tag{11}$$

According to the assumptions of the (M/M/1) model that completion times are exponentially distributed with parameter μ, the LAPLACE-transform of processing time should be equal to

$$\Phi_B^*(s) = \frac{\dfrac{\mu}{\mu + s}}{\Phi_R^*(s)} \tag{12}$$

For a given density of set-up times $\varphi_R(t)$, the LAPLACE-transform $\Phi_B^*(s)$ can be determined; inversion yields a function $\varphi_B(t)$ satisfying

$$\varphi_V(t) = \int_0^\infty \varphi_R(u) \varphi_B(t-u) \mathrm{d}u = \mu \cdot e^{-\mu \cdot t} \tag{9a}$$

However, the integral $\Phi_B(t)$ of this function $\varphi_B(t)$ is not a distribution of an non-negative stochastic variable. In particular, this can be proved for the following distributions of set-up times

- Exponential distribution
- General ERLANG distributions
- Hyperexponential distribution
- Equal distribution
- One-point distribution

This argument depends on the possibility to calculate the LAPLACE-transform of $\varphi_R(t)$ and to obtain the inverse of (12). Properties of the functions $\varphi_B(t)$ and $\Phi_B(t)$ obtained by inversion of (12) justify the conjecture that there are no densities of non-negative stochastic variables satisfying (12). That is, an exponentially distributed stochastic variable cannot be the sum of two non-negative random variables. But even if this conjecture does not hold, the model of KARMARKAR is valid only for a few, very special combinations of the distributions of set-up times and processing times.

These inconsistencies in KARMAKAR'S model may, however, be removed by dropping the assumption of a (M/M/1) queue and applying more general queueing systems.

4. Removal of the Inconsistencies in KARMARKAR'S Model

4.1. Completion Time as a Sum of Set-up and Processing Times

If we drop the assumption that completion times are exponentially distributed and assume that set-up and processing time are independent random variables, we can apply the formula of POLLACZEK/KHINTCHINE for the mean time in the system in a (M/G/1) queueing system (cf. ROTHER [1998]):

$$\bar{T} = \mathrm{E}(V) + \frac{\lambda \cdot [\mathrm{Var}(V) + [\mathrm{E}(V)]^2]}{1 - \lambda \cdot \mathrm{E}(V)} \tag{13}$$

where

$$\lambda = \frac{d}{q} \qquad \mathrm{E}(V) = \mathrm{E}(R) + \mathrm{E}(B) \qquad \mathrm{Var}(V) = \mathrm{Var}(R) + \mathrm{Var}(B)$$

In order to manage the set of parameters defined by KARMARKAR we assume that set-up times are exponentially distributed with rate $\alpha = 1/\tau$ and that processing times are exponentially distributed with rate $\beta = p/q$. Hence, completion times are double-exponentially distributed:

$$\varphi_V(t) = \frac{\beta \cdot \alpha}{\beta - \alpha} \cdot \left(e^{-\beta \cdot t} - e^{-\alpha \cdot t}\right. \tag{14}$$

with

$$\mathrm{E}(V) = \mathrm{E}(R) + \mathrm{E}(B) = \frac{1}{\alpha} + \frac{1}{\beta} = \tau + \frac{q}{p}$$

$$\mathrm{Var}(V) = \frac{1}{\alpha^2} + \frac{1}{\beta^2} = \tau^2 + \frac{q^2}{p^2}$$

The mean time a lot spends in the system is given by

$$\overline{T}=\left[\tau+\frac{q}{p}\right]+\frac{\left(\frac{d}{q}\right)\cdot\left[\tau^{2}+\frac{q^{2}}{p^{2}}+(\tau+\frac{q}{p})^{2}\right]}{2\cdot\left[1-\frac{d}{q}\cdot\left(\tau+\frac{q}{p}\right)\right]} \tag{15}$$

The relation between lot size q and mean time a lot spends in the system is plotted in Figure 2.

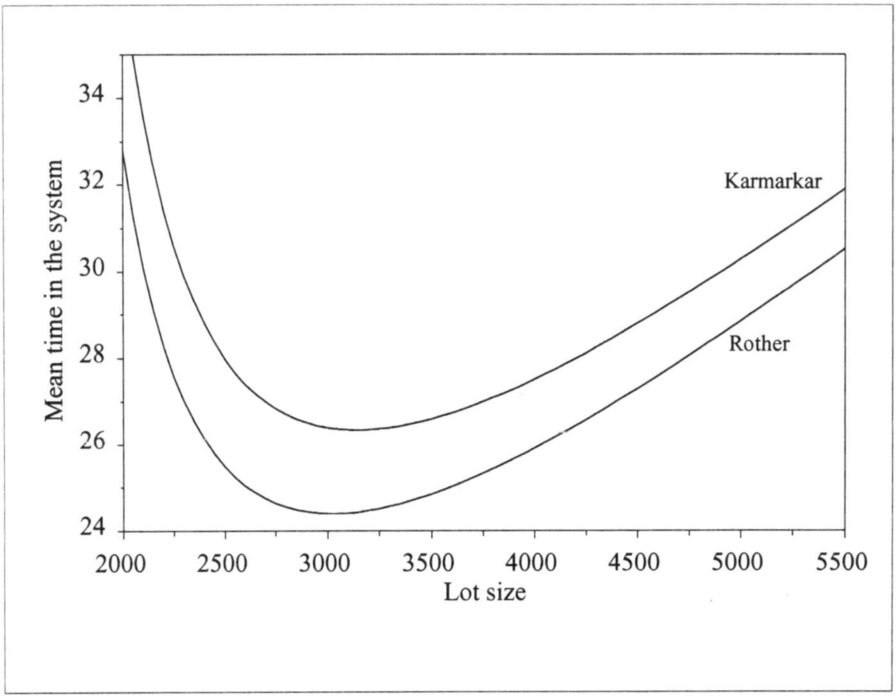

Fig. 2: Mean time in the system as a function of the lot size

Figure 2 shows, that Karmarkar overestimates the mean time spent by a batch in the system systematically; however, the shape of the function is equal in both models.

4.2 Processing Times of Batches as a Sum of Handling Times of Orders

Yet, replacing exponential completion times by the sum of exponential set-up and exponential processing times of batches does not remove all inconsistencies in KARMARKAR'S model: In his model, the processing times of the batches are assumed to be exponential with a rate indirectly proportional to the lot size. This implies, that the processing time of a lot is composed of processing times of the orders combined to the batch. Hence, processing time of a batch B is the sum of the processing times B_i of q orders

$$B = \sum_{i=1}^{q} B_i$$

In analogy to the argumentation in section 3 we claim that the distribution of a sum of independent, non-negative random variable cannot be exponential. Hence, the model developed above, which assumed that completion times are double-exponentially distributed, cannot be valid, as well.

This observation has, however, no effects on the applicability of the POLLAZEK/KHINTCHINE formula: We can calculate the expected value of processing times of batches as the sum of expected values of processing times of q orders:

$$\mathrm{E}(B) = \sum_{i=1}^{q} \mathrm{E}(B_i)$$

As mean processing times of all orders are equal, that means $\mathrm{E}(B_i) = \mathrm{E}(B_o)$, we have

$$\mathrm{E}(B) = q \cdot \mathrm{E}(B_o)$$

similarly, the variance of processing times of the batches is given by

$$\mathrm{Var}(B) = q \cdot \mathrm{Var}(B_o)$$

In order to be as close as possible to KARMARKAR'S model, we now assume that processing times of orders are exponentially distributed with mean

$$\mathrm{E}(B) = \frac{q}{p}$$

and variance

$$\mathrm{Var}(B) = \frac{q}{p^2}$$

The processing times of batches are q-ERLANG distributed.

Considering set-up times, we get for the mean and the variance of completion times:

$$\mathrm{E}(V) = \tau + \frac{q}{p}$$

$$\mathrm{Var}(V) = \tau^2 + \frac{q}{p^2}$$

In this case, the mean time spent by a batch in the system is given by

$$\overline{T} = \left[\tau + \frac{q}{p}\right] + \frac{\left(\frac{d}{q}\right) \cdot \left[\tau^2 + \frac{q}{p^2} + \left(\tau + \frac{q}{p}\right)^2\right]}{2 \cdot \left[1 - \frac{d}{q} \cdot \left(\tau + \frac{q}{p}\right)\right]} \tag{16}$$

The relation between lot size q and mean time in the system $\overline{T}$ is depicted in figure 3.

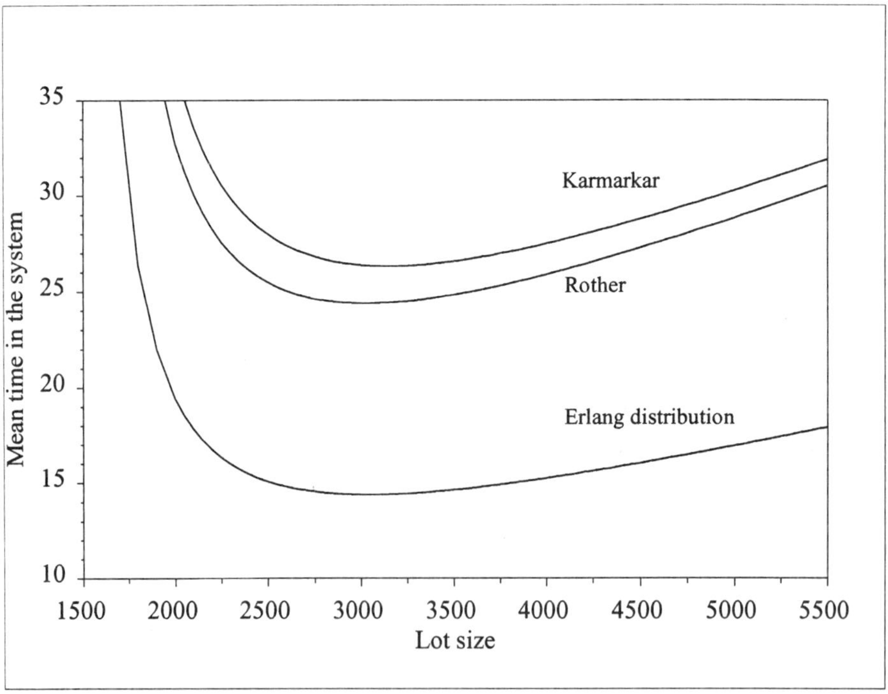

Fig. 3: Mean time in the system as a function of the lot size

The picture shows that KARMARKAR'S model as well as ROTHER'S model considerably overestimate the mean time a batch spends in the system. However, qualitative results of KARMARKAR'S model with respect to the shape of the function hold furthermore.

4.3 The Release of Batches as a POISSON Stream

KARMARKAR assumes that batches are release in a constant rate and that the mean time between the release of two batches is proportional to the lot size. Applying the (M/M/1) model of queueing theory, he assumes implicitly a POISSON stream of batches to be processed.

The assumption that the time between the release of two successive batches is proportional to the size of the batches lead to the following interpretation of the arrival process of orders:

(1) Orders arrive separately in random distances A_i.

(2) Orders are collected in an inventory till a stock of q orders is reached.

(3) As soon as a batch of size q is reached, it is released and enters the waiting line of batches to be processed.

These properties of the arrival process of orders and the release of batches has the following consequences:

(1) The time between the release of two successive batches is a sum of q independent random variables

$$A = \sum_{i=1}^{q} A_i$$

(2) According to the argumentation used to analyse completion times, it is not appropriate to assume that these random variables are exponentially distributed.

(3) If times between two successive arrivals are independent identically distributed random variables with expectation $\mathrm{E}(A_o)$ and variance $\mathrm{Var}(A_o)$, then we have

$$\mathrm{E}(A) = q \cdot \mathrm{E}(A_o) \qquad\qquad \mathrm{Var}(A) = q \cdot \mathrm{Var}(A_o)$$

In contrast to the models discussed in 4.1 and 4.2, we cannot apply the formula of POLLACZEK/KHINTCHINE any longer, as the interarrival times of batches are exponentially distributed. Hence we have to apply results of the (GI/G/1) model of queueing theory. Unfortunately, there exists no exact formula for the calculation of the mean time in the system for this model. Instead, we have to rely on approximations.

For example, FISCHER/HERTEL [1990, S. 81] give the following approximation for the mean time in the system in the case of a (GI/G/1) queueing model:

$$\bar{T} = E(V) + \frac{[\mathrm{E}(V)]^2}{2 \cdot [\mathrm{E}(A) - \mathrm{E}(V)]} \cdot [K \cdot \mathrm{C}^2(V) + \mathrm{C}^2(A)] \tag{17}$$

where

$$\mathrm{C}^2(A) = \frac{\mathrm{Var(A)}}{[\mathrm{E(A)}]^2} \quad \text{and} \quad \mathrm{C}^2(V) = \frac{\mathrm{Var(V)}}{[\mathrm{E(V)}]^2}$$

are the squared coefficients of variation of the interarrival times and completion times of the batches. Furthermore K is given by:

$$K = \left[\frac{\mathrm{E}(V)}{\mathrm{E}(A)}\right]^{1-\mathrm{C}^2(A)} \cdot [1 + C^2(A)] - C^2(A)$$

In the special case of exponentially distributed interarrival times of orders we have q-ERLANG distributed times between the release of two sucessive batches with

$$\mathrm{E}(A) = \frac{q}{d} \qquad \mathrm{Var}(A) = \frac{q}{d^2} \qquad C^2(A) = \frac{1}{q}$$

According to 4.2 we assume that completion times are q-ERLANG distributed as well, and that

$$\mathrm{E}(V) = \mathrm{E}(R) + \sum_{i=1}^{q} B_i = \tau + \frac{q}{p}$$

$$\mathrm{Var}(V) = \mathrm{Var}(R) + \sum_{i=1}^{q} \mathrm{Var}(B_i) = \tau^2 + \frac{q}{p^2}$$

$$\mathrm{C}^2(V) = \frac{\tau^2 \cdot p^2 + q}{(\tau \cdot p + q)^2}$$

The mean time in the system as a function of the lot size is plotted in figure 4 and 5. Figure 4 shows that this measure of performance is considerably lower than in the models discussed above. Neither KARMARKAR'S model nor the other models presented can be accepted as an approximation of the model suggested by KARMARKAR'S assumptions. In fact, mean time in the system diverges only for a very high utilisation of capacity – arrival rate very close to completion rate – notably from the completion times represented by the linear line in figure 5. This result can be supported by using the upper bound on mean time in the system given by (cf. FISCHER/HERTEL [1990, S. 81]:

$$\bar{T} \leq \mathrm{E}(V) + \frac{[\mathrm{E}(V)]^2}{2[\mathrm{E}(A) - \mathrm{E}(B)]} \cdot [\mathrm{C}^a(A) - \mathrm{C}^2(V)] \tag{18}$$

where

$$a = \frac{\mathrm{E}(A)}{0{,}4136 \cdot \mathrm{E}(V) + 0{,}0703486 \cdot \mathrm{E}(A)} \qquad \text{for} \qquad \mathrm{C}(A) < 1$$

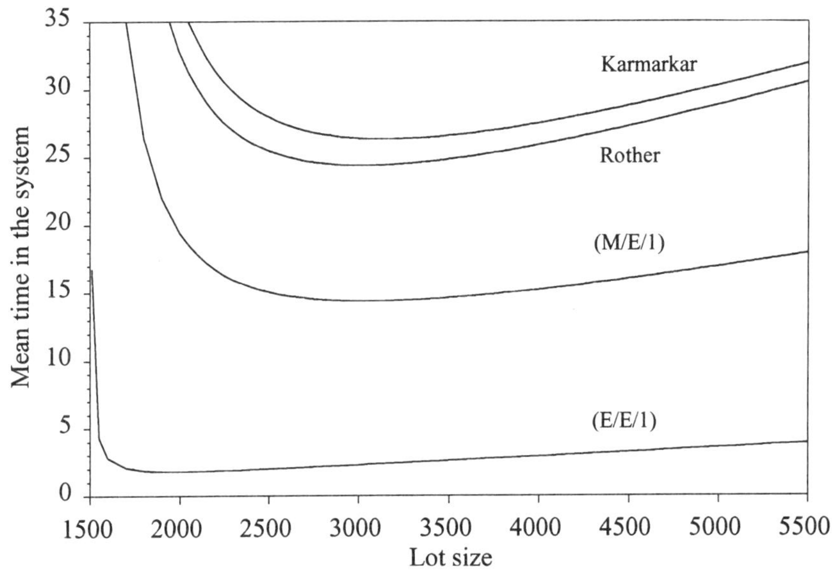

Fig. 4: Mean time in the system in the models discussed above

This surprising result can easily be explained by the following considerations:

(1) Completion times of lots are sums of $q+1$ exponentially distributed random variables. Summation of random variables results in a reduction of the standard deviation and the coefficient of variation; for large q the coefficient of variation tends to zero, fluctuations of processing times of orders and set-up times are levelled out.

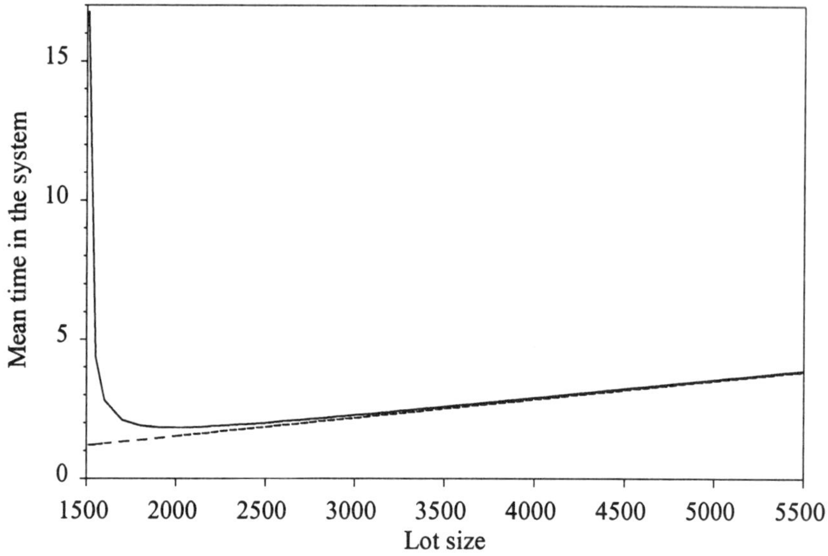

Fig. 5: Mean time in the system and processing times in the (G/G/1) model

(2) Interarrival times of lots are as well sums of q exponentially distributed random variables; the standard deviation and the coefficient of variation decrease with lot-sizes q. This effect is clearly demonstrated for the formula for the coefficient of variation of an q-ERLANG distributed random variable:

$$C^2(A) = \frac{1}{q}$$

Hence, for reasonable lot sizes, the problem can rather be approximated by a deterministic model than by a (M/M/1) queueing model.

5. Results

In the preceding sections, we disclosed a treble inconsistency between the definition of important parameters of KARMARKAR'S model and basic assumptions of the (M/M/1) queueing model applied:.

(1) Completion times of batches as a sum of set-up times and processing times cannot be exponentially distributed.

(2) Furthermore, processing times of batches as a sum of processing times of the orders combined to the lot cannot be exponentially distributed.

(3) Finally, times between the release of two successive batches as a sum of interarrival times of individual orders cannot be exponentially distributed.

Using well known approaches of queueing theory, these inconsistancies can easily be removed. In analogy to the original version of KARMARKAR'S model, we assumed that interarrival times and processing times of individual orders as well as set-up times are exponentially distributed. There are, however, technical assumptions to manage with the data of KARMARKAR'S model. The models of queueing theory applied enable us to cope with more general distributions.

Yet, it does not suffice to replace the (M/M/1) model of queueing theory by a more general one; in fact, we proved that queuing models are not suitable to describe the problem appropriately: The combination of orders to batches levels out fluctuations of interarrival times, processing times and set-up times, and result in a quasi-deterministic situation. To summarize, KARMARKAR'S approach can be adequately appreciated by citing SHAKESPEARE: „Much Ado About Nothing"

6. References

Ferschl, F., Zufallsabhängige Wirtschaftsprozesse, Wien (Physica) 1964

Fischer, K., Hertel, G., Bedienungsprozesse im Transportwesen, Berlin (Transpress) 1990

Karmarkar, U.S., Lot Sizes, Lead Times and In-Process Inventories, Management Science 33 (1987); S. 409-418

Kistner, K.-P., Die Substitution von Umlaufvermögen durch Anlagevermögen im Rahmen der Produktion auf Abruf, OR Spektrum 16 (1994); S. 125-134

Kistner, K.-P., Steven/Switalski, M., Warteschlangen-Netzwerke in der hierarchischen Produktionsplanung, OR Spektrum 12 (1990); S. 89-101

Lessing, G.E., Materialien zur Hamburgischen Dramaturgie, in: Witkowski, G., Lessings Werke, Bd. 5, Leipzig/Wien (o.J.), Bibliographisches Institut, Bd. 5; S. 400

Lindley, D.V., The Theory of Queues with a Single Stage Server, Proc. Cambridge Phil. Soc. 48 (1952); S. 277

Little, J.D.C., A Proof of the Queueing Formula L=λW, OR 9 (1061); S. 383

Rother, A., Substitution von Umlauf- durch Anlagevermögen, Diss. Bielefeld 1998

Solberg, J.J., A Mathematical Model of Computing Manufacturing Systems, Proceedings of the Fourth International Conference on Production Research, Tokio (1977); S. 1265-1275

Tempelmeier, H., Kapazitätsplanung für flexible Fertigungssysteme, ZfB 58 (1988); S. 963-980

Zimmermann, G. Quantifizierung der Bestimmungsfaktoren von Durchlaufzeiten und Werkstattbeständen, ZfB 54 (1984), S. 1016-1032

Analysis of MRP Policies with Recovery Options

Karl Inderfurth and Thomas Jensen

Faculty of Economics and Management
Otto-von-Guericke-University Magdeburg
e-mail:inderfurth@ww.uni-magdeburg.de

Abstract

The importance of product recovery aspects demands for integrating reuse and remanufacturing options into material requirements planning. In this paper (within the context of a single-stage system) a recovery option is analyzed which allows for the remanufacturing of reusable products or components. Depending on the source of product returns we consider two different scenarios of reverse logistics: external return flows of used products and internal flows of reworkable products generated by unreliable production processes. For both scenarios an extended MRP approach for material coordination is developed. It is shown that this so-called MRRP approach generates certain types of control rules, and that the structure of these rules depends on the way of integrating forecasted returns of products into the MRP context. These MRP based control rules, as far as possible, are compared with the optimal policy structure developed from approaches of stochastic inventory control for this remanufacturing system.

1 Introduction

In the recent years for economical, ecological and legal reasons firms faced a steadily growing pressure to increase their efforts to organize product and material cycles in order to reduce waste and at the same time to substitute primary production inputs (see e.g. THIERRY et al., 1995). Origins of return flows in these material cycles can be divided into external and internal sources. Whereas external return flows consist of used products or components which are collected from users and redistributed to the producers (e.g. photocopiers, TV-sets or cars), internal returns are generated by a production system itself, e.g. as by-product or as scrap products within not completely

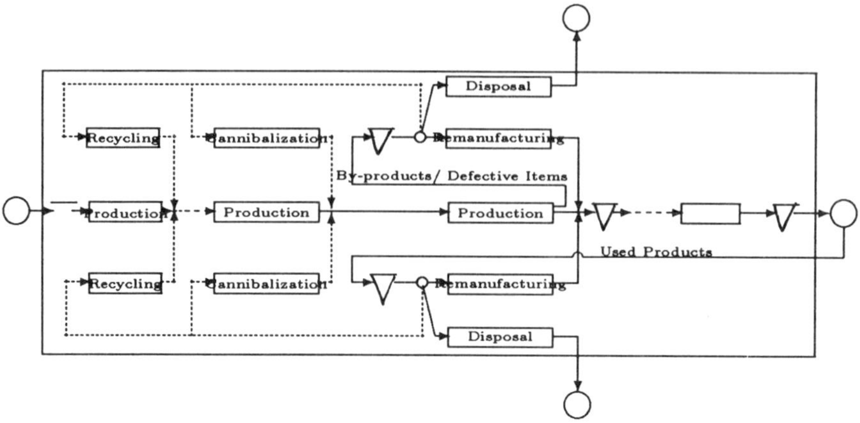

Figure 1: Multi-stage Production/Remanufacturing System with Return Flows

controllable production processes (e.g. in the chemical industry). A production/remanufacturing system with both types of return flows is depicted in Figure 1.

When designing a system of reverse logistics which enables to reuse high valuable components of the return flows, different recovery options can be used. THIERRY et al. (1995) categorized these reuse options depending on the required disassembly level. Whereas the recovery options 'cannibalization' and 'recycling' only use smaller portions of the recoverable products like components (cannibalization) or materials (recycling), 'repair', 'refurbishing' and 'remanufacturing' attend to bring each product as a unity to a certain quality level which makes the distinction between these options. While 'remanufacturing' means to recover products so that the quality standards of new ones are fulfilled, refurbished products are of a less rigorous quality level and repaired products are only brought up to a working order.

Product recovery management refers to the coordination of these recovery options and the involved functions such as collection, testing and reprocessing, and to the control of the flow of material and information connected to the underlying material cycles (see e.g. THIERRY et al. (1995)). On the other hand, an additional task of integration arises from the necessity to coordinate the flow of regularly produced and recovered items which perform alternative sources of procurement.

As a consequence when using recovery options the production system may be influenced by additional uncertainty caused by the return flows of used or defective products. This uncertainty concerns quantity and timing of reusables and, especially, the quality of the returned goods and the reliability of recovery processes. Apart from the more strategic problem of determining the optimal recovery option the main problem on the operational management level is the coordination of the different forward and reverse material flows (see FLEISCHMANN et al., 1997).

This task can be complicated in case of joint use of capacities from production and recovery operations which demands for the integration of capacity and time planning. In this paper we restrict our analysis to the problem of material planning facing possibly stochastic flows of reusables and treating remanufacturing as the predetermined available recovery option. As often proceeded in material coordination capacity aspects are not (explicitly) considered.

The increased complexity of material coordination within this context is due to the decision of how to use two alternative supply modes to increase the filling of the production pipeline together with a disposal option which can be used to decrease system stocks. In addition to this decision complexity both the remanufacturing and disposal option depend on the stochastic return flow, and at least for the remanufacturing option we may have to take into consideration lotsizing aspects. As a result of this complexity, the material coordination problem with return flows leads to a multi-stage, multi-dimensional stochastic dynamic decision problem.

One potential approach to tackle these material coordination problems is to extend the theoretical models of stochastic multi-stage inventory control. But as for multi-stage stochastic inventory control models without return flows in general cases no tractable solution procedures are available, this even more holds for the case when return flows and instationarities have to be integrated. Including return flows analytical results for periodic review models are only obtainable for simple single-stage models (see e.g. INDERFURTH, 1997). However, integrating external return flows in the continuous review case considerable analytical and numerical methods are developed (see e.g. SALOMON et al., 1994 / VAN DER LAAN, 1997 / VAN DER LAAN and SALOMON, 1997 / VAN DER LAAN et al., 1996 / VAN DER LAAN et al., 1996a), but the respective approaches are restricted to the optimization of the control parameters of predetermined control rules for simple stationary single-stage models.

Another way of dealing with the problem of integrating return flows is to coordinate reverse and forward material flows by using unsystematically selected ad hoc decision rules for planning recovery options (see e.g. FLAPPER, 1994). But this approach completely neglects the whole potential of using scientific decision support and especially lacks of satisfactory system performance if the flow of returned products has a considerable quantity and/or value.

As a third option the extension of the traditional Material Requirements Planning (MRP) concept might be an advantageous alternative to deal with these problems in a suitable way, both from a practical as well as from a theoretical point of view. The basic concept of the MRP logic is to determine production plans covering a time horizon of prespecified length within a periodically based rolling horizon environment (see e.g. VOLLMANN et al., 1992). The determination of the material requirements follows a stage by stage calculation beginning with the end-item stages thereby separating the computation of lotsizes and net-requirements at each stage. Whereas the planning procedure itself is a deterministic concept, based on estimations of the uncertain input data, prespecified buffering mechanisms such as safety stocks, and the updating of rolling schedules are used to protect against uncertainties within the production system and from external sources.

A major limitation of this planning concept besides not explicitly including uncertainty is the ignoring of capacities and the resulting problem of deviations between planned and realized leadtimes (for this aspect see e.g. BAKER, 1993, pp 605-613). In addition to this critique, buffering decisions are not coordinated with the calculation of lotsizes (see e.g. VAN DONSELAAR, 1989, pp 51-56) and the use of buffers is not integrated in the MRP planning concept in a suitable way just when operating in a stochastic environment. However, due to the serious limitations of alternative approaches to solve the complex material coordination problem, and because of the simplicity and wide-spread application of the MRP concept for material planning we feel that it is worthwhile to investigate if this concept can also be used in a straightforward way if recovery options amplify a production system.

For extending the MRP concept in order to coordinate recovery options for using return flows it is essential to include the planning of future return flows within the considered planning horizon. To be able to coordinate recovery and production actions furtheron realistic planned leadtimes for remanufacturing processes have to be specified. Based on cost and customer service considerations decision rules have to be developed to calculate lotsizes for remanufacturing orders, to determine disposal quantities and to specify the use of buffering mechanisms such as safety stocks in order to cope with the uncertainty from the return and demand side. Finally, planning of material requirements to be fulfilled from regular production and the use of different recovery options requires priority rules to coordinate the utilization of these different material sources.

Extending the MRP approach to a concept of Material Requirements and Recovery Planning (MRRP) the specific task of integration has to take place at those production stages where the recovered products meet the forward flow of materials. Whereas the other stages can be planned according to the traditional MRP concept, the stages which are directly connected to return flows have to be planned by applying extended calculations which integrate the return flows and available recovery options.

For these reasons in the sequel we will consider the material coordination problem for just a single stage of the system facing returns of products which can be remanufactured. We assume fixed and predetermined processing times for regular production and remanufacturing. Holding of safety stocks as applied buffering mechanism is used only for items within the forward material flow. Within this context in this paper we develop control rules to determine production, remanufacturing and disposal decisions based on deterministic cost considerations.

The rest of the paper is organized as follows. In the next section the used notation and the detailed assumptions characterizing the considered return flows, the available recovery options and the planning scenario are presented. In Section 3 we develop extended MRP calculations to integrate remanufacturing and disposal options applied to external return flows. Exploiting these calculations we derive equivalent MRRP control rules to specify the relevant decision variables. In Section 4 a similar analysis is performed for the case of internal returns. Taking up the results of the preceding two sections in Section 5 the structure of the developed MRRP rules are compared with the structure of optimal decision rules from Stochastic Inventory Control (SIC) as far as optimal SIC policies for the analyzed planning scenarios and assumptions are known. The paper concludes with a summary of the main results and suggestions for further research.

2 Material Coordination Problem with Returns

Following the arguments of the introductory section we will focus on a single-stage material coordination problem. Remanufactured items are assumed to meet the same quality standards as serviceable products which are regularly produced. Thus the (internal and external) requirements for these serviceables can be fulfilled from both sources of procurement, i.e. from ordinary production and from remanufacturing.

Returned items can be processed in two different ways. They can either be remanufactured or be discarded. A temporary third option exists by stocking reusable products (RP) for a time-span in a respective RP-inventory. Also for serviceable products (SP) stock-keeping in a SP-inventory is allowed.

According to the MRP concept periodic orders are released under a deterministic planning environment. For the material coordination problem with returns this means that in each planning period t of a finite planning horizon T decisions are made on planned orders for producing (POP_t), remanufacturing (POR_t) and disposing (POD_t) items with respect to forecasted gross requirements of serviceables (GR_t) and projected returns of reusable products (PR_t). In Figure 2 the extended single-level production system is displayed for the case that returns result from an external inflow of used products which are checked to fulfill the quality requirements to be remanufactured. The two circles in this figure correspond to the location of decision points in coordinating the material flows.

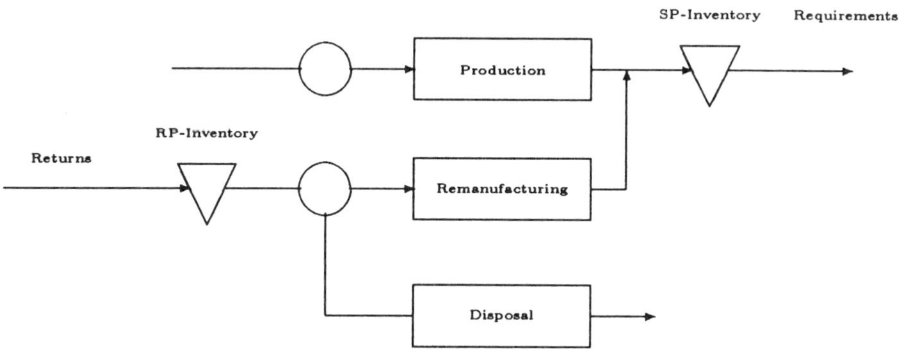

Figure 2: Production/Remanufacturing System with External Returns

To protect against uncertainties a prespecified amount of serviceable products has to be hold as a safety stock (SST). Hence, production and remanufacturing decisions have to assure that in each period the gross requirements are fulfilled and that the serviceables inventory does not fall below the safety stock level.

For both the production and remanufacturing process a fixed planned leadtime is taken into consideration which is assumed to have equal length (λ

periods). That means that it is assumed that remanufacturing and regular production take about the same processing time so that only cost aspects affect the priority setting with respect to both procurement options. Following the traditional MRP approach available capacity is incorporated in the leadtime specification and no additional capacity constraints are considered. All costs are assumed to be strictly proportional, i.e. we consider constant costs per unit for production (c_P), remanufacturing (c_R) and disposal (c_D) on the one hand, and constant costs per unit and per period for stock holding in the RP-inventory (h_R) and in the SP-inventory (h_S) on the other. No fixed cost components are incorporated, neither for production nor for remanufacturing or disposal.

The background of the internal returns case is a production system where due to a certain unreliability of the regular production process jointly with the serviceable parts by-products or defective items are produced which can be processed to serviceables by recovery operations. This situation is depicted in Figure 3 where it is shown that the returns are generated by the production decisions themselves.

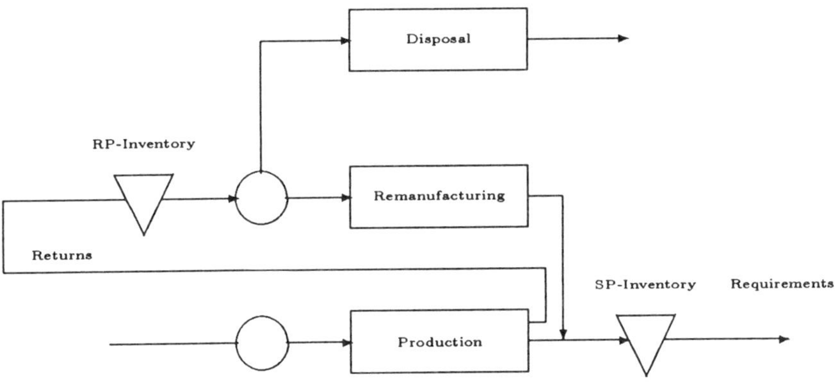

Figure 3: Production/Remanufacturing System with Internal Returns

When a production order is released only a certain fraction z (with $0 < z \leq 1$) of the production lot is assumed to be of serviceables quality. This means that one unit which is processed at cost c_P in the regular production facility yields z units of serviceables and $(1 - z)$ units of recoverable products (in future denoted by 'defective' items). Both types of products are available after production leadtime λ. The remanufacturing process itself is assumed to be completely reliable so that no defective items come out of this process.

Apart from the case of unreliable production it is assumed without loss of generality that in each process one unit of output needs exactly one unit of input material.

For an overview we summarize the notation introduced in this section:

POP_t	:	planned order release production (at the beginning of period t)
POR_t	:	planned order release remanufacturing at t
POD_t	:	planned order release disposal at t
GR_t	:	gross requirements in period t
PR_t	:	projected returns (available at the end of period t)
SST	:	safety stock of serviceable products
c_P	:	production cost per unit
c_R	:	remanufacturing cost per unit
c_D	:	disposal cost per unit
h_R	:	holding cost for returns per unit and period
h_S	:	holding cost for serviceables per unit and period
λ	:	production as well as remanufacturing leadtime
z	:	fraction of serviceables from production (in case of internal returns)
T	:	number of planning periods

Using this notation a straightforward extension of the traditional MRP approach for material coordination will be developed in the succeeding sections. For the presentation of the extended MRP-calculations some additional notation will be introduced where necessary.

3 MRRP Policies with External Returns

3.1 The Extended MRP Tableau

In order to integrate returns of items into a MRP scheme of material coordination additional steps have to be included in the regular MRP calculations. These steps consist of considering stocks of returned products and determining time and quantity for remanufacturing and disposal orders concerning these items. When using the common MRP tableau see (TERSINE, 1994, pp 348) additional rows have to be incorporated as it is shown in Table 1 (see also GUIDE and SRIVASTAVA 1997 for a similar extension).

Table 1: Extended MRP Tableau for Example 1

Period t			$PD(0)$	1	2	3	4	5
GR_t	:	gross requirements		10	10	10	10	10
SRP_t	:	scheduled receipts production		8	14			
SRR_t	:	scheduled receipts remanufacturing		5	4			
SOH_t	:	projected serviceables on hand	9	12	20	15	15	15
NR_t	:	net requirements		3	0	5	10	10
PR_t	:	planned returns		4	4	4	4	4
ROH_t	:	projected returns on hand	7	6	4	4	4	-
PRR_t	:	planned receipts remanufacturing		-	-	5	6	4
POR_t	:	planned order release remanufacturing		5	6	4	4	-
POD_t	:	planned order release disposal		0	0	0	0	-
PRP_t	:	planned receipts production		-	-	0	4	6
POP_t	:	planned order release production		0	4	6	6	-

Table 1 which also introduces some additional notation gives a numerical MRRP example (Example 1) for a case of a 5 period planning horizon where production and remanufacturing leadtimes are equal to 2 periods ($\lambda = 2$) and the safety stock amounts to 15 units ($SST = 15$). The figures in boxes are given problem data, the other figures are computed, in principle following to the well-known MRP rules. For extending these rules to the situation with returns we have to make some assumptions which will be discussed later on. For the example in Table 1 these assumptions are as follows:

(1) We use lot-for-lot production and remanufacturing. (2) Net requirements are - as far as possible - satisfied by remanufacturing orders before production orders are taken into consideration. (3) We will not use the disposal option. (4) Returned items not actually needed to fulfill demands for serviceables are stocked in the RP inventory. (5) Planned (expected) future returns are taken into account.

Considering the usual definitions that the projected inventory balances refer to the end of each period while the scheduled and planned receipts and order releases refer to the beginning, it is easy to follow the calculations in Table 1 beginning with the serviceables and returns inventory on hand in the past due period (PD=period 0). Due to the external character of the return flow there is no interaction between production and future planned returns. Different from the situation where no returns occur net requirements now are fulfilled from both sources of procurement taking into account that the remanufacturing source has priority. Since demands and requirements are chosen to be constant in the example we can see how the system approaches a steady state policy of remanufacturing 4 units and producing 6 units each period.

3.2 Basic Cost Considerations

According to the deterministic planning concept of MRP the question of how the decisions referring to the production, remanufacturing and disposal option are made is a matter of pure deterministic cost comparisons.

In general, since both production and remanufacturing costs are strictly proportional and since no capacity constraints are assumed to exist, a lot-for-lot ordering policy is economical for both types of serviceables procurement. A cost comparison of production and remanufacturing has to take into account that each returned unit which is not remanufactured has to be disposed of at a cost c_D. Thus, remanufacturing is only non-profitable if the cost c_R of recovering one unit is higher than the unit production cost c_P plus disposal cost c_D. Since in this case all returned items will be disposed of, we face a regular single source procurement problem where no integration of remanufacturing has to take place. So for $c_R > c_P + c_D$ traditional MRP can be used for material coordination.

On the other hand, if $c_R \leq c_P + c_D$ as assumed in the sequel, remanufacturing is always superior to regular production. Thus the priority rule for procurement prescribes to first use all returns available for fulfilling net requirements of serviceables before regular production orders are placed.

A question still open is under which cost conditions returned items should be discarded. This will be the case if such a surplus of returned goods exists that the holding costs are larger than the cost benefit $c_P + c_D - c_R$ of remanufacturing over regular production. Returned products will only be stocked in the RP-inventory if the respective holding costs are smaller than those for serviceables, i.e. $h_R < h_S$. Otherwise surplus returns which are not disposed of will immediately be remanufactured and stored in the SP-inventory at cost h_S. Thus the critical runout time for excess returns, denoted by τ, is

$$\tau = \left\lfloor \frac{c_P + c_D - c_R}{\min\{h_R, h_S\}} \right\rfloor \tag{3.1}$$

where $\lfloor x \rfloor$ is the largest integer smaller or equal to x.

Under these conditions returned items are discarded in any period t if they exceed a critical level $RMAX_t$ which results from the amount by which the expected requirements $ER^{\tau}_{t+\lambda}$ over τ periods from period $t+\lambda+1$ to $t+\lambda+\tau$ plus gross demand in period $t+\lambda$ and additional safety stock requirements exceed the projected serviceables on hand at the end of period $t+\lambda-1$:

$$RMAX_t = \max\{ER^{\tau}_{t+\lambda} + GR_{t+\lambda} + SST - SOH_{t+\lambda-1}, 0\} \tag{3.2}$$

The amount of projected requirements $ER^{\tau}_{t+\lambda}$ depends on respective forecasts for serviceables requirements and used product returns. It is different for alternative ways in which expected returns will be taken into account in the MRRP control procedure. This topic will be addressed in Section 3.5 where the approaches of reactive and proactive MRRP control are described.

3.3 MRRP-Formulas

With the cost considerations in the previous section similar to the situation of standard MRP application (see SEEGERSTEDT, 1996) we can give explicit formulas for the calculations used in the MRRP system described above. They reflect the computation of variables in the MRRP tableau for each period $t = 1, 2, \ldots, T$.

Since remanufacturing has priority over regular production we start with describing the remanufacturing decision in each period t which will depend on the relation of RP and SP holding costs. If holding costs of returned products are smaller ($h_R < h_S$) only as much available returned items will be ordered for remanufacturing as are needed to satisfy the net requirements in period $t+\lambda$. Otherwise (if $h_R \geq h_S$) all returns will be processed in the remanufacturing facility, unless they exceed the critical returns level $RMAX_t$. This leads to the following formulas for the planned order releases remanufacturing

$$POR_t = \begin{cases} \min\{ROH_{t-1}, NR_{t+\lambda}\} & \text{for} \quad h_R < h_S \\ \min\{ROH_{t-1}, RMAX_t\} & \text{for} \quad h_R \geq h_S \end{cases} \tag{3.3}$$

The size of the production order in period t is equal to that part of net requirements which is not fulfilled by remanufacturing

$$POP_t = \max\{NR_{t+\lambda} - POR_t, 0\} \tag{3.4}$$

The number of disposed items is given by the excess of projected returns on hand over the respective critical level

$$POD_t = \max\{ROH_{t-1} - RMAX_t, 0\} \tag{3.5}$$

Equations (3.3) to (3.5) perform the MRRP formulas for the decision variables. They are completed by formulas which explain the dynamic behavior of the MRRP inventory variables and define the size of net requirements which is expressed by

$$NR_t = \max\{GR_t + SST - SOH_{t-1} - SRP_t - SRR_t, 0\} \tag{3.6}$$

where SRP_t and SRR_t are given scheduled receipts stemming from production and remanufacturing orders before period 1.

The balance equation for serviceables is given by

$$SOH_t = SOH_{t-1} + PRP_t + PRR_t - GR_t \tag{3.7}$$

$$\text{with} \quad PRP_t = \begin{cases} POP_{t-\lambda} & \text{for} \quad t > \lambda \\ SRP_t & \text{for} \quad t \leq \lambda \end{cases} \tag{3.8}$$

$$\text{and} \quad PRR_t = \begin{cases} POR_{t-\lambda} & \text{for} \quad t > \lambda \\ SRR_t & \text{for} \quad t \leq \lambda \end{cases} \tag{3.9}$$

while for returns we find

$$ROH_t = ROH_{t-1} - POR_t - POD_t + PR_t \tag{3.10}$$

Furthermore, we face initial values SOH_0 and ROH_0 which represent the respective stock on hand in the past due period.

3.4 MRRP-Policies

By exploiting the MRRP formulas in (3.3) to (3.10) the expressions for the three decision variables POP_t, POR_t and POD_t can be transformed into decision rules consisting of comparisons of appropriately defined inventory positions with fixed critical inventory levels in each period t. In order to describe these expressions we have to define three different kinds of stock in the production/remanufacturing system:

x_{Rt} : stock on hand of returned products at the beginning of period t (with $x_{Rt} = ROH_{t-1}$)

x_{St} : inventory position of serviceable products at the beginning of period t (with $x_{St} = SOH_{t-1} + \sum_{i=1}^{\lambda} POP_{t-i} + \sum_{i=1}^{\lambda} POR_{t-i}$, where we define $POP_j = SRP_{j+\lambda}$ and $POR_j = SRR_{j+\lambda}$ if $j \leq 0$)

x_{Et} : echelon inventory position in the system at the beginning of period t (with $x_{Et} = x_{Rt} + x_{St}$).

Additionally we have to introduce two critical inventory levels S_t and D_t (with $S_t \leq D_t$) which are defined as

$$S_t = SST + \sum_{i=0}^{\lambda} GR_{t+i} \tag{3.11}$$

and

$$D_t = S_t + ER_{t+\lambda}^{\tau} \tag{3.12}$$

where $ER^{T}_{t+\lambda}$ refers to the amount of projected requirements mentioned in Section 3.2.

Parameter S_t corresponds to the inventory position in period t which is necessary to fulfill all requirements within the processing leadtime. Parameter D_t additionally contains the projected requirements within the critical runout time.

As shown in Appendix A, with these stock and parameter definitions in case of $h_R < h_S$ the MRRP decisions in (3.3), (3.4) and (3.5) can be formulated as

$$POP_t = \max\{S_t - x_{Et}, 0\} \tag{3.13}$$

$$POR_t = \min\{x_{Rt}, \max\{S_t - x_{St}, 0\}\} \tag{3.14}$$

$$POD_t = \max\{x_{Rt} - \max\{D_t - x_{St}, 0\}, 0\} \tag{3.15}$$

These kinds of decision rules correspond to inventory policies known from stochastic inventory control. Because each of the three decision variables depends on just one critical inventory parameter, we denote the complete set of rules by a (S, S, D) policy.

The production rule in (3.13) says that the echelon inventory position has to be raised up to inventory level S_t by additional production orders if it falls below this level. This means that parameter S_t plays the role of an order-up-to-level as it is known from production/inventory control without returns and with strictly proportional costs (see e.g. LEE and NAHMIAS, 1993). The remanufacturing rule in (3.14) describes that, if the order-up-to-level S_t just exceeds the serviceables inventory position, the available returned items are used to fill up this gap by remanufacturing. Finally, from the disposal rule in (3.15) it follows that as much units in the inventory of returned products are discarded as necessary to bring the echelon inventory position down to the stock level D_t if it exceeds this parameter. If the RP stock is not sufficient to decrease the echelon inventory down to level D_t all available returned items are disposed of. Thus parameter D_t can be interpreted as a dispose-down-to-level in the production/inventory system with returns.

In the case of comparatively high holding costs for returned products ($h_R \geq h_S$) returns are not stocked at all and the respective MRRP-formula (3.3) leads to a corresponding remanufacturing rule as follows

$$POR_t = \min\{x_{Rt}, \max\{D_t - x_{St}, 0\}\} \tag{3.16}$$

Under this rule remanufacturing of returned products is used to fill a gap between the dispose-down-to-level D_t (instead of S_t in (3.14)) and the serviceables inventory position. Production and disposal rule in (3.13) and (3.15), respectively, remain valid. Corresponding to the definition above we refer to this combination of decision rules as (S, D, D)-policy. This policy also holds in the case when no stockholding of returned goods is allowed (e.g. for technical or environmental reasons), thus forcing all returns either to be remanufactured or discarded at the beginning of each period. In this situation we only have two independent decision variables POP_t and POR_t, since for POD_t we get: $POD_t = x_{Rt} - POR_t$. So this policy can be denoted as a reduced two-parameter (S, D)-policy. For POP_t and POR_t the formulas (3.13) and (3.16), respectively, will hold.

3.5 Proactive vs. Reactive Planning

The computation of the projected requirements $ER^{\tau}_{t+\lambda}$ which are needed for the determination of the inventory parameter D_t in (3.12) still remains open. From the definition in Section 3.2 this value consists of all expected demands of serviceables for τ periods from period $t + \lambda + 1$ to $t + \lambda + \tau$ which could economically be satisfied by a surplus of returned items in the RP-buffer at the beginning of period t. Since also returns in the periods t to $t + \tau$ after remanufacturing could be used to fulfill demands in the above time span, the net demands for which a surplus of returns would be needed depend on the projected number of future returns which are taken into account within the planning procedure.

With respect to this procedure we find two different planning concepts. In practice we often face a conservative approach which says that uncertain return flows only should be taken into consideration as they emerge. That means that only those returns are regarded for planning purposes which are part of the actual RP-inventory, and no future expected returns are considered in each planning cycle, i.e. it is assumed that $PR_t = 0$ for all periods. This kind of planning will be denoted by reactive MRRP control. Given that future return expectations are ignored, the projected requirements in $ER^{\tau}_{t+\lambda}$ simply consist of the sum of all respective gross requirements within the critical time span:

$$ER^{\tau}_{t+\lambda} = \sum_{i=1}^{\tau} GR_{t+\lambda+i} \tag{3.17}$$

The alternative planning concept takes into consideration all expected future returns which can be used to fulfill future requirements after undergoing the remanufacturing process. This concept is denoted by proactive planning because it makes both remanufacturing and disposal decisions depend on possible employment of future returns. Cost minimizing usage of these returns consists of just-in-time remanufacturing to satisfy demand for serviceables λ periods ahead. Because returns in period t can be started to be remanufactured in period $t+1$ a net demand in a period $t+\lambda+j$ only occurs if we face: $\sum_{i=1}^{j} GR_{t+\lambda+i} > \sum_{i=1}^{j} PR_{t+i-1}$. Under these circumstances the projected total requirements for a time span from period $t+\lambda+1$ to $t+\lambda+\tau$ is equal to

$$ER^{\tau}_{t+\lambda} = \max\{\max_{1\leq j\leq \tau}\{\sum_{i=1}^{j} GR_{t+\lambda+i} - \sum_{i=1}^{j} PR_{t+i-1}\}, 0\} \tag{3.18}$$

This size of requirements can be assigned to a surplus of returned item in period t which are used to fulfill these demands after not more than τ periods of stockholding. If the planned returns are not larger than the corresponding requirements λ periods ahead (resulting in $\sum_{i=1}^{j} GR_{t+\lambda+i} > \sum_{i=1}^{j} PR_{t+i-1}$) the expression in (3.18) simplifies to

$$ER^{\tau}_{t+\lambda} = \sum_{i=1}^{\tau} GR_{t+\lambda+i} - \sum_{i=1}^{\tau} PR_{t+i-1} \tag{3.19}$$

In this case the dispose-down-to-level in (3.12) turns out to be

$$D_t = SST + \sum_{i=0}^{\tau} GR_{t+\lambda+i} - \sum_{i=0}^{\tau-1} PR_{t+i} \tag{3.20}$$

Due to the 5 assumptions made for Example 1 in Section 3.1 the decision variables in Table 1 can be calculated by using formula (3.13), (3.14), and (3.15). Control parameter S_t and D_t can be computed from (3.11) and (3.20) because of $PR_{t-3} < GR_t$ in the example. Assuming that $h_R \leq h_S$ and a runout time $\tau = 2$ (which is sufficient to fulfill assumption 4 in the example) the resulting values for S_t and D_t as well as the stock levels obtained for the inventory positions x_{Rt}, x_{St} and x_{Et} when applying the evaluated MRRP-policies are given in Table 2 for the periods 1 to 4. A comparison with Table 1 shows that classical MRRP calculations and application of MRRP policies lead to the same decisions.

Table 2: Decision parameters for the Example 1

Period t			1	2	3	4
x_{St}	:	serviceables inventory position	40	35	35	35
x_{Rt}	:	reusables on hand	7	6	4	4
x_{ET}	:	echelon inventory position	47	41	39	39
S_t	:	order-up-to-level	45	45	45	45
D_t	:	dispose-down-to-level	57	57	57	57
POP_t	=	$\max\{S_t - x_{Et}, 0\}$	0	4	6	6
POR_t	=	$\min\{x_{Rt}, \max\{S_t - x_{St}, 0\}\}$	5	6	4	4
POD_t	=	$\max\{x_{Rt} - \max\{D_t - x_{St}, 0\}, 0\}$	0	0	0	0

4 MRRP-Policies with Internal Returns

In this section the resulting MRRP-policies are analyzed when the return flows of reusable material are generated within the production system itself. Considering such endogenous sources of recoverable material is different from the case of external returns because the return flows of a certain period now depend on production decisions of preceding periods.

4.1 Extended MRP Tableau

To give a formalisation of the outcome of a production stage with unreliable production we assume a proportional yield process which is often observed in practice and also generally used in inventory models with stochastic yields (see e.g. YANO and LEE, 1995). According to this yield process following the logic of MRP as a deterministic planning concept an (estimated) fraction z of each released production lot POP_t is produced without defects while

$(1-z) \cdot POP_t$ units of the lot are defective. These defective parts form the return flows considered within the context of internal returns. Thus the planned receipts production PRP_t in period t are given by $z \cdot POP_{t-\lambda}$, while the residual order size $(1-z) \cdot POP_{t-\lambda}$ results in planned returns PR_{t-1} at the end of period $t-1$ (or, equivalently, at the beginning of period t).

Using these considerations an Example 2 of the MRRP-calculations for the case of internal returns is given in Table 3.

Table 3: Extended MRP-Tableau for Example 2

Period t			$PD(0)$	1	2	3	4	5
GR_t	:	gross requirements		10	10	10	10	10
SRP_t	:	scheduled receipts production		4	7			
SRR_t	:	scheduled receipts remanufacturing		5	4			
SOH_t	:	projected serviceables on hand	9	8	9	15	15	15
NR_t	:	net requirements		7	6	16	10	10
PR_t	:	planned returns		7	5	3	5	7
ROH_t	:	projected returns on hand	11	7	5	3	5	-
PRR_t	:	planned receipts remanufacturing				11	7	5
POR_t	:	planned order release remanufacturing		11	7	5	3	-
POD_t	:	planned order release disposal		0	0	0	0	-
PRP_t	:	planned receipts production		0	0	5	3	5
OPO_t	:	overplanned production orders		0	0	10	6	10
POP_t	:	planned order release production		10	6	10	14	-

The underlying data for setting initial inventories and past due released planned orders for serviceables and returns, safety stock and production and remanufacturing leadtimes are the same as in Example 1 given in Section 3.1. In addition to these input data for Table 3 we also refer to the five assumptions made for Example 1. For the yield rate we assume a constant estimation of $z = 0.5$. Using this forecast the row in the MRP tableau containing the scheduled receipts production now for each period $t \leq \lambda$ corresponds to those parts that are expected to arrive without defects from preceding production. The additional row OPO_t represents the overplanned production orders ($OPO_t = \frac{1}{z} \cdot PRP_t$) taking into account that an amount of $\frac{1}{z}$ units has to be ordered to receive one unit without defects. Since the planned returns are assigned to the end of the period before they are available for remanufacturing it should be noted that the projected returns on hand $ROH_0 = 11$ consist of the assumed initial inventory of 7 units like in Example 1 and the planned return quantity corresponding to a planned order release of 8 units at the beginning of period $t = -1$, which additionally results in a scheduled receipts production of 4 units in period $t = 1$.

Different from the results in the external return case it should be noted that with remanufacturing of internal returns for fulfilling demands the system does not approaches to a period by period steady state policy of remanufacturing and production orders. Instead a cyclical sequence of orders will be repeated with increasing planning horizon.

4.2 Basic Cost Considerations

In order to decide upon the amount up to which returned items are stored in the RP-inventory or are remanufactured instead of being disposed of, the costs which are connected with each of these options have to be compared with each other. These considerations are similar to the cost comparisons when analyzing external returns. But when considering the remanufacturing of internal returns we also have to take into account when comparing this alternative with the option of producing new products, that the latter option causes future return flows whereas we assume that the remanufacturing process works without defects. Considering the decision concerning the utilization of this future return flows remanufacturing is only profitable when the cost c_R of remanufacturing one item does not exceed the disposal cost c_D of one item plus the total cost c_T of producing one non-defective item and discarding the corresponding defective parts. Since for an outcome of one serviceable item $\frac{1}{z}$ units have to be released to the manufacturing process and $\frac{1}{z} - 1$ units are expected to be defective, these costs sum up to $c_T = \frac{1}{z} \cdot c_P + (\frac{1}{z} - 1) \cdot c_D$. Hence we face the condition $c_R \leq c_D + c_T = \frac{1}{z} \cdot (c_D + c_P)$ for the remanufacturing option to be cost effective compared with the regular production of new products for fulfilling requirements.

As in the case of external returns the decision of how many returned parts should be discarded depends on the projected requirements $E_{t+\lambda}^{\tau}$ during τ periods from $t + \lambda + 1$ to $t + \lambda + \tau$ with the critical runout time τ. Following the above cost argument the runout time τ in the case of internal returns is different from (3.1) and thus given by

$$\tau = \left\lfloor \frac{\frac{1}{z} \cdot (c_D + c_P) - c_R}{\min\{h_R, h_S\}} \right\rfloor . \tag{4.1}$$

Using this definition a critical level $RMAX_t$ as in (3.2) can be formulated which defines an upper limit beyond which available returned parts should be disposed of. However, it has to be noted that in the case of internal returns the projected requirements $E_{t+\lambda}^{\tau}$ might incorporate planned returns generated by endogenous production decisions.

4.3 MRRP-Formulas

Now we can give explicit formulas for the extended MRP calculations when integrating the decisions combined with the utilization of internal return flows from an unreliable production process.

Assuming cost superiority of remanufacturing over producing new items the decisions for planned order release remanufacturing are given just like in Section 3.1 for the case of external returns:

$$POR_t = \begin{cases} \min\{ROH_{t-1}, NR_{t+\lambda}\} & \text{for} \quad h_R < h_S \\ \min\{ROH_{t-1}, RMAX_t\} & \text{for} \quad h_R \geq h_S \end{cases} \tag{4.2}$$

As explained in Section 3.2 the number of items to be remanufactured depends on the relation of RP and SP inventory holding costs. Due to the perfect reliability of the remanufacturing process we find the same calculations as in Section 3.3.

For specifying the planned order release production which has to fulfill the net requirements which are not covered by remanufacturing, it is necessary to blow up these requirements according to an overplanning procedure in order to consider that only a fraction of the order is expected to be produced without defects. So, different from formula (3.4) POP_t here is given by equation (4.3).

$$POP_t = \max\left\{\frac{NR_{t+\lambda} - POR_t}{z}, 0\right\} \tag{4.3}$$

Identical to the case of external returns the quantity of returns available at the beginning of period t, which exceeds the critical level $RMAX_t$, is discarded, so that the planned order release disposal POD_t is given by

$$POD_t = \max\{ROH_{t-1} - RMAX_t, 0\}. \tag{4.4}$$

For the further MRRP calculations only some minor adjustments compared with the formulations given for external returns in Section 3.3 are necessary. For the net requirement NR_t still the expression in (3.6) holds. Furtheron, (3.7) describes the serviceables inventory balance equation. However, due to the difference of units released to and received from production instead of (3.8) we now have

$$PRP_t = \begin{cases} z \cdot POP_{t-\lambda} & \text{for} \quad t > \lambda \\ SRP_t & \text{for} \quad t \leq \lambda. \end{cases} \tag{4.5}$$

According to the assumed perfect reliability of the remanufacturing process equation (3.9) for PRR_t remains valid. With PR_t defined as planned returns available at the end of period t also balance equation (3.10) for the returns on hand ROH_t still holds.

Different from the situation with external returns PR_t will now depend on past production orders. According to the production leadtime of λ periods it is assumed that an order which is released in the beginning of period t will result in remanufacturable returns a the end of period $t + \lambda - 1$. So, in general, we get

$$PR_t = \begin{cases} (1-z) \cdot POP_{t-\lambda+1} & \text{for} \quad t > \lambda \\ (\frac{1}{z} - 1) \cdot SRP_{t+1} & \text{for} \quad t \leq \lambda. \end{cases} \tag{4.6}$$

However, this forecasting of returns only holds if we use a proactive planning approach as described in Section 3.5. Under a simple reactive planning procedure we ignore possible future occurrence of remanufacturable products so that planned returns are assumed to be $PR_t = 0$ for $t = 1, 2, \ldots, T$. Different from the case with external returns the planning approach has a major impact on the structure of the MRRP-policy since the returns-production dependency only plays a role when proactive planning is applied.

4.4 MRRP-Policies

For evaluating the given MRRP formulas in order to transform these calculations into MRRP control rules we have to separate two cases dependent on the planning procedure which is used to integrate (estimated) future return flows. We will see that ignoring future return flows within the MRRP calculations by using the reactive planning procedure will lead to decisions POP_t, POR_t and POD_t which are very similar to those obtained when using this planning approach in the external return case. However, due to the dependency between remanufacturing and production decisions using the proactive planning procedure will result in some structural different policies compared with the case of external returns.

4.4.1 Reactive Planning

In the case of reactive planning we assume $PR_t = 0$ for $t = 1, 2, \ldots, T$. Developing the MRRP policies the resulting decisions POP_t, POR_t and POD_t again depend on specific stock categories whose actual levels have to be compared with some critical inventory levels. These categories of stocks are the same as already introduced in Section 3.4 for the case of external returns. The available inventory of returned products x_{Rt} at the beginning of period t is defined by $x_{Rt} = ROH_{t-1}$. Stock level x_{St} defines the inventory position of serviceable products at the beginning of period t and both inventory types sum up to the available echelon inventory position $x_{Et} = x_{Rt} + x_{St}$ at the beginning of period t. The only difference compared with the case of external returns is in the definition of the inventory position of serviceable products x_{St}. Taking into account that only a fraction z of each released production quantity is produced without defects, x_{St} now is given by

$$x_{St} = SOH_{t-1} + z \cdot \sum_{i=1}^{\lambda} POP_{t-i} + \sum_{i=1}^{\lambda} POR_{t-i}. \tag{4.7}$$

Using these definitions of stocks in the system and the formulations of the critical inventory levels

$$S_t = SST + \sum_{i=0}^{\lambda} GR_{t+i} \tag{4.8}$$

and

$$D_t = SST + \sum_{i=0}^{\lambda+\tau} GR_{t+i} \tag{4.9}$$

which are identical to the formula (3.11) and (3.12) in case of reactive planning we get the following expressions for the three decision variables (for details see Appendix B.1). The remanufacturing decisions POR_t are given as in (3.14) and (3.16) respectively. Also disposal decisions POD_t are the same.

$$POR_t = \begin{cases} \min\{x_{Rt}, \max\{S_t - x_{St}, 0\}\} & \text{for} \quad h_R < h_S \\ \min\{x_{Rt}, \max\{D_t - x_{St}, 0\}\} & \text{for} \quad h_R \geq h_S \end{cases} \tag{4.10}$$

$$POD_t = \max\{x_{Rt} - \max\{D_t - x_{St}, 0\}, 0\}.$$

However, it should be noted that the inventory position x_{St} here is modified according to (4.7), and that the runout time τ used in the definition of D_t now is based on the cost comparison as given in (4.1).

Due to the impact of the imperfect reliable production process the production decisions POP_t obviously are different from the one described in the (S, S, D) and (S, D, D)-policy for external returns. Instead of a direct order-up-to production policy as found in (3.12), the production quantity now has to be increased by the expected amount of defect products in order to raise the echelon inventory position to the desired order-up-to-level S_t so that we get

$$POP_t = \max\left\{\frac{S_t - x_{Et}}{z}, 0\right\}. \tag{4.11}$$

So we find that in the case of reactive planning the structural results of the MRRP policy for external returns including an order-up-to and a dispose-down-to parameter are -with minor adjustments- still valid if the flow of returns is generated internally.

4.4.2 Proactive Planning

Analyzing the case when the proactive planning approach is used, future remanufacturing and disposal decisions different from the situation with reactive planning may depend on production decisions of former periods.

As explained above specifying the projected requirements $ER^{\tau}_{t+\lambda}$ used in the definition of the critical level $RMAX_t$ depends on the planning procedure which is used to account for the estimated return flows. Applying the proactive planning approach we have the same general expression (3.18) as in the case of external returns

$$ER^{\tau}_{t+\lambda} = \max\{\max_{1\leq j\leq \tau}\{\sum_{i=1}^{j} GR_{t+\lambda+i} - \sum_{i=1}^{j} PR_{t+i-1}\}, 0\}$$

Hence it is clear, that using $RMAX_t$ in the MRRP-calculations for the decisions POR_t and POD_t as in formula (4.2) and (4.4) respectively, these decisions are influenced by production decisions of former periods. However, it has to be noted that according to (4.6) the planned returns PR_t now still depend on former production orders. Furtheron, depending on the length of the runout time τ compared with the processing time λ, POR_t and POD_t may be affected by production decisions in periods $t' > t$ if $\tau > \lambda$. But considering that disposal actions are only taken if at the beginning of period t there are enough reusables available to cover the net requirements for τ periods ahead starting with period $t+\lambda+1$, we can conclude that no additional production orders are planned during the time span from period t to period $t+\tau-\lambda$ so that for the corresponding periods planned production orders and planned returns are equal to zero. Inserting the formula (4.6) for the planned returns into the definition of $ER^{\tau}_{t+\lambda}$ under these circumstances the projected requirements only depend on past production orders which generate returns proportional to the scheduled receipts production.

$$ER^{\tau}_{t+\lambda} = \max\{\max_{1\leq j\leq \tau}\{\sum_{i=1}^{j} GR_{t+\lambda+i} - (\frac{1}{z}-1)\cdot\sum_{i=1}^{j} SRP_{t+i}\}, 0\} \tag{4.12}$$

Different from the situation with external returns the external requirements in (4.12) now consist of both exogenous (GR_t) and endogenous (SRP_t) data. This fact complicates the derivation of respective decision rules. Unfortunately, evaluating the MRRP calculations for this general case will not lead to simple policy structures because of the multiple comparisons appearing in (4.12). But in the case of a considerably high yield rate z we will find that $\sum_{i=1}^{j} GR_{t+\lambda+i} > (\frac{1}{z}-1)\cdot\sum_{i=1}^{j} SRP_{t+i}$ holds so that (4.12) simplifies to the following expression:

$$ER^{\tau}_{t+\lambda} = \sum_{i=1}^{\tau} GR_{t+\lambda+i} - (\frac{1}{z}-1)\cdot\sum_{i=1}^{\tau} SRP_{t+i} \tag{4.13}$$

In this situation it is possible to give simple explicit control rules for the MRRP decisions. Evaluating the MRRP formulas (4.2) to (4.4) in connection with the other formulas belonging to the case of internal returns we are able to express the resulting MRRP policies using the already introduced inventory types x_{St}, x_{Rt} and x_{Et}. In addition to these stock categories we now need two additional categories x^{τ}_{Rt} and x^{τ}_{St}. x^{τ}_{Rt} is defined as the cumulated planned returns from period $t+1$ to period $t+\tau$ according to (4.14) and x^{τ}_{St} is defined as the sum of the serviceables and the described returns inventory position:

$$x_{Rt}^{\tau} = (\frac{1}{z} - 1) \cdot \sum_{i=1}^{\tau} SRP_{t+i} \tag{4.14}$$

$$x_{St}^{\tau} = x_{St} + x_{Rt}^{\tau} \tag{4.15}$$

Comparing these stock categories with the fixed critical inventory levels D_t and S_t the resulting decisions are given as (for details see Appendix B.2):

$$POR_t = \begin{cases} \min\{x_{Rt}, \max\{S_t - x_{St}, 0\}\} & \text{for} \quad h_R < h_S \\ \min\{x_{Rt}, \max\{D_t - x_{St}^{\tau}, 0\}\} & \text{for} \quad h_R \geq h_S \end{cases} \tag{4.16}$$

$$POD_t = \max\{x_{Rt} - \max\{D_t - x_{St}^{\tau}, 0\}, 0\}. \tag{4.17}$$

$$POP_t = \max\left\{\frac{S_t - x_{Et}}{z}, 0\right\}. \tag{4.18}$$

The critical inventory levels S_t and D_t are the same as in (4.8) and (4.9) for the procedure of reactive planning.

Different from this situation in the case of proactive planning the disposal decision now depends on a modified inventory position which includes serviceables and pipeline stocks of reusable items. The same holds for the remanufacturing decision, if stockholding of returns is favourable.

Resuming Example 2 presented in Table 3 in Table 4 we summarize the resulting values for the decision variables POP_t, POR_t and POD_t depending on the relevant inventory categories and the critical inventory levels S_t and D_t for 4 periods. Again we assume that $h_R < h_S$ and that the runout time is given by $\tau = 2$.

5 Optimal Policies

We know that due to its simplifications the MRP concept will usually not yield optimal control strategies for solving the stochastic dynamic manufacturing/remanufacturing problems. Nevertheless, in Section 3 and 4 we

Table 4: Decision parameters for Example 2

Period t			1	2	3	4
x_{St}	:	serviceables inventory	29	35	35	35
x_{ST}^{τ}	:	extended inventory position	36	35	35	35
x_{Rt}	:	reusables on hand	11	7	5	3
x_{ET}	:	echelon inventory position	40	42	40	38
S_t	:	order-up-to-level	45	45	45	45
D_t	:	dispose-down-to-level	65	65	65	65
POP_t	=	$\max\{\frac{S_t - x_{Et}}{z}, 0\}$	10	6	10	14
POR_t	=	$\min\{x_{Rt}, \max\{S_t - x_{St}, 0\}\}$	11	7	5	3
POD_t	=	$\max\{x_{Rt} - \max\{D_t - x_{St}^{\tau}, 0\}, 0\}$	0	0	0	0

derived the surprising result that the application of a straightforward extended MRP approach corresponds to applying control policies as they are well-known in a more simple form from stochastic inventory control (SIC) problems. So the question arises how much the MRRP rules are related to the optimal control policies for the combined production/remanufacturing problem. Unfortunately, comprehensive results are only available for the above considered problem with external returns.

5.1 Optimal Policies under External Returns

The original problem underlying the MRRP application is to find the optimal combined production, remanufacturing and disposal decisions in each period of a finite planning horizon which minimize the total expected costs under stochastic demands and returns. In order to account for the impact of stock-outs, different from the MRP approach where a predetermined safety stock is in operation a shortage cost component must explicitly be taken into consideration. Such a problem has to be formulated as a stochastic dynamic optimization problem which performs an extension of the traditional SIC problem by including returns as well as remanufacturing and disposal actions. Under the cost and leadtime assumptions of this paper it can be shown (see INDERFURTH, 1997) that the optimal control policy in each period has the following simple structure with 3 control parameters S_t, M_t and D_t (with $S_t \leq M_t \leq D_t$):

$$POP_t = \max\{S_t - x_{Et}, 0\} \tag{5.1}$$

$$POR_t = \min\{x_{Rt}, \max\{M_t - x_{St}, 0\}\} \tag{5.2}$$

$$POD_t = \max\{x_{Rt} - \max\{D_t - x_{St}, 0\}, 0\} \tag{5.3}$$

This so-called (S, M, D)-policy very much resembles to the MRRP-policy presented in (3.13) to (3.16). Only two differences show up. At first, while the policy structure for the production and disposal decision is identical, it deviates for the remanufacturing decision. Remanufacturing is optimally controlled by a specific (third) control parameter M_t which can be interpreted as a remanufacture-up-to-level. In the MRRP-policy this parameter is replaced by the parameter S_t or D_t, respectively, depending on the relation of the different holding costs. Secondly, the parameters S_t and D_t of the optimal control rule will normally differ from the MRRP-parameters. They depend on all cost parameters and on the whole distribution functions of the stochastic returns and demands. These parameters (and the third parameter M_t as well) can only be calculated numerically. It is not possible to derive simple closed formulas as in (3.11) and (3.12) for the MRRP-parameters. In case that stockholding of returned items is not allowed, it turns out that the optimal control rule from SIC is a two-parameter (S, D)-policy (see INDERFURTH, 1997), thus having completely the same structure as the MRRP-policy under these circumstances (see Section 3.4).

Finally, it should be noted that in the case of high remanufacturing costs ($c_R > c_P + c_D$) also in the stochastic case remanufacturing will never be economical and thus the problem reduces to controlling a conventional production system with proportional costs. As we know from inventory theory (see LEE and NAHMIAS, 1993) for such a system an order-up-to-S-policy is optimal. Applying the analysis of Section 3 it is easy to show that in this cost situation the MRP approach will also lead to this type of policy, thus resulting again in an identity of policies.

5.2 Optimal Policies under Internal Returns

Whereas facing external return flows at least for simple problems we are able to derive the structure of the optimal SIC policy, this is unfortunately not the case when considering internal returns. Although many attempts have been made to analyze different periodic inventory control models with stochastic demand and stochastic yield (for a review see LEE and YANO, 1995) the obtained results concerning the structure of optimal policies are still restricted to single-stage models with stochastic yield but without taking into account remanufacturing activities. For this situation HENIG and GERCHAK (1990) show that under quite general assumptions the optimal production policy in the multi-period case is of a more complex order-up-to type and has the following structure:

$$POP_t = \max\{S(x_{St}) - x_{St}, 0\} \tag{5.4}$$

This means that the order-up-to-level S is not a constant, but depends on the inventory position. In addition to this result for the single-period problem assuming a proportional yield model as in Section 4 HENIG and GERCHAK derive an approximate formula for the production quantity.

$$POP_t \approx \frac{1}{\hat{z}} \cdot \max\{S - x_{St}, 0\} \tag{5.5}$$

with $\hat{z} = \mu_z + \frac{\sigma_z^2}{\mu_z}$. This result shows that the production quantity approximately equals the difference between a critical order point S and the inventory position x_S divided by a factor $\hat{z}$ which depends on the variance σ_z^2 and the expectation μ_z of the distribution of the stochastic yield rate z. Interpreting as an estimation of the yield rate z in the MRRP calculations we obtain an identical structure as for the MRRP production decisions in Section 4 (e.g. formula (4.11)). The fact that instead of the serviceables inventory position the MRRP control rule depends on the echelon inventory x_{Et} is obviously due to the considered recovery option which is not integrated in the reported SIC approach. The second term $\frac{\sigma_z^2}{\mu_z}$ of the SIC yield factor $\hat{z}$ can be interpreted as a safety buffer to protect against the uncertainty of the yield rate.

6 Conclusions and Further Research

In this paper an extension of the traditional MRP concept was presented which enables to integrate external returns of used products as well as internal return flows by planning disposal and remanufacturing options in coordination with 'traditional' MRP-procurement decisions. For both considered types of reverse flows of reusables based on deterministic cost comparisons MRRP-calculations were developed. Transformations of these calculations to simple inventory control rules led us to the result that the structure of these rules are identical or very similar to those of the optimal stochastic control rules as far as these are known. Whereas the control parameters of these rules can be specified in a simple way, they usually will deviate from the optimal parameters. Furtheron, parameters as well as the structure of the developed control rules depend on the way of integrating forecasts of future return flows into the MRRP-calculations. Concerning this aspect the distinction between a proactive and a reactive planning approach was shown to have an influence on the structure and the parameters of the resulting control rules. Comparing the control rules for both types of returns we get the result that the structure of the rules developed in the case of internal return flows are more complex. This is obviously a consequence of the dependence of remanufacturing decisions on preceding production decisions in this situation. In our analysis the cases of external and internal returns have been treated separately. It is obvious that both cases can be considered simultaneously, and that the respective MRRP rules will be straightforward combinations in this situation.

For future research some aspects have to be analyzed in more detail. In order to be able to assess the service and cost performance of the extended MRP calculations they should be compared with the planning results obtained when implementing the decisions according to the optimal SIC rules. In addition to this investigation the influence of the planning approach concerning the integration of forecasted return flows has to be clarified by performing a comparative analysis of the proactive and reactive planning procedure. Whereas the presented analysis was restricted to scenarios with equal processing times for production and remanufacturing this strong assumption has to be relaxated in situations where processing times differ considerably. In such a generalized situation we get more complex control rules because the efficiency of the alternative procurement options in this case depends not only on pure cost considerations based on procurement and holding costs but also on additional leadtime effects. Because especially for remanufacturing operations we often find stochastic processing times, depending on the condition of the reusables, the assumption of deterministic processing times obviously is another critical aspect so that the performance of the MRRP-concept also has to be analyzed for situations with stochastic leadtimes. Another impact on the structure of the developed control rules is expected to be caused by introducing fixed costs for procurement and remanufacturing processes making it necessary that lot-sizing considerations have to be incorporated into the MRRP-calculations. Finally, the available options to (re)use flows of returned goods also should include disassembly options. Extending the

MRRP-concept to this aspect not only asks for the integration of a further option besides remanufacturing and disposal but also incorporates for the extension to a multi-level case because with this additional recovery option e.g. the question of an optimal disassembly-level has to be analyzed.

A MRRP Policies with External Returns

In Appendix A we prove the validity of the rules (3.13) to (3.15) formulated for the production, remanufacturing and disposal decisions. First we derive the decision rule (3.14) for planned order releases remanufacturing in case of $h_R < h_S$.

Starting with MRRP formula (3.3) we find

$$POR_t = \min\{ROH_{t-1}, NR_{t+\lambda}\} \quad \text{for} \quad t \geq 1 \tag{A.1}$$

express $NR_{t+\lambda}$ according to (3.6) and regarding that $SRP_t = SRR_t = 0$ for $t > \lambda$ as

$$NR_{t+\lambda} = \max\{GR_{t+\lambda} + SST - SOH_{t-1+\lambda}, 0\} \tag{A.2}$$

Repeated inserting of inventory balance equation (3.7) and regarding time lag expressions (3.8) and (3.9) leads to the following formula for $SOH_{t+\lambda-1}$ in (A.2)

$$SOH_{t+\lambda-1} = SOH_{t-1} + \sum_{i=1}^{\lambda} POP_{t-i} + \sum_{i=1}^{\lambda} POR_{t-i} - \sum_{i=0}^{\lambda-1} GR_{t+i} \tag{A.3}$$

where we use $POP_t = SRP_{t+\lambda}$ and $POR_t = SRR_{t+\lambda} \quad$ for $t \leq 0$.

With (A.3) $NR_{t+\lambda}$ in (A.2) can be written as

$$NR_{t+\lambda} = \max\{(\sum_{i=0}^{\lambda} GR_{t+i} + SST) - (SOH_{t-1} + \sum_{i=1}^{\lambda} POP_{t-i} + \sum_{i=1}^{\lambda} POR_{t-i}), 0\} \tag{A.4}$$

Using the definition of S_t and x_{St} in Section 3.4 we can rewrite (A.4) by

$$NR_{t+\lambda} = \max\{S_t - x_{St}, 0\} \tag{A.5}$$

Finally, replacing $NR_{t+\lambda}$ in (A.1) by (A.5) and employing the definition $x_{Rt} = ROH_{t-1}$ yields the POR_t-decision rule in (3.14)

In the case $h_R \geq h_S$ starting point is the second branch of MRRP-formula (3.3) with

$$POR_t = \min\{ROH_{t-1}, RMAX_t\} \tag{A.6}$$

From the definition of $RMAX_t$ in (3.2) it follows that by inserting $SOH_{t+\lambda-1}$ from (A.3) we find

$$\begin{aligned} RMAX_t &= \max\{(\sum_{i=0}^{\lambda} GR_{t+i} + SST + ER_{t+\lambda}^{\tau}) \\ &\quad -(SOH_{t-1} + \sum_{i=1}^{\lambda} POP_{t-i} + \sum_{i=1}^{\lambda} POR_{t-i}), 0\} \end{aligned} \tag{A.7}$$

Here, using the definition of D_t and x_{St} in Section 3.4 we can formulate

$$RMAX_t = \max\{D_t - x_{St}, 0\} \tag{A.8}$$

Replacing $RMAX_t$ in (A.6) by (A.8) and using $x_{Rt} = ROH_{t-1}$ results in decision rule (3.16).

Proving the validity of decision rule (3.13) for planned order releases production starts with the MRRP-formula (3.4)

$$POP_t = \max\{NR_{t+\lambda} - POR_t, 0\} \tag{A.9}$$

which, using the $NR_{t+\lambda}$ expression in (A.5), can be written as

$$POP_t = \max\{\max\{S_t - x_{St}, 0\} - POR_t, 0\} \tag{A.10}$$

Now we have to subsequently take into consideration the two different POR_t-decision rules in (3.14) and (3.16).

With the remanufacturing rule in (3.14) the production formula (A.10) results in

$$POP_t = \max\{\max\{S_t - x_{St}, 0\} - \min\{x_{Rt}, \max\{S_t - x_{St}, 0\}\}, 0\} \tag{A.11}$$

Here we have to differ between two cases:

$\boxed{1}$ $x_{Rt} \geq S_t - x_{St}$:

Due to $x_{Rt} \geq 0$ in this case we have $x_{Rt} \geq \max\{S_t - x_{St}, 0\}$, which exploiting (A.11) results in

$$POP_t = 0$$

$\boxed{2}$ $x_{Rt} < S_t - x_{St}$

Due $x_{Rt} \geq 0$ we get $S_t - x_{St} > 0$ and thus $x_{Rt} \leq \max\{S_t - x_{St}, 0\}$ which exploiting (A.11) for this case leads to

$$POP_t = \max\{S_t - x_{St} - x_{Rt}, 0\} = S_t - x_{St} - x_{Rt}$$

Using the definition $x_{Et} = x_{Rt} + x_{St}$, the results for both cases $\boxed{1}$ and $\boxed{2}$ can be combined to

$$POP_t = \max\{S_t - x_{Et}, 0\}$$

which is identical to decision rule (3.13).

With remanufacturing rule (3.16) production formula (A.10) turns out to be

$$POP_t = \max\{\max\{S_t - x_{St}, 0\} - \min\{x_{Rt}, \max\{D_t - x_{St}, 0\}\}, 0\} \quad \text{(A.12)}$$

Now we have to differentiate between three cases:

$\boxed{1}$ $x_{Rt} \geq D_t - x_{St}$:

Here due to $D_t \geq S_t$ we also have $x_{Rt} \geq S_t - x_{St}$ and furthermore, as above,
$x_{Rt} \geq \max\{D_t - x_{St}, 0\}$ and $x_{Rt} \geq \max\{S_t - x_{St}, 0\}$.
With these results we can exploit (A.12) and find

$$POP_t = 0$$

$\boxed{2}$ $S_t - x_{St} \leq x_{Rt} < D_t - x_{St}$:

In this case in a similar way we get

$$POP_t = \max\{\max\{S_t - x_{St}, 0\} - x_{Rt}, 0\} = 0$$

$\boxed{3}$ $x_{Rt} < S_t - x_{St}$:

In this case we have the same situation as with exploiting (A.11) above and therefore find the same result

$$POP_t = S_t - x_{St} - x_{Rt}$$

Obviously, the combination of all three cases again leads to

$$POP_t = \max\{S_t - x_{Et}, 0\}$$

Thus, the production decision rule (3.13) holds for both remanufacturing rules (3.14) and (3.16).

Finally, it has to be shown that decision rule (3.15) for planned disposal orders is valid.
Starting point is MRRP-formula (3.5)

$$POD_t = \max\{ROH_{t-1} - RMAX_t, 0\} \tag{A.13}$$

Using $x_{Rt} = ROH_{t-1}$ and replacing $RMAX_t$ by the expression in (A.8) results in

$$POD_t = \max\{x_{Rt} - \max\{D_t - x_{St}, 0\}, 0\}$$

This identical to the decision rule formulated in (3.15).

B MRRP Policies with Internal Returns

B.1 Reactive Planning

The derivation of the MRRP control rules using the reactive planning procedure is very similar to the analysis given in Appendix A.

Following the same steps as in Appendix A and using the PRP_t expression (4.5) instead of formula (3.8) we get the following formulas for $SOH_{t+\lambda-1}$ and $NR_{t+\lambda}$:

$$SOH_{t+\lambda-1} = SOH_{t-1} + z \cdot \sum_{i=1}^{\lambda} POP_{t-i} + \sum_{i=1}^{\lambda} POR_{t-i} - \sum_{i=0}^{\lambda-1} GR_{t+i} \tag{B.1}$$

$$NR_{t+\lambda} = \max\{(\sum_{i=0}^{\lambda} GR_{t+i} + SST) -$$

$$(SOH_{t-1} + z \cdot \sum_{i=1}^{\lambda} POP_{t-i} + \sum_{i=1}^{\lambda} POR_{t-i}), 0\} \quad \text{(B.2)}$$

Using the definition (4.8) of S_t and the modified definition (4.7) of x_{St} we can write $NR_{t+\lambda}$ as

$$NR_{t+\lambda} = \max\{S_t - x_{St}, 0\} \quad \text{(B.3)}$$

as in Appendix A. Furtheron inserting $SOH_{t+\lambda-1}$ from (B.1) and $ER_{t+\lambda}^{\tau}$ from (3.17), i.e.

$$ER_{t+\lambda}^{\tau} = \sum_{i=1}^{\tau} GR_{t+\lambda+i} \quad \text{(B.4)}$$

in the definition of $RMAX_t$ (see formula (3.2)) we get

$$RMAX_t = \max\{(\sum_{i=0}^{\lambda+\tau} GR_{t+i} + SST) - (SOH_{t-1} + z \cdot \sum_{i=1}^{\lambda} POP_{t-i} + \sum_{i=1}^{\lambda} POR_{t-i}), 0\}. \quad \text{(B.5)}$$

As in Appendix A with the definition of D_t from (4.9) this results in

$$RMAX_t = \max\{D_t - x_{St}, 0\}. \quad \text{(B.6)}$$

Inserting the expressions (B.6) and (B.3) for $RMAX_t$ and $NR_{t+\lambda}$ in (4.2) and (4.4) and substituting ROH_{t-1} by the introduced inventory position x_{Rt} the evaluation of the MRRP-formulas for POR_t and POD_t given in Section 4.3 is straightforward, as in Appendix A.

Evaluating the MRRP-formula for POR_t given in (4.3) using expression (B.3) for $NR_{t+\lambda}$ and inserting the two two derived remanufacturing decisions given in (4.10) we find in both cases the resulting production decision POP_t given in (4.11). Due to the overplanning this rule differs from the production decision in the external return case only by the additional division by the yield factor z.

B.2 Proactive Planning

In order to prove the formulas given in Section 4.4.2 for the assumption

$\sum_{i=1}^{j} GR_{t+\lambda+i} > \sum_{i=1}^{j} PR_{t+i-1}$ we start with the decision rule for the planned remanufacturing orders POR_t.

For $h_R < h_S$ this decision is given by

$$POR_t = \min\{ROH_{t-1}, NR_{t+\lambda}\}. \tag{B.7}$$

Inserting $NR_{t+\lambda} = \max\{S_t - x_{St}, 0\}$ as given in (B.3) and thus based on the modified definition of x_{St} as in (4.7) we get the corresponding formula for the decision rule in the same manner as in the case of external returns.

For $h_R \geq h_S$ we start with the formula

$$POR_t = \min\{ROH_{t-1}, RMAX_t\} \tag{B.8}$$

Inserting $SOH_{t+\lambda-1}$ as given in (B.1) into the formula for $RMAX_t$ (from (3.2)) we get:

$$\begin{aligned} RMAX_t &= \max\{(\sum_{i=0}^{\lambda} GR_{t+i} + SST + ER^{\tau}_{t+\lambda}) \\ &\quad -(SOH_{t-1} + z \cdot \sum_{i=1}^{\lambda} POP_{t-i} + \sum_{i=1}^{\lambda} POR_{t-i}), 0\}. \end{aligned} \tag{B.9}$$

Inserting $ER^{\tau}_{t+\lambda}$ from (4.13) in the next step we obtain:

$$\begin{aligned} RMAX_t &= \max\{(\sum_{i=0}^{\lambda+\tau} GR_{t+i} + SST) - (SOH_{t-1} + z \cdot \sum_{i=1}^{\lambda} POP_{t-i} \\ &\quad + \sum_{i=1}^{\lambda} POR_{t-i} + (\frac{1}{z} - 1) \cdot \sum_{i=1}^{\tau} SRP_{t+i}), 0\} \end{aligned} \tag{B.10}$$

Now using the definitions of the cumulated planned return flows x^{τ}_{Rt} in (4.14) and the extended inventory position x^{τ}_{St} (from (4.15)) the critical inventory level $RMAX_t$ is

$$RMAX_t = \max\{D_t - x_{St}^{\tau}, 0\} \tag{B.11}$$

with D_t as given in (4.9). Inserting this expression in (B.8) leads to the second branch of the decision rule for POR_t in (4.16).

Using the decision rule for POR_t we can derive the decision rule for POP_t according to (4.18). This leads to

$$POP_t = \frac{1}{z} \cdot \max\{\max\{S_t - x_{St}, 0\} - \min\{x_{Rt}, \max\{S_t - x_{St}, 0\}\}, 0\} \tag{B.12}$$

for $h_R < h_S$, whereas for $h_R \geq h_S$ we get the expression

$$POP_t = \frac{1}{z} \cdot \max\{\max\{S_t - x_{St}, 0\} - \min\{x_{Rt}, \max\{D_t - x_{St}^{\tau}, 0\}\}, 0\} \tag{B.13}$$

While (B.13) can be proved to be identical to (4.18) just as in the case of external returns in Appendix A, the prove of (B.14) makes it necessary to differ between three cases, which are slightly different from those in Appendix A:

[1] $x_{Rt} \geq D_t - x_{St}^{\tau}$:

Because of the assumption that $\sum_{i=1}^{j} GR_{t+\lambda+i} > (\frac{1}{z} - 1) \cdot \sum_{i=1}^{j} SRP_{t+i}$ we use the same arguments as in Appendix A and get

$$POP_t = 0$$

[2] $S_t - x_{St} \leq x_{Rt} < D_t - x_{St}^{\tau}$:

In a similar way we obtain

$$POP_t = \frac{1}{z} \cdot \max\{\max\{S_t - x_{St}, 0\} - x_{Rt}, 0\} = 0$$

$\boxed{3}$ $x_{Rt} < S_t - x_{St}$:

Again we have a similar situation as in the case of external returns and get the result

$$POP_t = \frac{1}{z} \cdot (S_t - x_{St} - x_{Rt})$$

The results for $\boxed{1}$, $\boxed{2}$ and $\boxed{3}$ are completely the same as the corresponding results in Appendix A. Thus a combination of all three cases leads to exactly the same decision rule

$$POP_t \quad = \quad \max \frac{1}{z} \cdot \{S_t - x_{Et}, 0\} .$$

which is identical to the rule in (4.18).

For the decision POD_t we use the definition of $x_{Rt} = ROH_{t-1}$ and formula (B.11) for $RMAX_t$. Inserting these formulas into the MRRP-expression in (4.4) directly results in the decision rule (4.17).

References

Baker, K.R. (1993): Requirements Planning. In: Logistics of Production and Inventory, Vol. 4 of Handbooks in Operations Research and Management Science (eds. S.C. Graves et al.): 571-627, Elsevier, New York.

Donselaar, K.H. van (1989): Material Coordination under Uncertainty. Ph.D Thesis, Eindhoven, The Netherlands.

Flapper, S.D.P. (1994): Matching Material Requirements and Availabilities in the Context of Recycling: An MRP-I Based Heuristic. In: Pre-Prints Eight International Working Seminar on Production Economics (eds. Grubbström, R.W. et al.): 511-519, Igls, Austria.

Fleischmann, M. and J.M. Bloemhof-Ruwaard, R. Dekker, E.A. van der Laan, Jo A.E.E. van Nunen, L.N. Van Wassenhove (1997): Quantitative Models for Reverse Logistics: A Review. European Journal of Operational Research, 103:1-17.

Guide Jr., V.D.R. and Srivastava, R. (1997): Buffering from Material Recovery Uncertainty in a Recoverable Manufacturing Environment. Journal of the Operational Research Society, 48: 519-529.

Henig, M. and Y. Gerchak (1990): The Structure of Periodic Review Policies in the Presence of Random Yield. Operations Research, 38: 634-643.

Inderfurth, K. (1997): Simple Optimal Replenishment and Disposal Policies for a Product Recovery System with Leadtimes. OR Spektrum, 19: 111-122.

van der Laan, E.A. (1997): The Effects of Remanufacturing Inventory Control. Ph.D Thesis, Ph.D-Series in General Management 28, Erasmus University Rotterdam, The Netherlands.

van der Laan, E.A. and M. Salomon, R. Dekker (1996): Product Remanufacturing and Disposal: A Numerical Comparison of Alternative Strategies. International Journal of Production Economics, 45:489-498.

van der Laan, E.A. and R. Dekker, M. Salomon, A. Ridder (1996a): An (s,Q) Inventory Model with Remanufacturing and Disposal. International Journal of Production Economics, 46-47:339-350.

van der Laan, E.A. and M. Salomon (1997): Production Planning and Inventory Control with Remanufacturing and Disposal. European Journal of Operational Research, 102: 264-278.

Lee, H.L. and St. Nahmias (1993): Requirements Planning. In: Logistics of Production and Inventory, Vol. 4 of Handbooks in Operations Research and Management Science (eds. S.C. Graves et al.): 3-55, North Holland, Amsterdam, The Netherlands.

Salomon, M. and E.A. van der Laan, R. Dekker, M. Thierry, A. Ridder (1994): Product Remanufacturing and its Effects on Production and Inventory Control. ERASM Management Report Series 172, Erasmus University Rotterdam, The Netherlands.

Segerstedt, A. (1996): Formulas of MRP. International Journal of Production Economics, 46-47: 127-136.

Tersine, R.J., (1994): Principles of Inventory and Materials Management. 4th ed., Prentice-Hall, New York.

Thierry, M.C. and M. Salomon, J. van Nunen, L. van Wassenhove (1995): Strategic Issues in Product Recovery Management. California Management Review, 37 (2): 114-135.

Vollmann, T.E. and W.L. Berry, D.C. Whybark (1992) Manufacturing Planning and Control Systems. 3rd ed., Irwin, Homewood, Illinois.

Yano, C.A. and Lee, H.L. (1995): Lot Sizing with Random Yields: A Review. Operations Research, 43: 311-334.

Bidding for Research Funds

Martin J. Beckmann

Technische Universität München

1 Introduction

Pure basic research produces nothing of value, that is of money value. Rather its product is a pure public good, not marketable, but freely available to any interested party. That at any rate is demanded by the "ethos of science".

The economic implication is that researchers, unable to sell a marketable product, must seek financing elsewhere: from private sponsors, foundations, universities or, as a last resort (but in practice often the first resort) government agencies. What matters, however, is not the nature of the donor but the institutional arrangements that define the donor's influence over the topics and methods of the research thus financed. It varies between the two extremes of no influence whatever, i.e., complete freedom for the researcher and the fixing of the research objective as a research project, the common practice in applied research or development.

Historically, it was the learned societies and academies that sought to influence the direction of research by announcing prizes for the solution or best answer to a specific problem (the "brachistochrone" or whether cultural development has improved mankind's happiness). Contemporary sponsors such as the NSF of the US will announce support to research in less specific but still well-defined areas, leaving the precise topic to be chosen by the applicant. In addition, there are sometimes government funds ear-marked for topics of national concern.

The award decision by the sponsoring agency will depend on any of the following: competence in the research area as demonstrated by previously published research, importance and technical feasibility of the proposed program and availability of resources and facilities at the research institution (NSF 1998). It is conceivable but hardly ever admitted, that research grants are allocated according to ethnic or geographic quotas or even in a purely random fashion.

It is universal practice nowadays that a researcher seeking financial support must submit an application describing his/her plans, expectations, background and the relevance and importance of the proposed work. In doing so, he/she must decide how much effort to put into the application. Risk of failure and hence wasted effort is borne by the researcher.

It is an often heard complaint that too much time is wasted, i.e., taken away from actual research in making grant applications, on onerous job often shifted to junior scientists in a university department, while the "principal investigator" sometimes contributes little more than his/her prestigious name to the enterprise.

This risk is even larger when competing for a prize that will be awarded for completed research. In this chapter we consider the first alternative, i.e., how much effort to put into an application for a research grant. For concreteness we will assume that the number of competitors is known and begin with the case of only two applicants. The scenario is then that of a two-person noncooperative nonzero sum game.

2 The Pure Strategic Game

Following Gottinger (1996) we distinguish the cases of a cursory from that of a thorough reading of the application by the funding agency or its referees. When read cursorily the chance of success depends on the funding agent finding something of appeal and interest in the proposal and this should be considered proportional to the length (quality) of the proposal which in turn would be proportional to the applicant's effort.

If x and y denote the two player's efforts, then player 1's chance of success $= \frac{x}{x+y}$ and his expected payoff is

$$\frac{x}{x+y} F - x$$

where F is the research fund competed for. We assume this to be the same for both applicants. This game, which is structurally equivalent to some advertising scenarios (Funke 1976) has a pure strategy solution.

$$\max_x \frac{x}{x+y} F - x \tag{1}$$

yielding

$$\frac{y}{(x+y)^2} F - 1 = 0 \tag{2}$$

and for player two

$$\frac{x}{(x+y)^2} F = 1 = 0 \tag{3}$$

$$x = y = \frac{(2x)^2}{F}$$

so that

$$x = \frac{F}{4}. \tag{4}$$

Thus each competitor puts in an effort worth one-fourth the prize, and the total equals half the intended reserch fund. Since each competitor has an equal chance in this game, choosing the winner at random would have produced the same result at no cost. Substituting the optimal strategies $x = y = \frac{F}{y}$ into the payoff function yields a value of $\frac{F}{4}$. Thus the opportunity of bidding for research funcs F opening a one-half chance of winning F by spending $\frac{F}{4}$ on a proposal is worth only one-fourth of the grant offered.

What if proficiencies differ in the sense that a proposal of given length x requires an effort ax, $a < 1$, while the rival's proposal y still needs an input y. Now

$$max_x \frac{x}{x+y} F - ax \tag{1a}$$

yields

$$\frac{y}{(x+y)^2} F = a$$

$$max_y \frac{y}{x+y} F - y$$

$$\frac{x}{(x+y)^2} F = 1 \tag{3}$$

so that

$$\frac{x}{y} = \frac{1}{a} > 1 \qquad \frac{x}{x+y} = \frac{1}{1+a} > \frac{1}{2} \tag{5}$$

$$\frac{x}{[(1+a)x]^2} F = 1$$

$$x = \frac{F}{(1+a)^2}$$

$$ax + y = \frac{F}{(1+a)} > \frac{F}{2} \tag{6}$$

While the chance of success is improved for the more proficient bidder, the total effort going into application is raised.

Suppose now that scientific reputation enters into the award process, perhaps by adding the length of the bibliography of the applicant (possibly with some weighting factor) to the length of the proposal in determining the chance of a favorable impression on the funding agent in the cursory review. Let a

and b denote this quantification of an applicant's scientific reputation so that the chance of success for player one is now

$$\frac{a+x}{a+x+b+y} \tag{7}$$

Player 1's optimal strategy is then to

$$max_x \frac{a+x}{a+b+x+s} F - x \tag{1b}$$

yielding

$$\frac{b+y}{(a+b+x+y)^2} F = 1 \tag{2b}$$

and for player 2

$$\frac{a+x}{(a+b+x+y)^2} F = 1 \tag{3b}$$

$$\frac{y+b}{(a+b+x+y)^2} = \frac{1}{F} = \frac{x+a}{(a+b+x+y)^2}$$

Effort plus reputation and hence probabilities are thus equalized through extra effort and hence are $\frac{1}{2}$. From

$$\frac{x+a}{4(x+a)^2} = \frac{1}{F} = \frac{y+b}{4(y+b)^2}$$

it follows that

$$x+a = y+b = \frac{F}{4} \tag{5b}$$

$$x+y = \frac{F}{2} - (a+b). \tag{8}$$

Total effort decreases with the role of prestige.

Finally, suppose that the funds of F_1, F_2 sought by the two competitors are unequal. Player 1 now aims to

$$max_x \frac{x}{x+y} F_1 - x \tag{1c}$$

yielding

$$\frac{y}{(x+y)^2} = \frac{1}{F_1} \tag{2c}$$

while player 2 seeking

$$max_y \frac{y}{x+y} F_2 - y$$

achieves

$$\frac{x}{(x+y)^2} = \frac{1}{F_2} \tag{3c}$$

From this

$$\frac{x}{y} = \frac{F_1}{F_2} \tag{9}$$

Efforts are proportional to the amounts sought. When $F_1 > F_2$ the first player's chance of success

$$\frac{x}{x+y} = \frac{\frac{F_1}{F_2}y}{(\frac{F_1}{F_2}+1)y} = \frac{F_1}{F_1+F_2} > \frac{1}{2} > \frac{F_2}{F_1+F_2} \tag{10}$$

Asking for more and choosing one's effort accordingly will thus raise an applicant's prospects. Modesty never pays in science.

3 A Game in Mixed Strategies

Suppose now that the sponsor or referees scrutinize the proposals thoroughly, and award the grant to the applicant with the better proposal, i.e., the one prepared with greater effort. The payoff function for player one is then

$$F\phi(x) - x \tag{11}$$

where

$$\phi(x) = Pr(y < x) \tag{12}$$

describes the mixed strategy of player two.

From now on let $F = 1$ without loss of generality. Let player one's mixed strategy be described by

$$\Psi(y) = Pr(x < y). \tag{13}$$

For each active x, i.e., x chosen with positive probability, the expected payoff must then be the same, equal to the value v_1 of the game for player one

$$\phi(x) - x = v_1. \tag{14}$$

For player two similarly

$$\psi(y) - y = v_2.$$

The symmetry of the game implies

$$v_1 = v_2 = v \qquad \text{(say)}.$$

When x is active throughout the interval

$$0 \leq x \leq 1$$

then

$$\phi(x) - x = \phi(0) - 0 = \phi(1) - 1 = 0 \tag{15}$$

so that the value of the game is zero. The optimal mixed strategies are identical

$$\phi(x) = x \qquad \psi(y) = y. \tag{16}$$

The average effort is now

$$\int_0^1 x d\phi(x) = \int_0^1 [1 - \phi(x)]dx = \int_0^1 (1 - x)dx = \frac{1}{2}. \tag{17}$$

Thus on the average an effort equal to half the grant is expended for a one-half chance of getting the grant causing the value of the game to be zero.

While researchers cannot expect any monetary surplus from entering such a competition, winning the grant will earn them prestige both directly and as a result of performing the intended research.

When $n-1$ competitors using the same mixed strategy $\phi(x)$ are bidding against player one, the expected payoff to any active strategy x is

$$\phi(x)^{n-1} - x = v. \tag{18}$$

Once more when all x in $0 \leq x \leq 1$ are active this implies

$$v = \phi(x)^{n-1} - x = \psi^{n-1}(0) - 0 = \phi^{n-1}(1) - 1 = 0 \tag{15a}$$

and

$$\phi(x) = x^{\frac{1}{n-1}} < x \quad \text{in} \quad 0 < x < 1 \tag{19}$$

showing that less effort is expended the greater n. The average effort is now

$$\begin{aligned} \int_0^1 x \quad \cdot \tfrac{d}{dx}(x^{\frac{1}{n-1}})dx &= \tfrac{1}{n-1} \int_0^1 x^{\frac{1}{n-1}} dx \\ &= \tfrac{1}{n-1} \, \tfrac{1}{\frac{1}{n-1}+1} = \tfrac{1}{n} \end{aligned} \tag{20}$$

Since each competitor puts in an average effort of $\frac{1}{n}$, the total is always equal to the value of the grant.

When player one is more proficient so that a proposal of length (and quality) x is achieved with effort ax, $a < 1$, then in the two-person each game active strategy x has a payoff

$$\phi(x) - ax = v_1$$

to player one equal to the value of the game. But player one can secure the grant with certainty by bidding

$$x = 1 + \epsilon.$$

and achieving

$$1 - a - \epsilon \tag{21}$$

If player two realizing this were to put in zero effort, player one could get the grant even cheaper by putting in any small but positive effort $\epsilon > 0$.

The correct strategy $Pr(y < x) = \phi(x)$ for player two, inferred from

$$\phi(x) - ax = v_1 = 1 - a, \tag{21a}$$

is

$$\phi(x) = 1 - a + ax \qquad 0 \leq x \leq 1$$

in which zero effort by player two has a discrete probability of $1 - a$. The value $v_1 = 1 - a$ is realized by player one by means of his mixed strategy as before

$$pr(x < y) = \psi(y) = y \quad 0 \leq y \leq 1,$$

while for player 2 the value is zero.

$$v_2 = \psi(x) - x = \psi(1) - 1 = 0$$

Both bidders are then active in the whole range $0 \leq x, y \leq 1$ and player two puts in zero effort with the discrete probability

$$\phi(0) = 1 - a. \tag{22}$$

When three bidders of unequal proficiency $a_1 < a_2 < 1$ compete, it can be shown that

$$v_1 = 1 - a_1 \quad v_2 = 1 - a_2 < v_1 \quad v_3 = 0.$$

Now let grants sought be different $F_1 > F_2$. Then the pure strategy $x_1 = F_2 + \epsilon$ secures the prize and the value of the game to player would be

$$v_1 = F_1 - F_2 - \epsilon.$$

The larger value $F_1 - F_2$ is realized by mixed strategies $\phi_2(x) = pr(y < x)$ and $\phi_1(y) = pr(x < y)$ in the range $0 \leq x, y \leq F_2$ yielding

$$F_1\phi_2(x) - x = v_1 = F_1\phi(F_2) - F_2 = F_1 - F_2$$

for player one and for player two

$$v_2 = F_2\phi_1(y) - y = F_2\phi_1(F_2) - F_2 = 0. \tag{23}$$

It is thus not economical for player one to enter the range $F_2 \leq x \leq F_1$. Once more aiming high is advantageous, achieving even a positive value of the game for the player seeking the larger grant.

To curb the demonstrated waste of effort and improve incentives by making bidding a game of positive value, let now the sponsor prescribe a limit m on the length of, and hence on the effort invested, in proposals.

$$0 \leq x, y \leq m.$$

Once more let the two applicants be equally qualified. For all active strategies x, y then

$$\begin{aligned} v_1 &= \phi(x) - x \\ v_2 &= \psi(y) - y \end{aligned} \tag{24}$$

The symmetry of the game implies

$$v_1 = v_2 = v \tag{25}$$

and so

$$\begin{aligned} \phi(x) &= v + x \\ \psi(y) &= v + y \end{aligned} \tag{24a}$$

The value v of the game is easily calculated: expected prize minus expected effort

$$v = \frac{1}{2} - \overline{x} \tag{26}$$

where the expected or average effort $\overline{x}$ is given by

$$\overline{x} = \int_0^m x dx + mpr(m) \tag{27}$$

Now

$$pr(m) = 1 - \phi(m) = 1 - m - v \tag{28}$$

using (24a).

Substituting (27) and (28) in (26)

$$\begin{aligned} v &= \tfrac{1}{2} - \tfrac{m^2}{2} - m[1 - m - v] \\ v &= \tfrac{1}{2} \cdot \tfrac{1}{1-m} \cdot (1 - m)^2 \\ &= \tfrac{1}{2}(1 - m). \end{aligned} \tag{29}$$

Assuming $x = 0$ to be active (24a) implies

$$pr(0) = \phi(0+) = v = \frac{1 - m}{2}$$

From (28)

$$pr(m) = 1 - \phi(m) = 1 - m - v = \frac{1-m}{2}$$

so that

$$pr(0) = pr(m)$$

and therefore

$$\overline{x} = \frac{m}{2} \tag{30}$$

as seen also from (29).

Imposing a "limit on the length" (and by implication quality) of applications is thus an effective way to reduce effort and enhance the value of the bidding game.

For $n > 2$ the value v of the game is the root (other than unity) of the algebraic equation

$$m + v = \frac{1}{n} + \frac{n-1}{m} \cdot (m+v)^{\frac{n}{n-1}} \tag{31}$$

It can be shown that v is positive and decreasing in n. The probability density of x decreases with x and as before $pr(0) > 0 \quad pr(m) > 0$.

Although the focus has been on pure basic research, the bidding strategies for research support and strategic considerations created thereby apply with equal force to applied research with expectations of positive profits (in addition to the funds obtained for doing the research).

When the value of the game is zero, in the absence of restrictions and asymmetries, it means that such grants in support of applied research offer no monetary incentive that might improve on the profit expectations of the researcher.

The game of seeking research funds, which should be just a preliminary to doing research, takes on a new face when getting grants is valued as an end in itself. Deplorably there is a recent tendency to attach prestige and measure a scholar's worth by his/her talent for obtaining money.

Just because modesty does not pay, we should give due recognition to those who succeed in research even without entering the game of getting money for research.

References

Gottinger, Hans W. (1996), "Competitive Bidding for Research," *Kyklos,* Vol. 49, Fasc. 3, 439-447.

Dixit, A. (1987), "Strategic Behaviour in Contests," *American Economic Review,* 77, 891-898.

National Science Foundation (1998), Grant Proposal Guide, Washington, DC, NSF 99-2.

Suzumura, K. (1995), *Competition, Commitment and Welfare,* Oxford: Clarendon Press.

Separate versus Joint Inventories when Customer Demands are Stochastic

Günter Fandel and Michael Lorth

FB Wirtschaftswissenschaft
FernUniversität Hagen

A. Introduction

Major effort within the operations research literature has been spent on the developments in the field of inventory theory and management. Whereas one strand focuses on modeling the inventory process and searching for optimal (in the sense of cost-minimizing) policies the other line of research concentrates on primarily practical issues such as demand and costs measurement, system design, relations among logistics and other industrial management functions, system management, and so on (Hax/Candea 1983, p. 128-129, recent reviews: Lee/Nahmias 1993; Federgruen 1993; Axsäter 1993; Bramel/Simchi-Levi 1997; Silver/Pyke/Peterson 1998).

This paper deals with a real world phenomenon that belongs predominantly to the second category. In some markets or industries one can observe that companies that purchase raw materials, intermediate or even finished products from outside suppliers do not stockpile inventories on their own but use a special service company for this purpose. For instance, in the German industrial Ruhr area many steel-using manufacturing firms, automakers or automotive suppliers purchase their different kinds of strip or sheet steel from a so-called "Stahlkontor" - a steel stockkeeper or wholesale firm that itself gets its supplies from the steel-producing companies. Besides, German pharmacies do not store just occasionally needed or irregular quantities of medicine but order those demands from a regional medicine wholesaler who is obliged to deliver the order on the same day. Moreover, a similar procedure can be found in the bookstore industry - but without the delivery time obligation.

All these examples have in common that the supplier does not deliver the products directly to the customers but to a wholesaler or a warehouse company that itself delivers the products to the different customers when an order is placed. The question that has to be answered in this paper is: why do those companies exist? In other words, is it economically advantageous to let the wholesaler or stockkeeper

build up a joint inventory for an item demanded by several customers instead of letting the customers store their orders in their own inventories?
Obviously, the answer cannot always be the same since, for example, in some cases there might be technological or geographical restrictions that make pooling the stockkeeping impossible or prohibitively expensive whereas in other cases no such restrictions exist. But even in the absence of technological or geographical restrictions, it might be questionable whether pooling individual demands and stocks induces positive cost advantages over separate stockkeeping.
To investigate this problem, we present a simple inventory model in which we take the standard way of determining the optimal policy for a one-item inventory in order to describe the different alternatives of stockkeeping in the case of two (or more) customers who face stochastic demand for the same item. Furthermore, we will give a criterion to decide when it is advantageous to hand over the inventory responsibility to a wholesaler or a warehouse keeper and in which cases the (customers') inventories should be separated. To explain by example the cost effects induced by going over from separate stockkeeping by the customers to joint stockkeeping by the wholesaler, the cost difference between both alternatives is calculated for normally distributed customers' demands and reasonable parameter values. The last section of the paper summarizes the results and brings up a short agenda for future work and desirable extensions of the analysis (see also Silver et al. 1998, p. 499, who provide a comprehensive overview of other research in this area).

B. A Model for Comparing Separate versus Joint Stockkeeping

I. The Basic Model

Suppose there are two customers A and B with stochastic demand[1] for the same single item which they purchase from the same supplier and which they store each in their own single-item inventory. The units of the item are assumed to be demanded one at a time or in small quantities, so that there are no great discrete stock reductions and differential calculus can be applied. The average individual demands in units during the planning horizon T are represented by the variables $\overline{X}_T^A$ and $\overline{X}_T^B$ respectively and stay approximately constant over time. Going along with standard stochastic inventory modeling (see, for instance, Tersine 1988, chapter 5; Hax/Candea 1983, chapter 4; Johnson/Montgomery 1974, chapter 2), we assume that it is possible to state the probability distributions of the individual demands. In addition, the individual demands in the respective periods are assumed stationary over time (i.e. the distribution parameters are time invariant)

---

[1] Stochastic demand means that the demand in any given interval of time is a random variable.

and independent from demand levels of previous periods, so that demand distributions in varying-length time periods can easily be obtained by the use of probability distribution convolutions.
Furthermore, suppose that both customers can alternatively get their supplies continuously from a warehouse keeper's inventory which, again, is built-up by discrete orders delivered by the single supplier. Then the warehouse keeper faces an average total demand of $\overline{X}_T^{A+B} = \overline{X}_T^A + \overline{X}_T^B$ in the planning horizon T.

Figure 1. Stochastic fixed order quantity inventory model

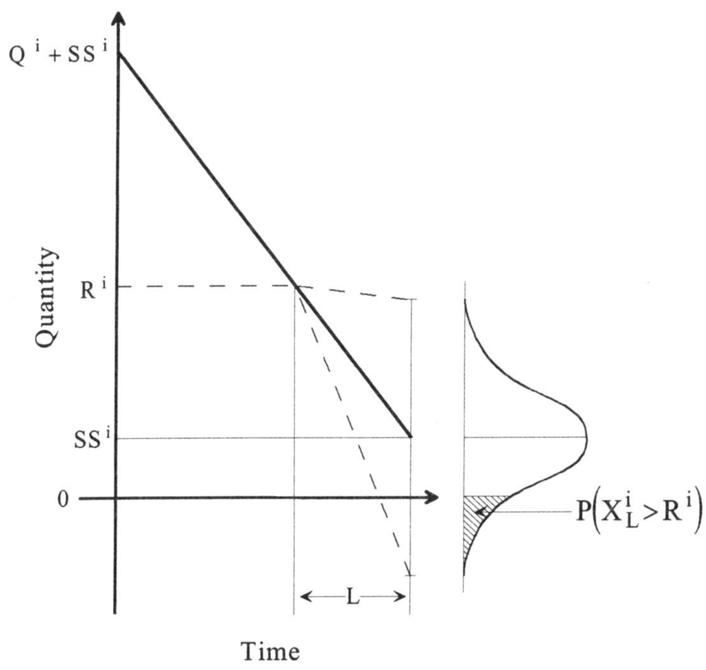

For simplicity, it is presumed that in the first case the customers, and in the second case the warehouse keeper respectively, follow a fixed order size inventory policy in which a fixed order quantity Q^i, $i = A, B$ or $i = A + B$, is ordered from the supplier every time when the reorder point R^i is reached.[2] In order to avoid a stockout because of a higher than expected demand until an order arrives after the

---

2 In real life, fixed order quantities are typically used whenever variable transport volumes or package sizes are unsuitable or prohibitively expensive.

(identical) constant[3] replenishment lead time L, the customers, and the warehouse keeper respectively, hold safety stocks SS^i in addition to working stocks (see Figure 1).

Nevertheless, it is possible that an actual lead time demand X_L^i, $i = A, B, A+B$, even exceeds the stock available for the replenishment period (reorder point R^i), i.e. that it exceeds the mean lead time demand μ_L^i plus the safety stock SS^i. Then a stockout (shortage) occurs, and this happens with probability $P\left(X_L^i > R^i\right)$ (see Figure 1). We assume that a stockout results in a backorder, i.e. that the customers' demands are satisfied upon initial receipt of either an expediting order or the next order of items to arrive (Tersine 1988, p. 187).[4] $E\left(X_L^i - R^i\right)^+$ denotes the expected stockout quantity during the lead time L.

II. The Optimal Inventory Allocation

In order to compare the situation of both customers holding their own inventory (first possible allocation of inventories) with a situation of a wholesaler or warehouse keeper building up a joint inventory for both individual demands (second possible allocation), the minimal expected relevant cost (i.e. order cost, holding cost, and stockout cost) TC^i, $i = A, B, A+B$, resulting from optimal inventory policy decisions in these two cases have to be determined. If the overall minimal expected cost of separate stockkeeping by the customers exceed the minimal expected cost of joint stockkeeping by the warehouse keeper, then a positive cost advantage

$$CA\left(TC^A, TC^B, TC^{A+B}\right) = TC^A + TC^B - TC^{A+B} \tag{1}$$

of joint over separate stockkeeping is generated, and, therefore, it is economically advantageous to let the warehouse keeper store the item. If the cost difference CA is negative, the customers should hold their own inventories.

The minimal expected relevant cost depend on the optimal inventory policy. Since the parameters R^i and Q^i completely define a fixed order size inventory system,

---

3 The assumption of a constant replenishment lead time is justified when the variation in lead time is small in relation to the average lead time, or if a definite lead time is assured by contract (Tersine 1988, p. 194).

4 For the case of a lost sale, see Tersine (1988), chapter 5, especially pp. 187, 203-206.

it is useful to calculate the optimal parameter values in the cost optimum. Applying these parameter values gives us the minimal expected relevant cost in the optimum.

The expected relevant cost TC^i consist of the order cost, the holding cost for the working stocks, the holding cost for the safety stocks, and the expected stockout cost. Suppose that there is no more than one outstanding order at any given time in the planning horizon T and that there are constant order cost c per order, constant holding cost h per unit of inventory held during the planning horizon T, and constant backordering cost b per unit of the item. Then we have the expected relevant cost in T (Tersine 1988, p. 249; Hax/Candea 1983, pp. 194-206; Johnson/Montgomery 1974, pp. 59-61):

$$(2)\ TC_T^i = \frac{\overline{X}_T^i}{Q^i} \cdot c + \frac{1}{2} \cdot Q^i \cdot h + SS^i \cdot h + \frac{\overline{X}_T^i}{Q^i} \cdot b \cdot E\left(X_L^i - R^i\right)^+,$$

$i = A, B, A + B$.

Substituting $SS^i = R^i - \mu_L^i$, taking the partial derivatives of the expected relevant cost in T with respect to the order quantity Q^i and the reorder point R^i, setting them equal to zero and reorganizing the equations yields the expressions for the cost-minimizing Q^{i*} and R^{i*} (Johnson/Montgomery (1974), pp. 59-66; Hax/Candea (1983), pp. 206-207):

(3) $$Q^{i*} = \sqrt{\frac{2 \cdot \overline{X}_T^i \cdot \left(c + b \cdot E\left(X_L^i - R^{i*}\right)^+\right)}{h}}$$ (optimum order quantity in units),

(4) $$P\left(X_L^i > R^{i*}\right) = \frac{Q^{i*}}{\overline{X}_T^i} \cdot \frac{h}{b}$$ (optimum probability of a stockout).

Unfortunately, these expressions are interdependent. So closed expressions for Q^{i*} and R^{i*} are not possible. Thus, to obtain the optimal pair $\left(Q^{i*}, R^{i*}\right)$ one has to use the following iterative procedure that converges to the optimum solution (Tersine 1988, p. 252; Johnson/Montgomery 1974, p. 61):

1. Assume $E\left(X_L^i - R^i\right)^+ = 0$.
2. Use equation (3) to compute Q^i.
3. Use the computed Q^i and equation (4) to determine $P\left(X_L^i > R^i\right)$ and R^i.
4. Use the computed R^i to obtain a value for $E\left(X_L^i - R^i\right)^+$.
5. Repeat step 2, 3, and 4 until convergence occurs.

Inserting the optimum values Q^{i*} and R^{i*} into equation (2) yields the minimal expected relevant cost $TC^{i}\left(c, h, b, P(.), E(.)^{+}, Q^{i*}, R^{i*}\right)$ which can be used to obtain the cost advantage CA and to find the optimal inventory allocation.

C. Calculation and Analysis of Cost Advantages

I. A Heuristic for the Calculation of Cost Advantages

So far, we are not able to describe general circumstances that favor joint against separate inventories since the above iterative procedure does not allow analytical considerations. Therefore, we have to make further assumptions and use simplifications to reduce the complexity and to avoid the interdependency respectively.

In a first step, it is supposed that the stockout cost per order cycle $b \cdot E\left(X_L^i - R^i\right)^{+}$ are considerably smaller than the order cost per cycle. Then one can approximate the optimum order quantity by the well-known EOQ formula

(5) $$\tilde{Q}^i = \sqrt{\frac{2 \cdot \overline{X}_T^i \cdot c}{h}},$$

and thus eliminate the interdependency between the order quantity and the reorder point. Inserting formula (5) into equation (2) yields the minimal expected relevant cost:

(6) $$TC_T^i = \sqrt{2 \cdot c \cdot h \cdot \overline{X}_T^i} + \left(R^i - \mu_L^i\right) \cdot h + \sqrt{\frac{\overline{X}_T^i \cdot h}{2 \cdot c}} \cdot b \cdot E\left(X_L^i - R^i\right)^{+},$$

with $i = A, B, A+B$ and R^i given by

(7) $$P\left(X_L^i > R^i\right) = \frac{1}{b} \cdot \sqrt{\frac{2 \cdot h \cdot c}{\overline{X}_T^i}}.$$

The first term in equation (6) gives the total working stock cost (order cost plus holding cost of the order quantity $\tilde{Q}^i$) in T. Note that these cost are equivalent to the optimum total cost in the deterministic economic order quantity model. The second term describes the holding cost for the safety stock, and the final expression gives the expected stockout cost incurred in T. We are now able to obtain the cost advantage CA of holding pooled stocks over separate stockkeeping:

$$CA = \sqrt{2 \cdot c \cdot h} \cdot \left(\sqrt{\overline{X}_T^A} + \sqrt{\overline{X}_T^B} - \sqrt{\overline{X}_T^A + \overline{X}_T^B} \right)$$

$$+ h \cdot \left(R^A + R^B - R^{A+B} \right)$$

(8)
$$+ b \cdot \sqrt{\frac{h}{2 \cdot c}} \cdot \left[\sqrt{\overline{X}_T^A} \cdot E\left(X_L^A - R^A\right)^+ + \sqrt{\overline{X}_T^B} \cdot E\left(X_L^B - R^B\right)^+ \right.$$

$$\left. - \sqrt{\overline{X}_T^A + \overline{X}_T^B} \cdot E\left(X_L^A + X_L^B - R^{A+B}\right)^+ \right].$$

The cost advantage term shows the three cost effects of allocating the inventory responsibility to the warehouse keeper or wholesaler. The first effect results from adapting the working stock to the total average demand to be satisfied during the planning horizon T from only one joint inventory. Suiting the safety stock level to the stochastic total lead time demand fluctuations gives the second cost effect. The third expression represents the stockout cost effect resulting from both adjusting the order frequency and the reorder point as well as convoluting the individual demand probability distributions when summing up the individual demand random variables. Obviously, the first term in equation (8) is non-negative because of the concavity of the square-root function. That means that the working stock cost always do not increase by pooling the average individual demands. Anyhow, the other effects are ambiguous, depending on the actual individual demand distributions and cost parameters. It is, therefore, necessary to analyze these cost effects by investigating the probability distribution impact.

II. The Probability Distribution Impact on Cost Advantages

Suppose that the customers' individual demands in T are distributed with mean μ_T^i, $\mu_T^i = \overline{X}_T^i$, and variance $\left(\sigma_T^i\right)^2$, $i = A, B$. Since the time period concerned is the replenishment lead time, it is necessary to convolute the demand distributions based on the planning horizon to the lead time period. Because of the assumptions made in section B of this paper, we get (Feller 1968, pp. 222, 230):

(9)
$$\mu_L^i = \frac{L}{T} \cdot \mu_T^i,$$

(10)
$$\left(\sigma_L^i\right)^2 = \frac{L}{T} \cdot \left(\sigma_T^i\right)^2 \text{ or } \sigma_L^i = \sqrt{\frac{L}{T}} \cdot \sigma_T^i,$$

with $i = A, B$. Furthermore, we have to calculate the mean and the variance of the joint (lead time) demand distribution in case that the warehouse keeper has got the inventory responsibility. Let the customers' individual demands be correlated with the correlation coefficient ρ^{AB}, $\rho^{AB} \in [-1;1]$.[5] Then the convoluted lead time demand distribution's mean and variance are given by (Feller 1968, pp. 222, 230):

(11) $$\mu_L^{A+B} = \mu_L^A + \mu_L^B,$$

(12) $$\left(\sigma_L^{A+B}\right)^2 = \left(\sigma_L^A\right)^2 + \left(\sigma_L^B\right)^2 + 2\cdot\rho^{AB}\cdot\sigma_L^A\cdot\sigma_L^B$$
$$\Rightarrow \quad \sigma_L^{A+B} = \sqrt{\left(\sigma_L^A\right)^2 + \left(\sigma_L^B\right)^2 + 2\cdot\rho^{AB}\cdot\sigma_L^A\cdot\sigma_L^B}.$$

Because $\rho^{AB} \in [-1;1]$, we have:

(13) $$\sigma_L^{A+B} \le \sigma_L^A + \sigma_L^B,$$

that means that the standard deviation σ_L^{A+B} of the convoluted demand distribution does not exceed the sum of the individual demands' standard deviations. For $\rho^{AB} < 1$, the standard deviation of the (joint) total demand falls even below the sum of the standard deviations of the individual demands. This effect, which is considered as diversification, is illustrated for $\sigma_L^A \le \sigma_L^B$ in Figure 2:

[5] Suppose that the customers' demands for the item in question (raw materials, intermediate or finished products) are deduced directly from the quantity of final products going to be sold by the customers on the market(s) for final products. Then a positive correlation between individual customer demands for the item typically occurs, ceteris paribus, when the customers' final products are complements, whereas a negative correlation usually results from the customers' final products being substitutes. (Note that this need not to be true if the market size is changing.)

Figure 2. Diversification of stochastic individual demand fluctuations for $\sigma_L^A \leq \sigma_L^B$.

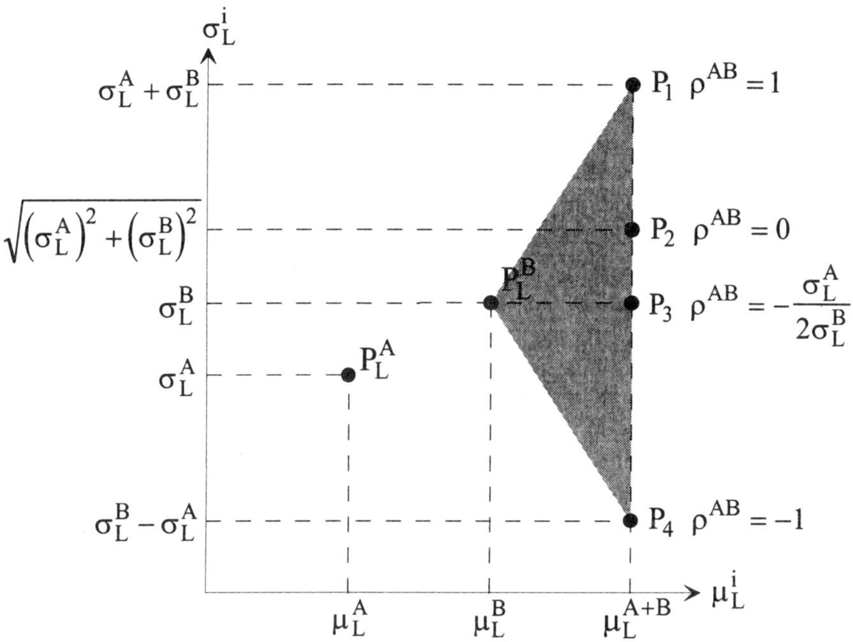

With decreasing correlation coefficients ρ^{AB}, the standard deviation σ_L^{A+B} of the total demand distribution decreases (which is shown by P_1 to P_4 in Figure 2). Considering this diversification effect, one would expect that the total cost of joint stockkeeping also decrease, so that a positive cost effect of pooling stocks is generated. Indeed, this expectation is well-founded since a wholesaler or warehouse keeper can always imitate the customers' ordering decisions which incurs the same total working stock cost as with separate inventories. But since in most cases (i.e. if $\rho^{AB} < 1$) the total lead time demand scatters less around its mean than both individual lead time demands together do, the warehouse keeper is able to save either holding cost for the safety stock or stockout cost. By optimizing the inventory policy the warehouse keeper can even improve upon his cost situation, so that, in summary, the total expected relevant cost cannot increase by pooling the individual demands and storing the item in only one joint inventory.[6]

6 This argument is similar to Williamson's idea of "Selective Intervention" which implies that one cannot get worse-off by merging two firms since "the resulting combined firm can [...] do everything that the two autonomous firms could do previously *and more*" (Williamson 1985, p. 133).

III. Calculating Cost Advantages for Normally Distributed Individual Demands

Let the customers' individual demands be normally distributed with mean μ_T^i and variance $\left(\sigma_T^i\right)^2$, $i = A, B$, and let the individual demands have a joint density being normal.[7] Then the total lead time demand in case that the warehouse keeper stores the item is normally distributed with mean μ_L^{A+B}, $\mu_L^{A+B} = \mu_L^A + \mu_L^B$, and variance $\left(\sigma_L^{A+B}\right)^2 = \left(\sigma_L^A\right)^2 + \left(\sigma_L^B\right)^2 + 2 \cdot \rho^{AB} \cdot \sigma_L^A \cdot \sigma_L^B$ (see section C.II and Feller 1971, p. 87). Using the cumulative (Gaussian) distribution function

$$F\left(X_L^i\right) = \int_{-\infty}^{X_L^i} f\left(\xi_i\right) d\xi_i = \Phi\left(\frac{X_L^i - \mu_L^i}{\sigma_L^i}\right), \tag{15}$$

with

$$f\left(X_L^i\right) = \frac{1}{\sqrt{2\pi}\sigma_L^i} e^{-\frac{1}{2}\cdot\left(\frac{X_L^i - \mu_L^i}{\sigma_L^i}\right)^2}, \tag{14}$$

we obtain the stockout probability

$$\begin{aligned} P\left(X_L^i > R^i\right) &= P^i\left(\frac{X_L^i - \mu_L^i}{\sigma_L^i} > \frac{R^i - \mu_L^i}{\sigma_L^i}\right) \\ &= 1 - \Phi\left(\frac{R^i - \mu_L^i}{\sigma_L^i}\right). \end{aligned} \tag{16}$$

Substituting $P\left(X_L^i > R^i\right)$ by inserting the optimum condition (7) into equation (16) and reorganizing gives the optimal reorder point

$$R^i = \mu_L^i + \sigma_L^i \cdot \Phi^{-1}\left(1 - \frac{1}{b} \cdot \sqrt{\frac{2 \cdot c \cdot h}{\overline{X}_T^i}}\right). \tag{17}$$

For convenience, we set

---

[7] The assumption of normally distributed demand requires the probability of negative demand being negligible. Hence, this assumption is justified when the coefficient of variation σ_T^i / μ_T^i is considerably small.

$$(18)\qquad 1-\frac{1}{b}\cdot\sqrt{\frac{2\cdot c\cdot h}{\overline{X}_T^i}}=s^i.^{8}$$

The expected stockout quantity during the lead time is defined as (Tersine 1988, p. 196; Hax/Candea 1983, p. 197):

$$(19)\qquad E\left(X_L^i-R^i\right)^+=\int_{R^i}^{\infty}\left(X_L^i-R^i\right)f\left(X_L^i\right)dX_L^i .$$

Using (17) and (18) and solving the integral in (19) yields

$$(20)\quad E\left(X_L^i-R^i\right)^+=\sigma_L^i\cdot\left[\frac{1}{\sqrt{2\cdot\pi}}\cdot e^{-\frac{1}{2}\cdot\left[\Phi^{-1}\left(s^i\right)\right]^2}-\Phi^{-1}\left(s^i\right)\cdot\left(1-s^i\right)\right].$$

Finally, the expected relevant cost can be derived by inserting the expressions (5), (17) and (20) into equation (6) and re-substituting for s^i:

(21)

$$TC^i=\sqrt{2\cdot c\cdot h\cdot\overline{X}_T^i}+h\cdot\sigma_L^i\cdot\Phi^{-1}\left(1-\frac{1}{b}\cdot\sqrt{\frac{2\cdot c\cdot h}{\overline{X}_T^i}}\right)$$
$$+\sqrt{\frac{\overline{X}_T^i\cdot h}{2\cdot c}}\cdot b\cdot\sigma_L^i\cdot\left[\frac{1}{\sqrt{2\cdot\pi}}\cdot e^{-\frac{1}{2}\cdot\left[\Phi^{-1}\left(1-\frac{1}{b}\cdot\sqrt{\frac{2\cdot c\cdot h}{\overline{X}_T^i}}\right)\right]^2}\right.$$
$$\left.-\Phi^{-1}\left(1-\frac{1}{b}\cdot\sqrt{\frac{2\cdot c\cdot h}{\overline{X}_T^i}}\right)\cdot\left(\frac{1}{b}\cdot\sqrt{\frac{2\cdot c\cdot h}{\overline{X}_T^i}}\right)\right]$$

This term, that encompasses the working stock cost, the holding cost for the safety stock, and the expected stockout cost, can be reduced to

(22)

$$TC^i=\sqrt{2\cdot c\cdot h\cdot\overline{X}_T^i}+\frac{1}{2}\cdot\sqrt{\frac{\overline{X}_T^i\cdot h}{c\cdot\pi}}\cdot b\cdot\sigma_L^i\cdot e^{-\frac{1}{2}\cdot\left[\Phi^{-1}\left(1-\frac{1}{b}\cdot\sqrt{\frac{2\cdot c\cdot h}{\overline{X}_T^i}}\right)\right]^2},$$

---

[8] Note that s^i is equivalent to the optimum probability of no stockout $P\left(X_L^i\le R^i\right)$. Thus, s^i can be interpreted as a service level that is endogenously determined.

showing in the second expression the overall "stochastic impact" on the expected relevant cost. Finally, inserting (22) for $i = A, B, A + B$ into equation (1) yields the cost advantage for normally distributed individual lead time demands
(23)

$$CA = \sqrt{2 \cdot c \cdot h} \cdot \left(\sqrt{\overline{X}_T^A} + \sqrt{\overline{X}_T^B} - \sqrt{\overline{X}_T^A + \overline{X}_T^B} \right)$$

$$+ \frac{1}{2} \cdot b \cdot \sqrt{\frac{h}{c \cdot \pi}} \cdot \left[\sqrt{\overline{X}_T^A} \cdot \sigma_L^A \cdot e^{-\frac{1}{2} \cdot \left[\Phi^{-1}\left(1 - \frac{1}{b} \cdot \sqrt{\frac{2 \cdot c \cdot h}{\overline{X}_T^A}} \right) \right]^2} \right.$$

$$+ \sqrt{\overline{X}_T^B} \cdot \sigma_L^B \cdot e^{-\frac{1}{2} \cdot \left[\Phi^{-1}\left(1 - \frac{1}{b} \cdot \sqrt{\frac{2 \cdot c \cdot h}{\overline{X}_T^B}} \right) \right]^2}$$

$$\left. - \sqrt{\overline{X}_T^A + \overline{X}_T^B} \cdot \sigma_L^{A+B} \cdot e^{-\frac{1}{2} \cdot \left[\Phi^{-1}\left(1 - \frac{1}{b} \cdot \sqrt{\frac{2 \cdot c \cdot h}{\overline{X}_T^A + \overline{X}_T^B}} \right) \right]^2} \right].$$

Note that this formula has been derived by using the simplifying assumption that the optimal order size can be approximated by the EOQ formula (5). Therefore, applying this formula presupposes that the stockout cost per order cycle $b \cdot E\left(X_L^i - R^i\right)^+$ are considerably smaller than the order cost per cycle c. In cases this is not true, this formula may not reveal the exact cost advantage of pooling the normally distributed individual demands and of storing the item in a joint inventory.

In section C.II we gave a reasoning for an always non-negative cost advantage. Unfortunately, the mathematical expression (23) describing the cost advantage is cumbersome to use and, therefore, does not allow to proof the above assertion for normally distributed individual demands in general. Furthermore, as stated previously, the derived formula is just an approximation of the actual cost advantage, so that deviations from the exact optimum may induce negative approximated cost advantages for parameter values ρ^{AB} close to 1.

Thus, to give an idea of the magnitude of such cost advantages, we will present a numerical example (see for some of the parameter values Tersine 1988, p. 197). Suppose there are two customers A and B whose annual demands for an item are normally distributed with means $\mu_{year}^A = \mu_{year}^B = 1800$ units and standard deviations $\sigma_{year}^A = \sigma_{year}^B = 900$ units. The lead time is assumed to be a half month, so that the expected lead time demands are given by $\mu_{0.5\ month}^A = \mu_{0.5\ month}^A = 75$ units, whereas calculating the lead time standard deviations $\sigma^{A}_{year} = \sigma^{B}_{year} = 900$ units. The lead time is assumed to be a half month, so that the expected lead time demands are given by $\mu^{A}_{0.5\ month} = \mu^{A}_{0.5\ month} = 75$ units, whereas calculating the lead time standard deviations leads to $\sigma^{A}_{0.5\ month} = \sigma^{B}_{0.5\ month} = 183{,}71$ units. Furthermore, it is assumed that the constant cost for placing an order are $c = \$30$. The constant annual holding cost per unit are $h = 30$ cents, and backordering one unit costs $b = \$1.00$. Now the cost advantage CA can be obtained by inserting the parameter values into formula (23) and choosing an appropriate value for the correlation coefficient ρ^{AB}. Repeating this procedure for different correlation coefficients and drawing the results into a diagram gives the following cost advantage function depending on ρ^{AB} (see Figure 3):

Figure 3. Exemplary cost advantage function depending on the correlation coefficien ρ^{AB}

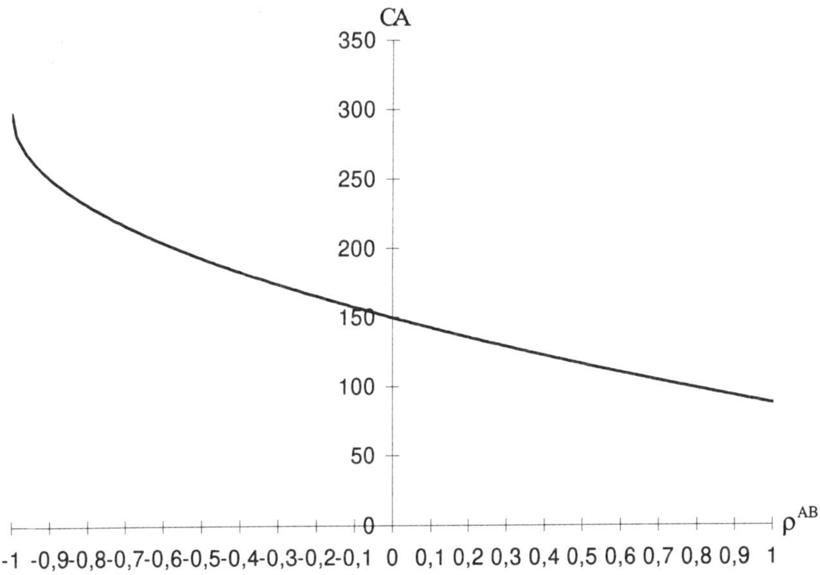

The maximal cost advantage of \$298.89 (resulting from expected total relevant cost of \$553.45 in case of separate stockkeeping minus expected relevant cost of only \$254.56 in case of joint inventories) occurs when $\rho^{AB} = -1$, i.e. when the individual demands are perfectly negatively correlated. In this case, neither safety stocks are held when the warehouse keeper has got the inventory responsibility nor stockout cost are incurred since - due to perfect diversification - the demand fluctuations are completely neutralized.

D. Conclusions

The analysis of a situation with two customers facing stochastic individual demand for the same item has shown that it is usually advantageous to allocate the inventory responsibility to a third party - a wholesaler or a warehouse keeper who is able to reduce the stochastic demand fluctuations and, thereby, the overall expected relevant cost using the diversification effect. This analysis is based on a set of assumptions about the actual cost situations and the prevailing inventory policy, though. In practice, these circumstances need not to be true since it is inappropriate in many cases to leave out, for instance, the transportation cost aspects of pooling inventories.
But even if the presented model is able to describe the actual situation, there are some further aspects unmentioned in the above analysis. For example, it could be useful to learn more about single cost effects and the trade-off between different costs. Furthermore, extensive comparative statics analysis is desirable in order to investigate how both the exact and the heuristic solution for the optimal order quantity and, by that, the calculated cost advantage depend on different parameter values. Thus, a lot of future work has remained to be done to analyze realistic phenomena and inter-firm relationships by means of operations research and applied statistics.

REFERENCES

Axsäter, S. (1993): Continuous Review Policies for Multi-Level Inventory Systems with Stochastic Demand. In: Graves, S. C.; Rinnooy Kan, A. H. G.; Zipkin, P. H. (Eds.): Logistics of Production and Inventory (Handbooks in Operations Research and Management Science: volume 4), North-Holland, Amsterdam, pp. 175-197.

Bramel, J.; Simchi-Levi, D. (1997): The Logic of Logistics: Theory, Algorithms, and Applications for Logistics Management, Springer, New York.

Federgruen, A. (1993): Centralized Planning Models for Multi-Echelon Inventory Systems under Uncertainty. In: Graves, S. C.; Rinnooy Kan, A. H. G.; Zipkin, P. H. (Eds.): Logistics of Production and Inventory (Handbooks in Operations Research and Management Science: volume 4), North-Holland, Amsterdam, pp. 133-173.

Feller, W. (1968): An Introduction to Probability Theory and Its Applications, volume I, third edition, revised printing, John Wiley & Sons, New York.

Feller, W. (1971): An Introduction to Probability Theory and Its Applications, volume II, second edition, John Wiley & Sons, New York.

Hax, A. C.; Candea, D. (1983): Production and Inventory Management, Prentice-Hall, Englewood Cliffs (N.J.).

Lee, H. L.; Nahmias, S. (1993): Single-Product, Single-Location Models. In: Graves, S. C.; Rinnooy Kan, A. H. G.; Zipkin, P. H. (Eds.): Logistics of Production and Inventory (Handbooks in Operations Research and Management Science: volume 4), North-Holland, Amsterdam, pp. 3-55.

Johnson, L. A.; Montgomery, D. C. (1974): Operations Research in Production Planning, Scheduling, and Inventory Control, John Wiley & Sons, New York.

Silver, E. A.; Pyke, D. F.; Peterson, R. (1998): Inventory Management and Production Planning and Scheduling, third edition, John Wiley & Sons, New York.

Tersine, R. J. (1988): Principles of Inventory and Materials Management, third edition, North-Holland, New York.

Williamson, O. E. (1985): The Economic Institutions of Capitalism: Firms, Markets, Relational Contracting, The Free Press, New York.

Optimal Macroeconomic Policies with and without the Monetary Instrument

Reinhard Neck

Department of Economics
University of Klagenfurt

Sohbet Karbuz

IEA/OECD 332
Paris Cedex

Abstract

In this paper, we show by example how techniques of econometrics and operations research can be used to give answers to macroeconomic policy problems. We consider the question of the design of macroeconomic policies, both with and without money supply as an instrument. Using the optimum control algorithm OPTCON, we determine approximately optimal stabilization policies for Austria for the period 1993 to 2000 within the framework of a problem of quantitative economic policy. An intertemporal objective function is minimized subject to the constraints of the macroeconometric model FINPOL2, estimated for Austria using 3SLS. Exogenous variables of the model are forecast by time series methods. The results show that optimal budgetary policies can improve upon the performance of the Austrian economy with respect to some policy objectives as compared to a simulation using extrapolations of policy variables. It is shown that optimal policies depend strongly on the assumptions made about the exogenous variables, which reflect alternative scenarios of global economic developments. In all cases considered, it turns out that the results for the objective variables are very close to each others in scenarios with and without active (optimizing) monetary policy.

1. Introduction

Methods of statistics and operations research have been frequently used to provide answers to questions posed by decision-makers within a firm or at the level of economic policy-making. Recently, they are increasingly being integrated into decision support systems which ideally should be user-friendly tools for practical decision-making. Most of these decision support systems are based on rather simple models of the firm or the economy under consideration and don't use very sophisticated mathematical methods (see, e.g., Buede 1993). In particular, most of these decision support systems do not take into account dynamic relations between economic variables and their consequences for decision-making.

On the other hand, there is by now a large bulk of research, accumulated over the past thirty years, on optimal decision-making over time, starting from dynamic programming and Pontryagin's maximum principle. These optimum control methods have been used in various theoretical studies to determine optimal intertemporal decisions for many problems in economics and operations research (e.g., Feichtinger and Hartl 1986). For actual problems of policy-making at the macroeconomic level, however, an analytical approach has only limited relevance, because these problems are usually characterized by a great number of constraints as embodied in an econometric model of medium or large size. Therefore, simulation analyses and numerical methods of dynamic optimization are the only means to solve problems of actual macroeconomic policy-making.

In this paper, we use an algorithm for determining optimal policies for nonlinear dynamic models to deal with the problem of designing optimal macroeconomic (fiscal and monetary) policies for Austria. We choose an approach of quantitative economic policy to determine numerically optimal budgetary and monetary policies for the nineties by minimizing an intertemporal objective function subject to the constraints given by an econometric model called FINPOL2. The objective function penalizes deviations of objective variables from their desired ("ideal") values. Exogenous variables of the model are forecast over the planning horizon, which is assumed to be 1993 to 2000, using time series methods. Optimal macroeconomic policies are calculated over this time horizon using the optimum control algorithm OPTCON. As the forecasts of the exogenous variables are rather uncertain, we conduct a sensitivity analysis of optimal policies with respect to the assumptions about the developments of these variables. It turns out that the design of optimal budgetary policies depends strongly upon the assumptions about the exogenous variables, in particular exports and import prices. Hence, optimal policies for the small open economy of Austria are to be regarded as contingent upon the assumed future developments of the world economy. Policy recommendations based on optimum control experiments therefore must be treated with great caution. On the other hand, the results are robust with respect to whether monetary policy is used as an active policy instrument in addition to fiscal policy or not. This indicates that monetary policy does not have an important potential role in stabilizing the Austrian economy.

2. The Econometric Model FINPOL2

The model FINPOL2 is based on traditional Keynesian macroeconomic theory in the sense of conventional IS-LM/aggregate demand-aggregate supply models.

Stochastic behavioral equations for the demand side include a consumption function, an investment function, an import function and an interest-rate equation as a reduced-form money market model. Prices are largely determined by aggregate demand variables. Disequilibrium in the labor market, as measured by the excess of unemployed persons over vacancies, is modelled to depend on the real GDP growth rate and the rate of inflation, embodying both an Okun's law-type relation and a rudimentary Phillips curve. The main objective variables of Austrian economic policies, such as real GDP, the labor market disequilibrium variable (related to the rate of unemployment), the rate of inflation, the balance of payments and the ratio of the federal net budget deficit to GDP, are related directly or indirectly to those fiscal and monetary policy instruments which are used as control variables, namely to federal budget expenditures and revenues and to money supply.

The model, which is dynamic and nonlinear, was estimated first by OLS and then by simultaneous equations estimation methods using annual data over the period 1965 to 1992. Data have been obtained from the Austrian Institute of Economic Research (WIFO). All real data have dimension Billions of 1983 Austrian Schillings. The estimates and test statistics together with ex-post simulation results suggest that the model provides a reasonable account of the development of economic variables in the recent past. Here we use the estimates of the parameters obtained by three-stage least squares; the software package PC TSP, Version 4.2B has been used for estimating and simulating the model. Details of the estimation results are contained in Neck and Karbuz (1994).

3. The Optimum Control Approach

In the theory of quantitative economic policy, macroeconomic policy problems are often considered as problems of optimizing an intertemporal objective function under the constraints of a dynamic system. Optimum control theory has been used in several studies to determine optimal policies for econometric models (e.g., Chow 1975, 1981; Kendrick 1981). Here we use the algorithm OPTCON (Matulka and Neck 1992); it determines approximate solutions of optimum control problems with a quadratic objective function and a nonlinear multivariable dynamic model. The objective function is quadratic in the deviations of the state and control variables from their respective desired values. The dynamic system is required to be given in a state space representation.

For our simulation experiments, we choose the planning horizon as 1993 to 2000. Among the variables whose deviations from desired values are to be penalized, we distinguish two categories: First, there are five "main" objective variables which are of direct political relevance in assessing the performance of the Austrian economy. These are the rate of inflation ($PV\%_t$), the labor market excess supply variable (UN_t) as a measure for involuntary unemployment, the rate of growth of real GDP ($YR\%_t$), the balance of current account (LBR_t), and the federal net budget deficit as percentage of GDP ($DEF\%_t$). In all experiments, 2% p.a. is considered as the desired rate of inflation ($PV\%_t$), 3.5% p.a. as the desired real growth rate ($YR\%_t$), and the desired levels for labor market excess supply (UN_t) and the balance of current account (LBR_t) are set equal to zero. For the deficit variable, we assume that the aim is to consolidate the federal budget deficit gradually such that the desired value of $DEF\%_t$ is reduced by 0.3 percentage points each year, from the historical value of 3.27% in 1992 down to 0.87% in 2000.

Second, we introduce a category of "minor" objective variables. These include real private consumption, real private investment, real imports of goods and services, the nominal rate of interest, real GDP, real total aggregate demand, the domestic price level, the price level of public consumption, nominal public consumption, and nominal public-sector net tax revenues, as well as the policy instrument (control) variables federal budget net expenditures (NEX_t), federal budget tax receipts (BIN_t) and money supply ($M1_t$). We take 1992 historical values of these "minor" objective variables (except for the rate of interest) to be given and postulate desired growth rates of 3.5% p.a. for the planning horizon for all real variables, desired growth rates of 2% p.a. for the price level variables, and desired growth rates of 5.5% p.a. for the nominal variables. The rate of interest has a desired constant value of 7 for all periods.

In the weight matrix of the objective function, all off-diagonal elements are set equal to zero, and the main diagonal elements are given weights of 10 for the "main" objective variables and of 1 for the "minor" objective variables. The state variables that are not mentioned above get weights of zero, thus being regarded as irrelevant to the hypothetical policy-maker. The weight matrix is assumed to be constant over time.

The algorithm OPTCON assumes the values of the non-controlled exogenous variables to be known in advance for all time periods of the planning horizon. In addition, starting values are required for the control variables for all time periods to initialize the iterative determination of their optimal values. For a simulation over a future planning horizon, projections (forecasts) of the exogenous (controlled and non-controlled) variables are needed. Here we use extrapolations of these variables for the years 1993 to 2000 calculated from linear stochastic time series models of the ARMA (mixed autoregressive-moving average process) type. After several trials and applying the usual diagnostic checking procedure for the time series under consideration, we decided to model federal budget expenditures (NEX_t) by an ARMA (2,1) process, federal budget revenues (BIN_t) by an ARMA (2,2) process, money supply ($M1_t$) by an ARMA (2,1) process, the import price level (PM_t) by an ARMA (1,1) process, real exports of goods and services (XR_t) by an ARMA (2,3) process, and the inventory change variable IIR_t by an AR (1) process.

The forecasts from these time series models imply moderate growth of the fiscal policy variables. The extrapolation implies that the federal budget deficit gets stabilized and falls gradually from 70.3 billions AS in 1993 to 60.5 billions AS in 2000, which is a very optimistic forecast. The development of the foreign sector variables PM_t and XR_t is even more optimistic: PM_t grows only by 1% p.a. or less, and XR_t grows by 5 to 7% p.a. IIR_t is positive but falling. Money supply $M1_t$ grows by 5 to 5.8% p.a.

4. Projected vs. Optimal Budgetary Policies

As a first step, the model was simulated over the years 1993 to 2000 using the extrapolations of all (control and non-controlled) exogenous variables from the time series models as input. This amounts to a dynamic forecast of the endogenous variables of the model; no optimization is involved in this projection. Next, we performed two optimization experiments as detailed in the previous section. Here again the projections of the non-controlled exogenous variables from the time series models are used as inputs, being assumed to be known for certain, but the values of the policy instruments are determined endogenously as (approximately) optimal under the assumed objective function. In this paper, we report about the results of deterministic optimization experiments only, i.e., the stochastics in the parameters of the econometric model and the additive disturbances are neglected. This simplifies the calculations of optimal policies considerably. From comparisons between optimal deterministic and optimal stochastic policies (reported elsewhere), we can conclude that their differences are not big provided the latter are based on the full estimated covariance matrix of the econometric model's parameters; hence we do not lose much information when neglecting the stochastics.

As we want to explore the optimal design of macroeconomic policies with and without active use of the monetary instrument, two optimization experiments are run: First, fiscal and monetary policy instruments (NEX_t, BIN_t, $M1_t$) are determined within the optimum control algorithm to minimize the objective function jointly ("active" monetary policy). This scenario can be interpreted as a policy design by a government acting in accordance with an independent or dependent central bank, who do not primarily care about the external value of the currency. Monetary policies like this have sometimes be pursued by central banks of small open economies, such as Switzerland, but never in Austria. On the other hand, the second optimization experiment regards only fiscal policy instruments (NEX_t and BIN_t) as control variables; money supply (M1t) is considered as an exogenous non-controlled variable, i.e., the forecasts from the time series model are used ("inactive" monetary policy). This scenario can be interpreted as a continuation of the monetary policies followed in the past by Austrian monetary authorities, which amounted to pegging the Austrian Schilling to the Deutschmark ("hard-currency policy"). A similar regime (with still less discretion for the

Austrian central bank) will prevail in the European Economic and Monetary Union, which started January 1, 1999. In any case, in this scenario Austria disposes of the monetary policy instrument for purposes of discretionary stabilization policy; only the budget is an active instrument of Austrian policy-makers.

The results of these three simulation experiments are shown in Tables 1, 2 and 3, respectively. For lack of space, only the results of the instrument variables (NEX_t, BIN_t and $M1_t$), the "main" objective variables, and (in Table 1) the two exogenous variables PM_t and XR_t reflecting global developments are given.

Table 1: Projected Values of Instruments, Exogenous Variables and Dynamic Forecasts of "Main" Objectives

year	NEX_t	BIN_t	$M1_t$	PM_t	XR_t	$PV\%_t$	UN_t	$YR\%_t$	LBR_t	$DEF\%_t$
1993	698.067	627.727	318.606	105.548	742.006	1.606	6.584	-1.073	-2.467	3.575
1994	742.229	673.814	336.990	106.674	788.905	2.286	5.604	4.434	26.617	3.245
1995	787.368	717.833	355.402	107.762	844.893	2.779	3.884	7.372	47.454	2.975
1996	835.620	767.266	375.266	108.814	887.021	2.782	3.276	4.925	48.349	2.694
1997	885.821	818.224	396.046	109.829	938.410	2.985	2.595	5.517	51.552	2.434
1998	938.909	873.143	418.061	110.811	989.843	3.059	2.215	4.978	50.802	2.171
1999	994.498	930.966	441.264	111.759	1045.287	3.163	1.886	5.035	50.233	1.919
2000	1053.056	992.592	465.770	112.675	1103.351	3.252	1.618	5.027	48.768	1.669

The projection scenario forecasts a recession for 1993 (or actually a continuation of the recession from 1992). Starting in 1994, however, a period of relatively high growth is projected, which is clearly above the one obtained on average during the eighties. The labor market excess supply variable (UN_t) falls gradually, with only slightly rising inflation ($PV\%_t$). High surpluses are obtained for the balance of trade (LBR_t), particularly from 1995 on, and the deficit variable $DEF\%_t$ falls gradually. The optimistic forecasts for the following years are primarily due to the favorable prospects of world market developments as expressed by the time series extrapolations for Austrian real exports and import prices.

In spite of the already optimistic picture of the future development of the Austrian economy provided by the projected forecast, there is still some scope for optimal stabilization policy, as can be seen from the optimization experiments. In particular, optimal fiscal and (when active) monetary policies are more countercyclical than projected ones and imply smoother time paths of the endogenous variables of the model. The recession of 1993 is avoided by expansionary monetary and especially budgetary policies. Federal budget expenditures (NEX_t) are clearly higher, federal budget revenues (BIN_t) are lower

Table 2: Optimal Values of Instruments and "Main" Objectives, Monetary Policy Active

year	NEX_t	BIN_t	$M1_t$	$PV\%_t$	UN_t	$YR\%_t$	LBR_t	$DEF\%_t$
1993	734.641	581.421	326.892	2.063	4.807	1.996	-22.144	7.196
1994	769.752	639.456	340.949	2.597	4.112	4.632	-7.253	5.671
1995	789.774	698.940	355.651	2.753	3.454	4.943	9.858	3.644
1996	833.577	746.124	373.033	2.658	3.428	3.365	12.669	3.282
1997	870.066	806.048	390.509	2.712	3.278	3.769	22.733	2.238
1998	907.822	870.236	409.455	2.681	3.279	3.390	32.310	1.229
1999	937.960	934.985	430.907	2.692	3.245	3.502	44.772	0.091
2000	959.630	974.370	457.717	2.838	2.920	4.423	55.274	-0.416

Table 3: Optimal Values of Instruments and "Main" Objectives, Monetary Policy Inactive

year	NEX_t	BIN_t	$PV\%_t$	UN_t	$YR\%_t$	LBR_t	$DEF\%_t$
1993	734.899	580.978	2.063	4.808	1.995	-22.139	7.229
1994	770.048	639.118	2.597	4.113	4.631	-7.241	5.698
1995	789.985	698.810	2.753	3.454	4.944	9.870	3.657
1996	833.675	746.234	2.658	3.427	3.365	12.680	3.282
1997	870.003	806.430	2.712	3.277	3.770	22.741	2.223
1998	907.555	870.856	2.681	3.278	3.392	32.312	1.200
1999	937.482	935.682	2.693	3.243	3.506	44.753	0.055
2000	959.079	974.821	2.840	2.916	4.431	55.209	-0.444

than both projected and desired levels of these variables. This results in a positive growth rate, lower unemployment, only slightly higher inflation, but distinctly higher deficits of the trade balance and the federal budget as compared to the projection. Also in 1994 optimal stabilization policies can be characterized as expansionary, with similar (though weaker) effects on the objective variables. The values of the instrument variables in 1995 and 1996 are close to those of the projection, with slightly more expansionary tax policy. From 1997 on, optimal monetary and budgetary policies are restrictive as compared to the projection.

This results in lower growth, higher unemployment and lower inflation than in the reference scenario. The surplus of the trade balance starts increasing some years later than in the projection. The federal budget gets fully consolidated, with a balanced budget in 1999 and even a surplus in 2000.

If we compare the results of the two optimization runs (Table 2 and 3), it is astonishing how similar the results for the scenarios with active and inactive monetary policies are. Active monetary policy (Table 2) implies more expansionary (higher) money supply than projected (Table 1) until 1995 and more restrictive (lower) money supply afterwards. As regards fiscal policies, both budgetary instruments act in a slightly less expansionary way (lower NEX_t, higher BIN_t) until 1995 and in a slightly less restrictive way (higher NEX_t, lower BIN_t) from 1996 on in the scenario with active monetary policy. This can be interpreted to mean that with the loss of the monetary policy instrument, the fiscal policy instruments have to take over its tasks and have to intensify their discretionary activities. However, this does not pose a large burden upon these instruments. Or, to put it the other way round, an active monetary policy is not very helpful in stabilizing the Austrian economy, as the results for all other variables are very similar to those obtained under an inactive monetary policy. This result might provide some justification for the "hard-currency policy" of Austria since the early eighties and for the decision to enter the European Monetary Union: loss of monetary sovereignty does not prevent achieving stabilization policy goals, as fiscal policy is the more effective instrument.

5. Optimal Policies under Different Assumptions about Exogenous Variables

The optimization experiments described in the previous section shows that the performance of the Austrian economy can be improved by countercyclical budgetary and (to some extent) monetary policies. When such a result is to be communicated to actual policy-makers, its robustness with respect to the underlying assumptions should be checked first. To do so, we have conducted several alternative optimum control experiments, using alternative values of the parameters of the objective function (weights, discount rate, planning horizon, desired values of objective variables). The results, which are reported elsewhere, show that in most cases optimal policies are quite similar to those of the previous experiment. On the other hand, one might expect optimal policies to depend upon the assumptions made about future developments of the world economy as expressed by the forecasts of the non-controlled exogenous variables of our model, in particular real exports (XR_t) and import prices (PM_t). It is well known from theoretical and empirical studies that macroeconomic developments in a small open economy like Austria are crucially influenced by global business cycles; hence, optimal national budgetary and monetary policies should depend on them, too. Moreover, the forecasts of the exogenous variables obtained from the time series models are rather unreliable, providing another reason for exploring the influence of alternative assumptions about global developments upon optimal Austrian budgetary policies.

Among the exogenous variables of the model FINPOL2, import prices (PM_t) and real exports of goods and services (XR_t) are most interesting. We have also conducted some simulations with alternative time paths of inventory changes (IIR_t), but their results (both the projections and the optimization experiments) do not differ much from those given in Tables 1, 2 and 3. The same is true if we use results from other ARMA specifications for PM_t and XR_t. Therefore, we decided to use arbitrary annual growth rates for import prices and real exports to construct alternative global scenarios. First, we assume both PM_t and XR_t to grow by 3% annually over the time horizon considered (1993 to 2000). This means higher growth of import prices and lower growth of real exports than implied by the time series models and can be characterized as a more "pessimistic" scenario. For the projection simulation, we still use the values of the control variables as given in Table 1; also the same values as in the previous simulation were used for IIR_t. The results are shown for the projection (dynamic forecast) and the two optimization runs in Tables 4, 5 and 6, respectively.

Comparing these results with those of Tables 1, 2 and 3, we see considerable differences. In the projection (with unchanged budgetary policies), the lower growth rate of real exports implies a slowdown of Austrian economic activity, as can be seen in the lower growth rate ($YR\%_t$) and the higher unemployment rate (UN_t) in Table 4. Although the federal budget deficit remains the same in nominal terms, its ratio to GDP ($DEF\%_t$) is higher than in the previous simulation due to the lower denominator of this ratio. In spite of the lower exports, the current account (LBR_t) shows higher surpluses than before, which is due to the endogenous reduction of imports implied by lower domestic demand. Although import prices rise more than in the previous simulation, the Austrian inflation rate ($PV\%_t$) is lower because of the offsetting effect of reduced demand.

Tables 5 and 6 show that the optimal reaction of Austrian budgetary policies (given the postulated objective function) is highly expansionary: Federal expenditures (NEX_t) are always considerably higher, federal revenues (BIN_t) are always considerably lower than in the projection (Table 4). Apart from the first year, where the expansionary course of budgetary policies is kept at a more moderate level now, this is also true when compared with the optimal policies of the previous (more "optimistic") scenario (Tables 2 and 3). The result of these policies is a much better performance than in the projection with respect to growth and unemployment at the expense of higher inflation, deficits of the current account and considerably higher budget deficits (up to 270 billions ATS or 8.2% of GDP in 2000). Especially these budget deficits will not be sustainable in the long run, but this aspect cannot be taken into account in a short-run Keynesian model like FINPOL2.

Table 4: Projected Values of Exogenous Variables and "Main" Objectives, "Pessimistic" Scenario

year	PM_t	XR_t	$PV\%_t$	UN_t	$YR\%_t$	LBR_t	$DEF\%_t$
1993	108.556	738.063	2.576	6.376	-0.832	-3.233	3.561
1994	111.812	760.205	2.557	6.550	0.629	16.298	3.363
1995	115.167	783.011	2.615	6.329	1.789	33.496	3.280
1996	118.622	806.501	2.689	5.963	2.395	47.539	3.072
1997	122.180	830.696	2.758	5.599	2.620	58.811	2.885
1998	125.846	855.617	2.813	5.307	2.620	68.183	2.663
1999	129.621	881.286	2.850	5.101	2.529	76.534	2.442
2000	133.510	907.724	2.876	4.966	2.434	84.511	2.206

Table 5: Optimal Values of Instruments and "Main" Objectives, "Pessimistic" Scenario, Monetary Policy Active

year	NEX_t	BIN_t	$M1_t$	$PV\%_t$	UN_t	$YR\%_t$	$LBR\%_t$	$DEF\%_t$
1993	706.804	592.455	332.847	2.775	5.191	0.395	-17.550	5.461
1994	763.685	613.829	353.022	3.008	4.775	3.237	-14.794	6.733
1995	811.601	644.571	372.841	3.108	4.381	3.419	-14.674	7.037
1996	860.859	675.359	393.618	3.185	4.069	3.398	-16.499	7.321
1997	914.428	705.344	415.393	3.257	3.801	3.443	-19.990	7.718
1998	974.565	736.829	437.545	3.328	3.555	3.533	-25.107	8.194
1999	1044.250	779.256	458.604	3.362	3.408	3.366	-30.972	8.536
2000	1121.448	853.735	476.387	3.253	3.653	2.225	-33.475	8.157

The results for 1993 show that there is also an intertemporal trade-off for optimal policies: When policy-makers know that they will be confronted with a prolonged period of lower global growth, as is the case in this scenario, they will use their instruments in a more cautious way at the beginning of the planning period than in the previous scenario where the recession ends after the first year. Similar (and even more expansionary) policies are prescribed as optimal in scenarios where a zero growth rate for real exports is assumed.

Table 6: Optimal Values of Instruments and "Main" Objectives, "Pessimistic" Scenario, Monetary Policy Inactive

year	NEX_t	BIN_t	$PV\%_t$	UN_t	$YR\%_t$	LBR_t	$DEF\%_t$
1993	707.040	591.614	2.774	5.193	0.386	-17.524	5.513
1994	764.206	612.656	3.007	4.778	3.234	-14.740	6.810
1995	812.315	643.167	3.108	4.384	3.418	-14.598	7.127
1996	861.711	673.785	3.184	4.071	3.399	-16.408	7.418
1997	915.412	703.643	3.257	3.802	3.444	-19.891	7.819
1998	975.683	735.113	3.327	3.556	3.533	-25.001	8.293
1999	1045.457	777.784	3.361	3.410	3.362	-30.845	8.624
2000	1122.538	852.916	3.251	3.658	2.214	-33.295	8.217

The comparison between the scenarios with active and inactive policies shows again the low effectiveness of monetary policies in this model of the Austrian macro economy. In the active monetary policy regime (Table 5), money supply is more expansionary (higher by 3 to 6 percent) than in the inactive monetary policy regime (see the values for $M1_t$ in Table 1), but fiscal policies are only slightly less expansionary to achieve approximately the same effect on the endogenous target variables. Forsaking discretionary monetary policy hence does not entail a loss for stabilization purposes also in a more "pessimistic" global environment.

Quite different outcomes are obtained if we assume a scenario of "global expansion". For this purpose, we assume both import prices (PM_t) and real exports (XR_t) to grow by 6% per year over the entire time horizon. Given experiences of the recent past, such a development is highly unlikely in the near future; it is simulated here just for the purpose of pointing out the effects of a very "optimistic" view about a sustained global boom on optimal policies for Austria. The main results are shown in Tables 7 to 9. From the projection results (Table 7), it can be seen that under unchanged budgetary and monetary policies, this scenario leads to an overheating of the Austrian economy, with high growth, high inflation and especially excess demand for labor (negative values of UN_t from 1996 on). In this case, the optimal reaction of budgetary policies (Tables 8 and 9) consists in a drastic reduction of budget deficits, leading eventually to considerable surpluses in the federal budget in the second half of the planning period. This is brought about both by low federal expenditures and high taxes. These restrictive policies reduce real growth and inflation and lead to an equilibrium in the labor market. Again, the demand-side effects dominate, as has to be expected from the structure of our Keynesian model FINPOL2. Budgetary policies are a very effective instrument in

Table 7: Projected Values of Exogenous Variables and "Main" Objectives, Scenario of "Global Expansion"

year	PM_t	XR_t	$PV\%_t$	UN_t	$YR\%_t$	LBR_t	$DEF\%_t$
1993	111.717	759.560	4.163	4.616	4.275	7.785	3.361
1994	118.420	805.134	4.691	2.992	6.884	28.422	2.941
1995	125.526	853.442	5.207	1.290	8.082	38.211	2.641
1996	133.057	904.648	5.659	-0.168	8.298	38.309	2.274
1997	141.041	958.927	6.023	-1.295	8.087	30.859	1.963
1998	149.503	1016.463	6.298	-2.116	7.759	17.972	1.665
1999	158.473	1077.450	6.496	-2.694	7.458	1.292	1.403
2000	167.982	1142.097	6.634	-3.098	7.235	-18.107	1.165

Table 8: Optimal Values of Instruments and "Main" Objectives, Scenario of "Global Expansion", Monetary Policy Active

year	NEX_t	BIN_t	$M1_t$	$PV\%_t$	UN_t	$YR\%_t$	$LBR\%_t$	$DEF\%_t$
1993	731.160	604.056	315.360	4.407	3.307	5.891	-8.081	5.708
1994	756.273	672.980	326.624	4.675	2.462	5.257	6.477	3.414
1995	781.214	744.222	338.304	4.889	1.867	4.937	21.488	1.384
1996	804.664	825.316	350.316	5.034	1.497	4.558	38.055	-0.706
1997	822.599	920.531	363.125	5.105	1.346	4.063	57.630	-3.072
1998	827.577	1025.689	378.680	5.120	1.371	3.583	81.497	-5.725
1999	809.969	1111.142	401.659	5.185	1.267	3.964	107.615	-7.985
2000	777.187	1102.417	439.161	5.599	0.109	7.347	122.800	-7.625

this context, but their optimal design is crucially dependent on the assumed developments in the world economy. Monetary policy, when active (Table 8), also reacts restrictively, but can again be seen to be a comparatively ineffective instrument for stabilization purposes.

Table 9: Optimal Values of Instruments and "Main" Objectives, Scenario of "Global Expansion", Monetary Policy Inactive

year	NEX_t	BIN_t	$PV\%_t$	UN_t	$YR\%_t$	LBR_t	$DEF\%_t$
1993	731.271	604.298	4.408	3.305	5.899	-8.102	5.702
1994	756.173	673.699	4.675	2.459	5.258	6.437	3.380
1995	780.834	745.514	4.890	1.866	4.937	21.432	1.321
1996	803.910	827.274	5.034	1.496	4.557	37.987	-0.799
1997	821.365	923.157	5.106	1.346	4.063	57.556	-3.192
1998	825.783	1028.754	5.121	1.369	3.587	81.404	-5.865
1999	807.715	1113.996	5.187	1.261	3.977	107.456	-8.118
2000	775.042	1104.044	5.603	0.095	7.374	122.484	-7.709

6. Concluding Remarks

In this paper, we have used a medium-size macroeconometric model of the Austrian economy to calculate optimal budgetary and monetary policies for the years 1993 to 2000 for a given objective function. If we compare the results of the optimization runs to simulations with extrapolations of policy instruments used as inputs, optimal policies turn out to be more countercyclical and to dampen the amplitude of business cycle fluctuations. If this is in fact a goal of economic policy-making, using an optimum control approach within a framework of quantitative economic policy might be recommended to political decision-makers and their advisers as an instrument to generate insights into possibilities for improving policy-making. However, alternative assumptions about the development of non-controlled exogenous variables reflecting global developments have been shown to change optimal budgetary policies considerably. Monetary policies, on the other hand, do not exert much effect on macroeconomic objective variables in this Keynesian model of the small open economy of Austria, as can be seen from the comparisons of the active and inactive monetary policy regimes. Obviously, more research is needed, especially to build more elaborate econometric models, before policy proposals can be derived which can be implemented for actual political decisions. So far, the reliability of policy recommendations depends strongly on the quality of the forecasts for the exogenous variables, and great caution is required in interpreting results from optimization experiments for policy purposes.

References

Buede, D. (1993): Aiding Insight: Survey Decision Analysis. OR/MS Today, April 1993, 52-60.

Chow, G.C. (1975): Analysis and Control of Dynamic Economic Systems. Wiley, New York.

Chow, G.C. (1981): Econometric Analysis by Control Methods. Wiley, New York.

Feichtinger, G., Hartl, R.F. (1986): Optimale Kontrolle oekonomischer Prozesse. De Gruyter, Berlin.

Kendrick, D. (1981): Stochastic Control for Economic Models. McGraw-Hill, New York.

Matulka, J., Neck, R. (1992): OPTCON: An Algorithm for the Optimal Control of Nonlinear Stochastic Models. Annals of Operations Research 37: 375-401.

Neck, R., Karbuz, S. (1994): Optimal Stabilization Policies for the Nineties: A Simulation Study for Austria. In: Kaylan, A.R. et al. (Eds.): Proceedings of the European Simulation Symposium 1994, I. SCS, Istanbul, 214-218.

Acknowledgement

Financial support from the "Jubilaeumsfonds der Oesterreichischen Nationalbank" (project no. 6917) and from the Ludwig Boltzmann Institute for Economic Analysis is gratefully acknowledged. Karbuz acknowledges support from the Institute for Advanced Studies, Vienna. The views expressed are not necessarily those of the IEA/OECD.

Dynamic Economic Models of Optimal Law Enforcement

Gustav Feichtinger

Institute for Econometrics, Operations Research and Systems Theory
Vienna University of Technology, Austria

Abstract

Since Becker's (1968) seminal work on crime and punishment economists see a task in the optimal allocation of resources to reduce illegal behaviour. In some follow-up studies Becker's approach, which is essentially *static*, has been extended by including *intertemporal* aspects. It turns out that efficient law enforcement in a dynamic context is a sophisticated task revealing some important and new aspects of optimal crime control. In particular, we will stress that *optimal control theory* and *dynamic games* are tools being suitable for investigating *dynamic* extensions of law enforcement.

One issue of the present paper is to show how the influence of reference groups to micro-behaviour may result in multiple equilibria. This 'density-dependence' and other inherent non-linearities imply the existence of thresholds separating basins of attractions for optimal paths. Instead of providing a systematic framework we illustrate our approach by several interesting examples of optimal law enforcement. In particular, our game-theoretic approach of law enforcement contains only a collection of preliminary ideas and unsolved examples rather a than general competitive approach to crime and punishment. We hope, however, that this material is useful for future work in a more systematic optimal dynamic law enforcement.

1. Introduction

'Crime' is a heterogeneous set of phenomena that are not only of serious social consequences but also economically very important. Criminal activities range widely from murder and burglary to tax evasion and environmental offenses. Crimes generate damages and harm and put billions of dollars in to the pockets of offenders. Significant public and private resources are spent in order to prevent offenses and to apprehend and convict offenders. This raises the question, how many resources and how much punishment should be used to enforce law. In his *economic* approach to crime and punishment, Becker (1968) put it more strangely:

'How many offenses should be permitted and how many offenders should go unpunished?'

Since Becker's work on crime and punishment, economists see a task in the optimal allocation of resources to reduce illegal behaviour. In particular, this *economic approach* should help to determine an efficient allocation of a given budget to apprehend offenders, to treat them, and to prevent offenses.

Although 'crime' is an economically important activity, it is often elusive from an economist's point of view. The lack of reliable data for reasons whatsoever suggest the necessity of modeling in the economic of crime.

Crime control generally has also received a considerable amount of attention from the *operations research* community and quantitative methods generally, including all of the criminal career modeling (see, e.g., Blumstein and Cohen, 1973, Blumstein et al., 1978, and Blumstein and Nagin, 1981), selective incapacitation, and recently the trend toward longitudinal individual level analyses (see, e.g., Leung, 1995). We also refer to two interesting surveys of Maltz (1994, 1996).

Our main reference, however, is the path-breaking analysis of Gary S. Becker and his followers. According to Becker (1968), the authorities have to determine the amount of resources to prevent offenses and to apprehend offenders. Moreover, for those convicted the punishment which fits the crime has to be ascertained. In particular, Becker tries to find those expenditures on law enforcement and punishments that minimize the social loss. This loss is the sum of damages, costs of apprehension and conviction, and costs of carrying out the punishments. The analysis of the optimality conditions yields numerous interesting insights into efficient control of illegal behaviour.

Several other scientists took up Becker's ideas and extended them in different ways. Let us briefly mention some selected follow-up work of Becker.

In a model of optimal enforcement by Malik (1990) offenders can engage in activities that reduce the probability of being caught and fined. As in other extensions (such as the one by Polinsky and Shavell (1991) where wealth varies among individuals, or the model by Bebchuk and Kaplow (1993) who consider the possibility that individuals are not all equally easy to apprehend) the optimal fines turn out to be less than those proposed by Becker. Polinsky and Shavell (1992) find that the optimal fine equals the harm, properly inflated for the chance of not being detected, plus the variable enforcement cost of imposing the fine.

In contrast with Becker, Akiba (1991) shows that an increase in the subjective probability of apprehension (or severity of punishment) does not necessarily lead to an unambiguously negative effect on crime. And Shavell (1990) tries to answer the question if one should also punish attempts and argues that the punishment of attempts increases deterrence by expanding the set of circumstances in which sanctions are imposed.

Becker's approach and most follow-up models in the literature on optimal punishment theory are confined to a *static* set-up. However, the severity of „crime“ we will face tomorrow depends, at least in part, on the law enforcement strategy choosen today.

Leung (1991) showed that Becker's result that the optimal fine should be a multiple of the social costs is no longer valid in a dynamic environment. In contrast to the existing deterrence models which are based on a static framework and thus have to ignore recidivism (which is, in fact, a serious shortcoming), Leung (1995) can - through his micro-dynamic approach - incorporate recidivistic behaviour into his more general deterrence model. Among other things, the analysis confirms the familiar result that an increase in the certainty of punishment is more deterrent-effective than an increase in the severity. Such micro-dynamic extensions of Becker's static framework provide a useful platform for various research possibilities, e.g. that punishment depends on the offender's prior criminal record rather than on the offense rate at arrest time, problems of recidivism, etc.

Davis (1988) models on offender's choice of optimal crime rate if an increase in this rate lowers the expected time until detection. He studies implications of his model for the optimal enforcement of laws.

The paper is organized as follows. In section 2 we present a fairly general intertemporal optimization model providing a framework for an appropriate dynamic extension of Becker's static economic modeling of crime and punishment. As it has been demonstrated in several studies, economic modeling of crime and its control often leads to multiple equilibria. A more detailed mathematical formulation of the model is deferred to an appendix. In section 3, 'density-dependence' is identified as an important cause for nonlinearities implying multiple equilibria. In particular, the existence of separating thresholds or critial levels is discussed. Section 4 contains a (certainly non-exhaustive) sample of such effects of law enforcement which seem to be surprising (at least at the first look). An economic analysis of crime and punishment has to take into consideration that offenders act as rational agents. The complete paradigm amounts to a *dynamic game* between a law enforcement agency, offenders and victims. Section 5 illustrates the differential game approach by several examples. Finally, section 6 concludes with some remarks which might be valuable for future work in the dynamic economic modeling of crime and law enforcement.

2. Optimal Law Enforcement in an Intertemporal Setting

Let us start with some rather general observations on intertemporal optimization.

Virtually every optimization model starts with three questions:

- *What* should we do?
- *How* can we do it?
- What are the *constraints* to reach our goal?

The first point refers to the target which one tries to reach. The second question is that of the decision possibilities. The third ingredient deals with the impact of these decision variables on the reachability of a specific aim.

Thus, we *firstly* determine the social costs which arise for a law enforcement agency. These costs are the sum of the damages, costs of apprehension and conviction, and costs of carrying out the punishments imposed. These three components of the social loss generated by offenses have been discussed in detail by Becker (1968); see also below.

Second, let us turn to decision instruments. The authority's main economic decision variable are its expenditures on policy, courts etc. which help to determine the probability that an offense is uncovered and that the offenders are apprehended and convicted. In the simplest version the size of the punishment for those convicted and the form of the punishment are assumed to be constant.

The *third* issue are the constraints describing how the instrumental variables influence the social costs. In the dynamic case this refers to modeling the impact of the decision instruments on the change of the number of offenses. In the basic model (described below) this means the effect of law enforcement expenditures on the conviction probability and from those further to the number of offenses[1].

In particular, the following *dynamic* extension of Becker's *static* supply function of offenses[2] has been proposed by Caulkins (1990, 1993a) and others in the

---

[1] By assuming that each offender commits a constant number of offenses per unit time we may identify the number of offenses with those of the offenders.

[2] Becker (1968) assumes a static supply function relating the number of offenses by any person to his/her probability of conviction and to the punishment. In reality, however, the

context of a macro-dynamic description of the movement of dealers into and out of local drug markets under police enforcement. Comparing the dealers with firms and illicit drug markets with industries, where free entry and exit ensures zero long-run profit, it is proposed that the rate of change of offenders depends on the expected utility from illegal activity compared with that from legal work. To model such a framework it is assumed that the potential criminals become offenders as soon as their individual utility expected from committing a crime exceeds the (average) income from an alternative, but legal activity. If their utility is smaller than the reservation wage, criminals will lower or even stop the number of offenses[3].

In addition to that, the dynamics of offenders is reduced by the rate of apprehended criminals.

Using such an offender's dynamics, Feichtinger et al. (1997) minimize the total discounted stream of social losses (as described above). By applying optimal control theory (whose importance in a dynamic approach of crime and punishment is discussed at the end of this section) they are able to prove an interesting 'threshold behaviour' of optimal law enforcement policies. In particular, this means that there exists a critial level for offenses, denoted by N_c, in the following sense. If the initial number of offenders N(0) is *above* N_c, then there is long-run 'high' equilibrium (i.e. a long-run steady state which is a saddle point) which is gradually approached along the stable manifolds (both from below and above as long as N(0) is greater than the threshold N_c). In economic terms, this means that the intertemporal trade-off between the damage from offenses and the law enforcement and punishment costs yields an upper (interior) equilibrium. This result answers the question 'how many offenses should be permitted' posed by Becker (1968) and mentioned at the begin of section 1. In addition to Becker, our dynamic analysis provides the optimal time path of law enforcement illustrated in Fig. 1 by the thick black curves. It turns out that its structure makes economic sense.

However, if N(0) is *below* the critical level N_c then it is optimal to eradicate crime, i.e. it pays to enforce until the illegal market collapses. The steady-state equilibrium is at the (lower) boundary, and the law enforcement expenditures increase first, but finally decrease (see Fig. 1). For details see Feichtinger et al.

---

number of criminals at a certain time depends not only on the conviction probability and the fine at that time but also on the law enforcement in the past.

[3] Note that the driving mechanisms of a such a system dynamics exhibits a certain similarity with the well-known replicator dynamics (see, e.g., Hofbauer and Sigmund, 1998).

(1997) [4]. A brief description of the model is given in the appendix of the present paper.

The very reason for this threshold-dependent optimal enforcement policy is a special non-linearity originating in the dependence of the conviction probability on the law enforcement expenditure *per offender* (see also the discussion in section 3)[5]. In most cases, it is the convexity of the Hamiltonian with respect to the state variable(s) implying this interesting result. However, it has been recently stressed, that the economically important threshold property is compatible with strict concavity (Wirl and Feichtinger, 1998).

The model sketched above may be seen as a first step to extend Becker's static approach to an intertemporal setting. A more realistic analysis has to take into consideration that the law enforcement agency has available a diverse array of interventions with which it seeks to mitigate the consequences of crimes. Let us just mention two of them in addition to enforcement by police and courts: treatment of offenders and prevention. The relative efficacy of these instruments depends on the pattern in which the criminal activity considered varies over time.

It is an interesting fact that the use of illicit drug shows an inherent *epidemic* pattern. Behrens et al. (1997ab) have pointed out that for a number of illicit drugs a period of quiescence is typically followed by rapid escalation, a plateau, finally, and a gradual decline of drug consumption. It is quite plausible that the *optimal mix* of interventions will be different for different levels of drug use. An important research question is how the optimal mix of instruments might vary over time. For a given budget, we could ask whether the ratio of spending financial resources on prevention and spending on treatment should be higher at the beginning of a planning period than later on.

---

[4] The occurence of multiple equilibria which are separated by thresholds is quite common in economic models. Skiba (1978) discussed such critical values, but his proof is incomplete. A first proof of existence was given by Dechert and Nishimura (1983); see also Long et al. (1997) as well as Wirl and Feichtinger (1998). Note that the 'optimal' control jumps in N_c, i.e. it is not unique in this point.

[5] Such thresholds occur in several economic models of crime; see Kort et al. (1995) and Tragler et al. (1997, sect. 6).

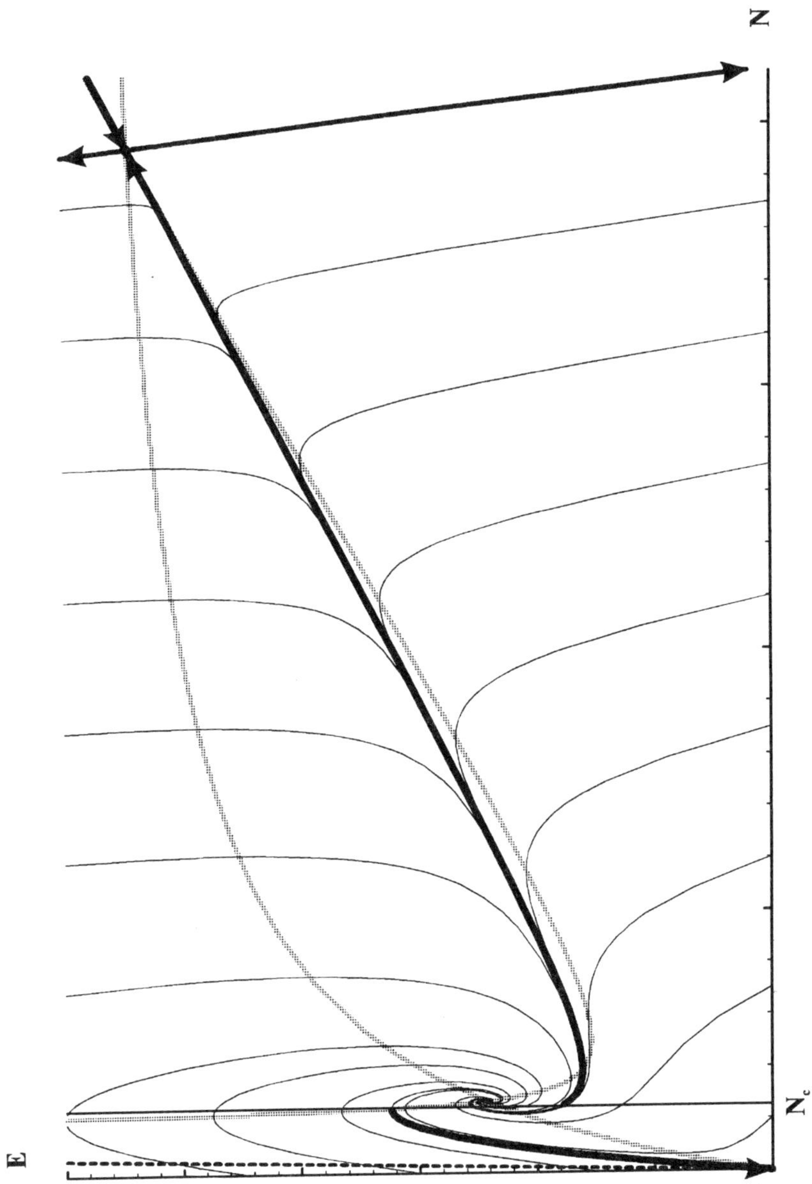

Fig. 1: Phase portrait of the state-control space, i.e. of the (N,E)-diagram. The basins of attraction of the low 'equilibrium (instable focus) and the 'high' equilibrium (saddle-point) are separated by the critical level N_c.

To answer this question one has to specify, among other issues, how imitation of offending depends on the available array of interventions. Preventive measures must interfere with the positive feedback effect of a network of juvenile offenders. Generally, it is a hard task to model both the 'inflow' and the 'outflow' of the offenders. Clearly, prevention dampens the initiation to drug use, while treatment increases the outflow of offenders, and enforcement does both. To specify the functional relationships in the dynamic supply of offenders one has to know how the socio-economic mechanisms are working. Beside of that, psychological, institutional, cultural and other variables will influence the number of offenders over time. A good example of the state of the art on the impact of enforcement and treatment on illicit drug consumption has recently been given by Tragler et al. (1997). The work of these authors illustrates how a more realistic system dynamics than the aforementioned replicator-like one can be identified and validated (at least partially) by empirical data.

In what follows we will describe a solution procedure which is well-suited for obtaining results on optimal enforcement polices as well as on the optimal mix of instruments of controlling offenses. The most efficient instrument in the tool-kit of intertemporal optimization models for the analysis of dynamic economic models is the maximum principle of Pontryagin and his associates. The main advantage of this solution procedure is its powerful capability to yield important *qualitative* insights into the structure of the optimal paths. More specifically, this means that the optimality conditions allow to derive a geometrical, i.e. qualitative description of the shape of the solution trajectories without solving these conditions quantitatively (either analytically or, mostly, numerically). The qualitative approach of the maximum principle also implies the *robustness* of the solution paths in the following specific sense. The structure of the optimal trajectories does only depend on the qualitative properties of the underlying functions, like monotonicity, concavity etc. but *not* on the specific form of those model functions.

Let us give an example of this very important fact which represents essentially the main reason of the ubiquitous application of the maximum principle in dynamic economics. In our basic model of dynamic law enforcement (briefly discussed above) the conviction probability depends on the per capita law enforcement expenditures, i.e. on the expenditures for police and courts divided by the number of offenders (or offenses). Clearly, it holds that this probability increases with per capita expenditures. Beyond that, however, it turns out that the structure of the optimal law enforcement policy is similar without respect of the special form of this function. In particular, it can be shown that a concavity shaped conviction probability yields essentially similar solutions as a linear one. Although the concavity assumption seems to be more realistic (decreasing efficiency of marginal conviction probability), a linear probability has been chosen for our analysis, since it is mathematically more tractable (see also Feichtinger et al., 1997).

It is this robustness property of the maximum principle (in the aforementioned specific sense) which guarantees its importance in dynamic socio-economics. The chronical *deficit of empirical* data which prevails particularly in the economic modeling of crime does not allow to estimate neither the specific form of most functional relations nor the parameters. A striking example for this (sad but realistic) fact is provided by the dynamics of illicit drug consumers under the influence of enforcement, prevention and treatment (see Tragler et al. 1997). Although one has estimates of most of the model parameters based on empirical data, the selection of the special functions is often a matter of taste (and experience). Fortunately, the structure of the model solution frequently does not depend on this selection.

To summarize, it must be admitted that we only consider highly stylized models. However, although the dynamic models considered are simplified to an extent that they only are 'caricatures of the reality' they are anything else but useless. On the contrary, their simplicity allows us to exploit their optimality conditions such that substantial qualitative statements on the structure of the solution paths may be derived.

3. How the Macro Level Influences Microbehaviour: An Excursion to Non-linearity

We might ask for the very reason of the 'threshold behaviour' of optimal law enforcement expenditures in the basic model discussed in section 2. Since the dependence of the optimal paths on the initial condition is due to the existence of *multiple equilibria* the question shifts to this property. Examining our model it is easily seen that the property is due to the dependence of the conviction probability on the total number of offenders N (beside those of E). Thus, the *macro* level, N, influences the *individual* conviction probability p.

This idea is of general importance in socio-economics. Before we illustrate this fact, let us very briefly mention the impact of such dependencies of micro-characteristics on the macro environment. It turns out that it is this dependence which creates *nonlinearities* being rich enough to generate complex solution structures. There are virtually dozens of examples in which the macro level influences micro characteristics. Actually, in the literature those effects are well-known. Some decades ago Schelling (1978) has already discussed 'micromotives and macrobehavior'.

In population dynamics and ecology the influence of a reference group or the environment to individual rates is also well-known and denoted as *'density-dependence'*. An interesting example fitting formally in our paradigm is the explanation of the *Easterlin cycle* in a simple nonlinear Leslie model by Samuelson (1976). By assuming that the age specific fertility rates depend negatively on the stocks, i.e. on the number of potential mothers, Samuelson's model is able to generate persistent oscillations.

Let us now focus to the macro-micro impact in the economics of crimes. In his excellent survey on the economics of corruption Andvig (1991) assumes that the utility an individual receives from a given action depends on the choices of others in that individual's reference group. For instance, in an environment where corruption is the norm it would be not rational to 'stay clean'. The general idea is conveyed through what Andvig calls a *Schelling diagram* (see Schelling, 1973, p. 388). Since the application in corruption is extensively described by Andvig (1991, p. 69-75), it is not repeated here. Instead we focus on two questions which Andvig tries to approach by using Schelling's diagram (Andvig, 1991, p. 59):

- Why do corruption levels vary rather strongly across nations and regions?

- How is it possible to explain that not more people are corrupt or clean?

The explanation hinges on the fact already mentioned above that the profitability of engaging in a corrupt transaction depends on the number of other people who do it, i.e. on the size of the reference group (and, more generally, on its structure).

It should be noted that Akerlof's (1980) theory of social customs to explain the existence of involuntary unemployment can be used to explain the persistence of corruption (see Dawid and Feichtinger, 1996a). Again the main assumption is that moral feelings of guilt by breaking the rules or social norms decrease as the number of rule breakers increases.

In his model Akerlof (1980) assumes that there exists a code of honour where the fraction of people believing in the code always adapts towards the fraction of people actually obeying it. A similar approach using social customs may be used to study the phenomenon that on one hand corruption is present in almost any organisation but on the other hand some people always stay honest; see Dawid and Feichtinger (1996a). Bicchieri and Rovelli (1995) show for a dynamic population model that the transition from a corrupt to a honest equilibrium is possible if there are some people in the population who stay honest all times.

Another example for the idea that reference groups may be important in economic behaviour has been suggested by Schlicht (1981). He shows that small changes in profitability of corruption may cause large changes in observed behaviour.

As result of those ideas we conclude that the same kind of agents within the same kind of socio-economic system may through their *interaction* generate different levels of crime. Thus, models including social interactions in the specific sense described above typically possess *multiple equilibria*. This might provide a theoretical explanation of the empirical fact that offense levels and enforcement rates differ regionally and with respect to other characteristics.

Density-dependencies occur not only in biology and demography but also in various fields of sociology and economics. By social interactions, we refer to the idea that the utility an individual receives from a given action depends on the choice of other persons in a reference group. Recently, Brock and Durlauf (1995) developed a stochastic model to describe these spillover effects covering a wealth of charming examples. In the same spirit argue that social interactions can explain large differences in community crime rates.

One of the most interesting research avenues in the economics of crime seems to be the combination of the influences of the macro level to micro behaviour with intertemporal aspects of crime control. The already existing work in that direction suggests that substantial progress could be expected in the design of optimal law enforcement policies. In particular, threshold mechanisms and other inherent non-linearities generate multiple equilibria including boundary equilibria, instabilities and even more complex behaviour.

4. Some Surprising Effects of Law Enforcement

Law enforcement causes several, sometimes surprising and unintended or even contradicting, reactions. Basically, all enforcement efforts are intended to reduce the rate of offense.

The impact of anti-corruption campaigns depends crucially on certain non-linearities which are typical for epidemic processes like the spread of corruption. The threshold structure and multiplicity of equilibria suggest that after strong "cleaning measures" at the beginning of an anti-corruption campaign the momentum may move the system beyond the unstable equilibrium to a "clean" state. On the other hand the instability implies that even small shocks may lead the system dynamics to a high corruption level trap (compare Andvig, 1991).

A mechanism by which strict enforcement can increase crime is when conviction limits future labour market opportunities. Young males commit crimes for whatever reasons, but they typically 'mature out' of criminality. However, if while they are young, they are arrested and convicted of crime, particularly a felony, that black market may follow them for the rest of their lives, affecting their ability to get a job. This effect is all the stronger if they serve time in prison. Then, at older ages, crime will be relatively more appealing than it be otherwise would be because their licit labour market earning opportunities are more limited. That is something which can be analysed in a dynamic model.

Focusing on markets of illicit drugs, one might think that enforcement of prohibition will deter individuals from consumption and purchase and, consequently, reduce the trade of drugs. However, repression and an increase of repression, respectively, can, e.g., change the specific way of transaction. Dealers will try to avoid or reduce sales to strangers and, nevertheless, create long-lasting vendor-customer relationships. In turn it becomes more difficult for the police to discover drug markets. The risk of high punishments can result in an increased willingness for violence and threats to force maintenance of sales levels.

Benson and Rasmussen (1991), Benson et al. (1992) and Sollars et al. (1994) investigate the relationship among illicit drug use, property crime, police resources, and the allocation of police resources in models using data from the Florida counties. In general, people believe that drug offenders attempting to finance their habits are often responsible for property crimes, thus implying that increasing drug enforcement should reduce property crimes. Increasing drug enforcement might affect the property crime rate (and, by implication, the aggregate crime rate) in a different way, however: this kind of reallocation of given scarce police resources results in diminished rate of deterrence to commit property crimes and, as a result, an increase in the numbers of these crimes. Besides, an increase of drug enforcement in general implies higher prices of illicit drugs, requiring users to acquire greater resources which again may lead to increasing rates of offenses (cf. also Braun and Diekmann, 1993). More recently Dworak et al. (1998) developed a dynamic model in which they showed that the amount of drug enforcement expenditures depend both on the parameter settings, mainly the elasticity of demand of the drug and the social costs of drug use, as well as on the initial value of number of users.

Potential customers could be motivated to first-time consumption by offering them prices below the common price in the market while, on the other hand, the already addicted customers will face higher prices due to the increased risk of the suppliers. Higher prices can force the consumers of concern to commit thefts or get engaged in drug dealing themselves in order to finance their daily demand of a addictive illegal substance. This "terrible franchising system" (Wichmann, 1993) leads to an increased number of suppliers and, subsequently, to an enlarged group of consumers. This "snowball effect" seems to be challenging from a mathematical point of view.

There exist several reports concluding that a higher enforcement rate might lead to an increase of criminal offenses. Caulkins (1993b), e.g., points out that under plausible conditions applying so-called "zero-tolerance" policies (i.e. policies that impose fixed stiff sanctions for possession of any positive amount of an illicit drug, no matter how small the peculiar quantity are) can actually encourage users to consume more, not less, than they would if the punishment increased in proportion to the quantity.

Braun and Diekmann (1993) describe how a highly restrictive drug policy can result in a higher cumulative demand and lower prices of illicit drugs than a more liberal policy would do. One central problem of drug control is to evaluate the impact of enforcement on the illicit drug market, i.e. on the amount of the transactions, the situation of the addicts, the number of dealers. Braun and Diekmann (1993) provide an interesting survey on inefficiencies on illicit drug markets and negative side effects generated by repressive enforcement. They claim that neither a complete decontrol nor the opposite are optimal options. Concluding we can also say that increased enforcement can strengthen the power of the dealers in a market without lowering the amount of drugs consumed.

Another interesting aspect which occurs not only in case of illicit drugs but in all kinds of street crime is the fact that if jurisdiction is relatively tolerant to some type of crime and if neighbouring areas become relatively tougher on this crime, the tolerant jurisdictions will experience increasing crime activity (see Rasmussen et al. (1993) for a drug-related paper). These geographic effects lead to a kind of spatial prisoner's dilemma which could, for example, be analysed with the help of Cellular Automata (cf. Nowak and May, 1993).

5. About a Game-Theoretic Approach of Law Enforcement

To obtain a realistic assessment of the enforcement's impact on criminal behaviour the authority has to include the offender's reaction to crime control. A complete economic analysis of crime and punishment should take into consideration the fact that offenders act as (bounded) rational economic agents. Thus, a multi-agent decision model seems to be the appropriate framework instead of the single decision maker (unilateral) approach mostly used up to now. To study the strategic interaction between criminals and law enforcement agents in an intertemporal setting, the theory of dynamic games provides the suitable framework.

To exemplify such a paradigm the representative offender is interpreted as first player whose decision variable is the intensity of his/her criminal activity considered. This player tries to maximize the discounted expected utility stream taking into consideration that the risk of being apprehended and convicted increases with his/her offense rate. The second player, the law enforcement agency, interacts with the criminal individual(s) via the conviction probability which also depends on the expenditures spent for enforcement. As in the optimal control scenario, this agent minimizes the discounted total stream of social losses over a planning period.

For such a game (or similar, more general competitive interactions of offenders and law enforcement agencies) various solution concepts should be calculated (open-loop, feedback, Stackelberg) and compared with each other. Up to now, however, only one-sided partial analyses have been carried out. This means that it has been studied one the one hand how law enforcement intensity depends on a given level of offending, and one the other hand how offending activities react on law enforcement and punishment for the latter (see, e.g. Caulkins 1993b, and Fent et al. 1997). Although such 'partial approaches' might yield valuable insight they are only preliminary steps to a complete game-theoretic analysis[6].

Based on a simple intertemporal optimization of an optimal pilfering thief by Sethi (1979), Feichtinger (1983) considered a differential game of one thief versus the police. In his model a risk-averse offender 'plays' against police whose objective function incorporates convex costs of law enforcement, a one-shot utility at the time of arrest and imprisonment costs. The probability that the offender is arrested at time t depends not only on the offending rate but also on the rate of law enforcement. The analysis delivered some interesting insight into the qualitative behaviour of Nash equilibria. A remarkable asymmetry of the solutions has been shown: whereas the optimal law enforcement rate always increases, the monotonicity behavior of the thief depends on the constellation of the parameters, mainly on the elasticity of the utility functions.

In Dawid et al. (1996) a conflict between a potential criminal offender and a law enforcement agency is studied. The model is a two-stage extensive form game with imperfect information. It is shown that in equilibrium the offense rate and the law enforcement rate in the first period are always less or equal than the offense rate in the second period. The fact that both offense and enforcement rates are monotonically non-increasing from stage to stage is also established for multistage games, and it is shown that this property disappears if recidivistic behavior is present.

In general the nature of the interaction between criminals and law enforcers implies that the actions of the opposing side are neither easy to determine nor to anticipate. Thus it seems to be appropriate to model these interactions as a game between bounded rational players with a lack of information. Results and techniques from evolutionary game theory may be used to study the evolving

---

[6] A recent extension of the second reference is given by Fent et al. (1998).

behaviour of such a system of interacting individuals. For example, Antoci and Sacco (1995) use the well known replicator dynamics to describe the changing behaviour of a population where each individual can decide in each period whether (s)he will act honestly or corrupt. In order to generate realistic models, it may be necessary to consider systems which can not be dealt with analytically. In this case, Genetic Algorithms or other population based simulation tools could be used to study the behaviour of such a system numerically. An example of this approach has been recently provided by Behrens and Dawid (1996). They model a game theoretic situation between dealers in an illicit open air drug market and crack-down officers within the framework of Genetic Algorithms. These heterogeneous populations rapidly converge towards a homogenous Nash-equilibrium. The success of the crackdown critically depends on the maximum possible enforcement activity and the minimum income of dealers from their illegal activity.

Wirl et al. (1997) analyzed a differential game between a corrupt agent and a law enforcement agency (or the tabloid press with market power). It turns out that the open-loop Nash equilibrium is not unique. The long run strategies are not constant but may follow a persistent limit cycle. The model provides an example of a dynamic game in which complex behaviour holds already in a one state model. In fact, indeterminacy is a generic property of the dynamics game.

Dawid and Feichtinger (1996b) studied a differential game between a (representative) dealer and the drug police. By using rather stylized assumptions they are able to calculate a Markov-perfect equilibrium. It turns out that a foresighted authority should attack the drug problem from the demand side and put much effect in treatment measures.

While law enforcement agents can be subsumed as one player in a first crude approximation this is by no means true for offenders. It is clear that the assumption of the *representative* criminal is an artifact pretending a homogeneity in the offender population which virtually never occurs. Dealers of illicit drugs, addicts, in general criminals are sometimes disorganized and atomized. In that case they cannot implement strategies that involve sacrifices for some members of their group even if they benefit the group as a whole. Even in organized criminality there are mostly several competing organizations ('gangs') making the concept of a two-per-son game elusive.

The conclusion of this state of the art is simply that dynamic games should and will play an important role in the future development of the economics of crime. To conclude this section let us consider the following dynamic game (see Fig. 2).

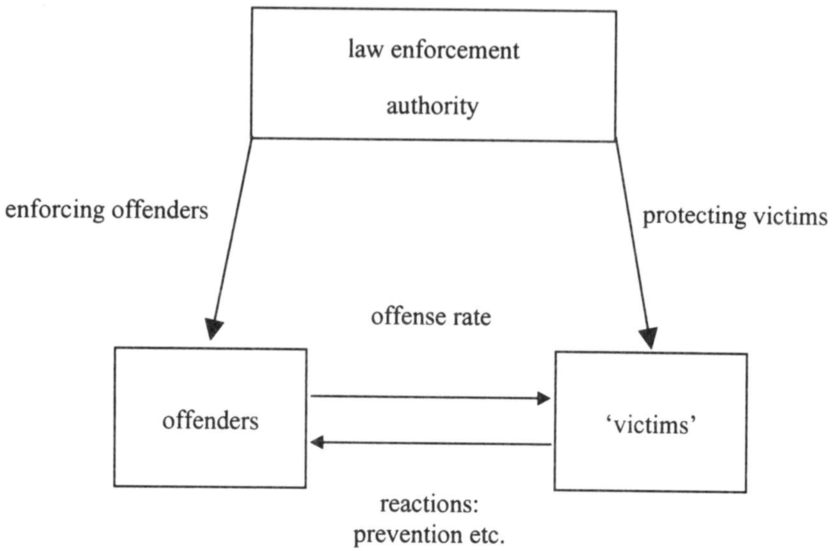

Fig. 2: A stylized scheme of a three-person non-zero sum dynamic game between a law enforcement agency, the population of offenders and the 'victims'.

A law enforcement authority tries to interfere the interaction between criminals and 'victims'. Here we have set quotation marks, since, among others, we are particularly interested in so-called victimless crimes. Consider, e.g., the symbiosis of illicit drug dealers and addicts which urgently need each other. Another example of such a positive feedback is corruption where the interaction between bribers and bribes would lead to a persistent growth of this evil without an intervention of the authority in this loop. Even by simplifying to a representative offender and a representative 'victim' the resulting three-person sum game is rather complex and too complex to allow a calculation of Markov-perfect solutions without substantial (and mostly unrealistic) simplifications.

A more realistic interpretation of this paradigm is to consider two interacting populations, one of offenders and the other is formed by 'victims'. They are controlled by a single player, i.e. the law enforcement agency. An appropriate analysis could model the interaction of the two populations in terms of evolutionary games, while the interfering agency is 'hierarchically above' the game between the populations.

6. Concluding Remarks and Hints for Further Work

The main message of our brief survey is that ignoring intertemporal aspects of the economics of crime and law enforcement is not suitable anymore due to recent advances in modeling.

An effective analysis has to take into consideration that offenders act as rational agents. The complete paradigm amounts to a game between three competitors, namely offenders, victims and law enforcement agencies.

Inherent nonlinearities, e.g. to the impact of reference groups on microbehaviour, may generate optimal law enforcement strategies which will provide economic explanations of variations in crime frequency. Among others, rather surprising results can be derived in dynamic settings.

By reviewing the existing literature in the economics of crime and punishment, two striking features can be observed. First, there seem to be two different 'strings' of papers in law enforcement literature which are virtually not connected to each other. One is in the tradition of the Chicago school of economics and has been originated by Becker's path-breaking 68' paper. The other line of research was done by operations researchers and management scientists and is connected mainly with names like Blumstein (see the list of references), Larson (1972) and others. It seems that the separation of both research avenues is rather an institutional matter than a substantial one.

Second, and more important, a newcomer in this field might be surprised about the lack both of *dynamic* aspects as well as *game-theoretic* approaches in the economics of crime. Although there exist already a couple of papers on both issues, neither time nor strategic interactions seem to be mainstream law and economics. The purpose of the present paper is to collect some arguments to change this situation towards a more efficient approach to cope with criminality.

In our opinion it would be an interesting and promising research strategy to apply instruments of dynamic optimization to a dynamic set-up of law enforcement. In section 2 it has been argued that optimal control techniques (in particular the maximum principle) can be applied to this inherently intertemporal field.

Aside from the intertemporal aspects of crime the second important feature of law enforcement which has not yet found due attention, is the *competitive* aspect. An adequate complete analysis of crime control has to take into consideration that law enforcement is not a problem with a single decision maker. Beside of the law enforcement authority (police or court, respectively) the offenders faced with the risk of being apprehended have to decide how intensive their illegal activities should be. Among other things, the optimal enforcement depends on the cost of catching and convicting offenders, the nature of punishment, and the responses of offenders to changes in enforcement etc. Their responses which are important for the question of deterrence are inherently a game-theoretic issue. Another problem which essentially asks for a game-theoretic treatment is the assessment of the effect of various punishment policies on the individual offense rate. Thus, the analysis of Caulkins (1993b) on zero-tolerance policies of drug consumption could be revisited and extended in a (Stackelberg) game framework. Combing the strategic interaction of the offender and the policemen with the intertemporal aspect amounts to the tool-kit of dynamic game theory (see section 5).

Let us now turn to another important possibility to extend the modeling in crime and law enforcement, namely to the heterogeneity of the offender population. Up to now most models in the field consider a homogenous group of criminals or, what is the same, deal with a representative offender.

However, when modeling the behaviour of people towards some special kind of crime one should think of the possibility of splitting the group of offenders into several subgroups characterised by different offending propensities or 'crime levels'.

Especially in the case of drug control, this inclusion of heterogeneous aspects seems to be crucially important. The non-discriminating attitude of law enforcement agencies towards drug users with regard to what kind of drugs they use (i.e., users of "light" drugs such as marijuana are usually punished equally heavy as users of "heavy" drugs such as cocaine, heroin, etc.) leads to the unintentional fact that users of light drugs tend to enter the group of heavy users, because the ratio between their costs and their utilities from drug use is too similar to that of heavy users. On the other hand, the familiar arguments of politicians are to stress the enforcement of light drugs, i.e. to prevent an enlargement of the group of novice users. One could also distinguish users of the same drug based upon their frequency of use. A simple dichotomous distinction between light and heavy users of the same illicit substance might help to understand the mechanisms of their contradictive influence to nonusers, which are responsible for the occurrence of a drug epidemic (see Behrens et al., 1997a,b).

A worthwhile task would be the construction of a model measuring the impact of enforcement on the consumption to assess the effectiveness of the whole spectrum of drug control policies (differentiated by the degree of repression). Assume that each non-user has a certain threshold to become a user of light drugs and the same is true for the transition to heavy drugs. Then Granovetter and Soong's threshold model for collective behaviour provides an appropriate framework to describe the dynamics between these three groups (see Granovetter and Soong, 1986). In a recent rational choice approach, Braun (1995a,b) shows that threshold distributions and threshold equilibria may result from benefit-cost distributions and network properties. Since the fact that individual transition behaviour is influenced by threshold mechanisms depending on the individual's social environment is empirically supported, the threshold approach should provide a useful framework for modeling the enforcement dynamics. Braun's threshold idea could yield a basis to compare the efficiency of enforcement policies for light drug control in the Netherlands and Germany or Austria, say.

Appendix

This appendix contains a brief description of the optimal law enforcement model sketched already in section 2.

Consider a law enforcement agency whose aim is to minimize the total discounted stream of social losses

$$\min_{E(.)\geq 0} J[E(.)] = \int_0^\infty \exp(-rt)[D(N(t)) + C_1(E(t)) + C_2(N(t), E(t))]dt. \tag{A.1}$$

The number of offenders[7] at time t, N(t), is the state variable, whereas the law enforcement rate E(t) acts as control variable[8]. The discount rate $r > 0$ measures the time preference rate and is assumed to be constant.

As in Becker's (1968) static analysis the social cost can be divided into three components:

- the damage D(N) caused by offenders,
- the cost of apprehension and conviction, $C_1(E)$,
- the cost of punishment, $C_2(N, E)$.

The cost functions D(N) and $C_1(E)$ increase monotonically and are convex with respect to N and E, respectively. Together with $C_2(N, E)$, they are assumed to be sufficiently smooth. For a more detailed discussion see Becker (1968) and Feichtinger et al. (1997).

---

[7] By assuming a homogeneous population of offenders we may identify the number of offenses per time unit with that of the offenders.

[8] The enforcement rate E transforms the input of manpower, material and capital to an amount of police and court activities per time unit (compare Becker, 1968).

For simplicity the cost functions are specified as follows[9]

$$D(N) = N^2, \quad C_1(E) = \frac{c}{2}E^2, \quad C_2(N,E) = dE.$$

To derive the dynamics of offenders already sketched in section 2 we denote by y the income an offender draws from the illegal activity, and by p the probability that an offense will result in a conviction. Assuming for simplicity a linear utility function, $u(y) = y$, and a constant fine, $f = 1$, the expected utility of an offense is given by

$$\mathbb{E}(u) = y - pf = y - p.$$

The key assumption driving the model is that the conviction probability depends on the law enforcement rate per offender, $e = E/N$, in a concave manner, i.e. $p = p(e)$ with

$$p'(e) > 0, \quad p''(e) \le 0.$$

Now we are able to specify the dynamics of the offenders as follows

$$\dot{N}(t) = \kappa[\beta - p(e(t))] - \alpha p(e(t))N(t), \tag{A.2}$$

where β = y-w, w being the average wage rate of the legal activity. Clearly, β must be positive. The proportionality constant κ adjusts the dimension in the r.h.s. of (A.2). Without loss of generality we set $\kappa = 1$. The rate α refers to imprisonment of the convicted offenders.

Again for simplicity it is assumed that

$$p(e) = pe$$

with constant slope $p > 0$.

To satisfy $0 \le p(e) \le 1$ we have $0 \le e \le p^{-1}$, i.e. the inequality

$$N(t) - pE(t) \ge 0 \tag{A.3}$$

---

[9] See Feichtinger et al. (1997) for a justification of the cost function C_2.

must be satisfied for all t. Note that this constraint corresponds to the dashed line in Fig. 1.

To avoid a singularity, we introduce a (very small) level of undetectable offenders, $\underline{N} > 0$, which adds the inequality

$$N(t) - \underline{N} \geq 0 \tag{A.4}$$

for all t. For simplicity this constraint is not shown in Fig. 1.

To summarize, the authority wants to minimize the total social loss in (A.1) subject to the state dynamics (A.2) for a given initial state $N(0) = N_0 \geq 0$. This provides a deterministic optimal control problem with infinite planning horizon, one state variable (N), one control (E), a mixed path constraint (A.3) and a pure state constraint (A.4). Note that for $C_1'(0) = 0$, which is satisfied for $C_1(E) = (c/2)E^2$, the non-negativity of the control variable E is automatically satisfied.

Some results on the (N,E) phase portrait of this intertemporal optimization model are mentioned in section 2. For a detailed analysis we refer to Feichtinger et al. (1997). It can be shown that the qualitative behaviour of the solution, e.g. the existence of a critical point N_c, is rather robust with respect to the specification of the model functions.

References

Akerlof, G.A. (1980): A theory of social custom, of which unemployment may be one consequence. The Quarterly Journal of Economics 94, 749-775

Akiba, H. (1991): The deterrent effect reconsidered: the minimum-time approach. The Journal of Socio-Economics 20(2), 181-192

Andvig, J.C. (1991): The economics of corruption: a survey. Studi economici 43(1), 57-94

Antoci, A., Sacco, P.L. (1995): A public contracting evolutionary game with corruption. Journal of Economics 61(2), 89-122

Bebchuk, L.A., Kaplow, L. (1993): Optimal sanctions and differences in individuals' likelihood of avoiding detection. International Review of Law and Economics 13, 217-224

Becker, G.S. (1968): Crime and punishment: an economic approach, Journal of Political Economy 76, 169-217.

Behrens, D., Caulkins, J.P., Tragler, G., Haunschmied, J.L., Feichtinger, G. (1997a): A dynamic model of drug initiation: implications for treatment and drug control. Forschungsbericht 213 des Instituts für Ökonometrie, OR und Systemtheorie, TU Wien, Dezember (forthcoming in Mathematical Biosciences)

Behrens, D., Caulkins, J.P., Tragler, G., Feichtinger, G. (1997b): Controlling the US cocaine epidemic: finding the optimal mix of drug prevention and treatment. Forschungsbericht 214 des Instituts für Ökonometrie, OR und Systemtheorie, TU Wien, Dezember

Behrens, D., Dawid, H. (1996): Genetic learning on illicit drug markets: can it lead to a crackdown? Forschungsbericht 206 des Instituts für Ökonometrie, OR und Systemtheorie, TU Wien, Dezember

Benson, B.L., Rasmussen, D.W. (1991): Relationship between illicit drug enforcement policy and property crimes. Contemporary Policy Issues 9(4), 106-115

Benson, B.L., Kim, I., Rasmussen, D.W., Zuehlke, T. W. (1992): Is property crime caused by drug use or by drug enforcement policy? Applied Economics 24(7), 679-692

Bicchieri, C., Rovelli, C. (1995): Evolution and revolution. Rationality and Society 7(2), 201-224

Blumstein, A., Cohen, J. (1973): A theory of the stability of punishment. Journal of Criminal Law and Criminology 64(2), 198-207

Blumstein, A., Nagin, D. (1981): On the optimum use of incarceration for crime control. Operations Research 26(3), 381-405

Blumstein, A. et al. (eds) (1978): Deterrence and Incapacitation: Estimating the Effects of Criminal Sanctions on Crime Rates. National Academy of Sciences, Wash DC

Braun, N. (1995a): Individual thresholds and social diffusion. Rationality and Society 7(2), 167-182

Braun, N. (1995b): The threshold model revisited. Submitted to Journal of Mathematical Sociology

Braun, N., Diekmann, A. (1993): Drogenschwarzmarkt und KonsumentInnensituation: Einige Ergebnisse der Berner Szenebefragung. Drogalkohol 17, 161-182

Brock, W.A., Durlauf, S.N. (1995), Discrete choice with social interactions I: theory. Working Paper 95-10-084, Santa Fe Institute

Caulkins, J.P. (1990): The Distribution and Consumption of Illicit Drugs: Some Mathematical Models and Their Policy Implications. Ph. D. Dissertation, M.I.T.

Caulkins, J.P. (1993a): Local drug markets' response to focused police enforcement. Operations Research 41(5), 848-863

Caulkins, J.P. (1993b): Zero-tolerance policies: do they inhibit or stimulate illicit drug consumption? Management Science 39(4), 458-476

Davis, M.L. (1988): Time and punishment: an intertemporal model of crime. Journal of Political Economy 96(2), 383-390

Dawid, H., Feichtinger, G. (1996a): On the persistence of corruption. Journal of Economics 64, 177-193

Dawid, H., Feichtinger, G. (1996b): Optimal allocation of drug control efforts: a differential game analysis. Journal of Optimization Theory and Applications 91, 279-297

Dawid, H., Feichtinger, G., Jorgensen, S. (1996): Crime and law enforcement: a multistage game. Forschungsbericht 201 des Instituts für Ökonometrie, OR und Systemtheorie, TU Wien, August (forthcoming in Annals of Dynamic Games)

Dechert, W.D., Nishimura, K. (1983): A complete characterization of optimal growth paths in an aggregated model with a non-concave production function. Journal of Economic Theory 31(2), 332-354

Dworak, M., Feichtinger, G., Tragler G., Caulkins, J.P. (1998): On the effect of drug enforcement on property crime. Forschungsbericht 215 des Instituts für Ökonometrie, OR und Systemtheorie, TU Wien, Jänner (forthcoming in Journal of Economics)

Feichtinger, G. (1983): A differential games solution to a model of competition between a thief and the police. Management Science 29(6), 686-699

Feichtinger, G., Grienauer, W., Tragler, G. (1997): Optimal dynamic law enforcement. Forschungsbericht 197 des Instituts für Ökonometrie, OR und Systemtheorie, TU Wien, September

Fent, T., Feichtinger, G., Tragler, G. (1998): A dynamic Stackelberg game of offending and law enforcement. Forschungsbericht 219 des Instituts für Ökonometrie, OR und Systemtheorie, TU Wien, Juni

Fent, T., Zalesak, M., Feichtinger, G. (1997): Optimal offending in view of the criminal record. Forschungsbericht 198 des Instituts für Ökonometrie, OR und Systemtheorie, TU Wien, Oktober

Granovetter, M., Soong, R. (1986): Threshold models of interpersonal effects in consumer demand. Journal of Economic Behavior and Organization 7, 83-99

Hofbauer, J., Sigmund, K. (1998): Evolutionary Games and Population Dynamics. Cambridge University Press, Cambridge

Kort, P., Feichtinger, G., Hartl, R.F., Haunschmied, J.L., (1998): Optimal enforcement policies (crackdowns) on a illicit drug market. Optimal Control Applications and Methods 19, 169-184

Larson, R.C. (1972): Urban Police Patrol Analysis. MIT Press, Cambridge, MA

Leung, S.F. (1991): How to make the fine fit the corporate crime? An analysis of static and dynamic optimal punishment theories. Journal of Public Economics 45(2), 243-256

Leung, S.F. (1995): Dynamic deterrence theory. Economica 62, 65-87

Long, N.V., Nishimura, K., Shimomura, K. (1997): Endogenous growth, trade, and specialization under variable returns to scale: the case of a small open economy. In: Jensen, B., Wong, K. (Ed.): Dynamics, Economic Growth and International Trade. Michigan University Press

Malik, A.S. (1990): Avoidance, screening and optimum enforcement. RAND Journal of Economics 21(3), 341-353

Maltz, M.D. (1994): Operations research in studying crime and justice: its history and accomplishments. In: Pollack, S.M. et al. (Eds.): Handbooks in OR & MS 6. 201-262

Maltz, M.D. (1996): From Poisson to the present: applying operations research to problems of crime and justice. Journal of Quantitative Criminology 12(1)

Nowak, M.A., May, R.M. (1993): The spatial dilemmas of evolution. International Journal of Bifurcation and Chaos 3(1), 35-78

Polinsky, A.M., Shavell, S. (1991): A note on optimal fines when wealth varies among individuals. The American Economic Review 81(3), 618-621

Polinsky, A.M., Shavell, S. (1992): Enforcement costs and the optimal magnitude and probability of fines. Journal of Law & Economics 35(1), 133-148

Rasmussen, D.W., Benson, B.L., Sollars, D.L. (1993): Spatial competition in illicit drug markets: the consequences of increased drug law enforcement. Review of Regional Studies 23(3), 219-236

Samuelson, P.A. (1976): An economist's non-linear model of self-generated fertility waves. Population Studies 30, 243-247

Schelling, T.C. (1973): Hockey helmets, concealed weapons, and daylight saving: a study of binary choices with externalities. Journal of Conflict Resolution 17(3), 381-428

Schelling, T.C. (1978): Micromotives and Macrobehavior. Norton, New York

Schlicht, E. (1981): Reference group behaviour and economic incentives: a remark. Zeitschrift für die gesamte Staatswissenschaft 137, 125-127

Sethi, S.P. (1979): Optimal pilfering policies for dynamic continuous thieves. Management Science 25(6), 535-542

Shavell, S. (1990): Deterrence and the punishment of attempts. Journal of Legal Studies 19(2), 435-466

Skiba, A.K. (1978): Optimal growth with a convex-concave production function. Econometrica 46(3), 527-539

Sollars, D.L., Benson, B.L., Rasmussen, D.W. (1994): Drug enforcement and the deterrence of property crime among local jurisdictions. Public Finance Quarterly 22(1), 22-45

Tragler, G., Caulkins J.P., Feichtinger, G. (1997): Optimal dynamic allocation of treatment and enforcement in illicit drug control. Forschungsbericht 212 des Instituts für Ökonometrie, OR und Systemtheorie, TU Wien, Dezember (forthcoming in Operations Research)

Wichmann, S. (1993): Gesetze der Ökonomie. Wirtschaftswoche 47(44), 50-59

Wirl, F., Feichtinger, G. (1998): Conditions for and existence of unstable equilibria in concave intertemporal optimizations. Working Paper, Otto-von-Guericke University of Magdeburg

Wirl, F., Novak, A., Feichtinger, G., Dawid, H. (1997): Indeterminacy of open-loop Nash equilibria: the ruling class versus the tabloid press. In: Ben-Haim, Y.: Uncertanty: Models and Measures. Akademie-Verlag, 124-136

List of Contributors

Martin Beckmann
Institut für Angewandte Mathematik und Statistik
Technische Universität München
Arcisstraße 21, D-80333 München
Brown University
Providence Rhode Island

Lutz Beinsen
Institut für Volkswirtschaftslehre
Karl-Franzens-Universität Graz
Universitätsstraße 15/F4, A-8010 Graz
e-mail: lutz.beinsen@kfunigraz.ac.at

Helmut Beran
Institut für Systemwissenschaften
Johannes-Kepler-Universität Linz
Altenbergstraße 69, A-4040 Linz
e-mail: helmut.beran@jk.uni-linz.ac.at

Gerhart Bruckmann
Zehenthofgasse 11, A-1190 Wien

Günther Fandel
FB Wirtschaftswissenschaft
Fernuniversität Hagen
Feithstraße 140/AVZ II, Postfach 940, D-58084 Hagen
e-mail: guenter.fandel@fernuni-hagen.de

Gustav Feichtinger
Institut für Ökonometrie und Operations Research
Technische Universität Wien
Argentinierstraße 8, A-1040 Wien
e-mail: or@e119ws1.tuwien.ac.at

Karl Inderfurth
Fakultät für Wirtschaftswissenschaft, Lehrstuhl BWL VI
Otto-von-Guericke-Universität Magdeburg
Postfach 4120, D-39016 Magdeburg
e-mail: inderfurth@ww.uni-magdeburg.de

Thomas Jensen
Fakultät für Wirtschaftswissenschaft, Lehrstuhl BWL VI
Otto-von-Guericke-Universität Magdeburg
Postfach 4120, D-39016 Magdeburg,
e-mail: jensen@ww.uni-magdeburg.de

Klaus-Peter Kistner
Fakultät für Wirtschaftswissenschaften
Universität Bielefeld
POB 100131, D-33501 Bielefeld
e-mail: kkistner@wiwi.uni-bielefeld.de

Carola Kratzer
Institut für Statistik, Ökonometrie und Operations Research
Karl-Franzens-Universität Graz
Universitätsstraße 15/E3, A-8010 Graz

Wilhelm Krelle
Institut für Gesellschafts- und Wirtschaftswissenschaften
Rheinische Friedrich-Wilhelms-Universität Bonn
Adenauerallee 24-42, D-53177 Bonn,
e-mail: krelle@solo.lenne35.uni-bonn.de

Ulrike Leopold-Wildburger
Institut für Statistik, Ökonometrie und Operations Research
Karl-Franzens-Universität Graz
Universitätsstraße 15/E3, A-8010 Graz,
e-mail: ulrike.leopold@kfunigraz.ac.at

Shuangzhe Liu
Institut für Statistik und Ökonometrie
Universität Basel
Holbeinstraße 12, CH-4051 Basel
e-mail: liu@iso.iso.unibas.ch

Michael Lorth
FB Wirtschaftswissenschaft
Fernuniversität Hagen
Feithstraße 140/AVZ II, Postfach 940, D-58084 Hagen
e-mail: michael.lorth@fernuni-hagen.de

Reinhard Neck
Institut für Wirtschaftswissenschaften
Universität Klagenfurt
Universitätsstraße 65-67, A-9020 Klagenfurt
e-mail: reinhard.neck@uni-klu.ac.at

Georg Pflug
Institut für Statistik, Operations Research und Computerverfahren
Universität Wien
Universitätsstraße 5/9, A-1010 Wien
e-mail: pflug@eos.smc.univie.ac.at

Wolfgang Polasek
Institut für Statistik und Ökonometrie
Universität Basel
Holbeinstraße 12, CH-4051 Basel
e-mail: wolfgang@iso.iso.unibas.ch

Angi Rösch
Seminar für Ökonometrie und Statistik
Ludwig-Maximilians-Universität München
Akademiestraße 1/I, D-80799 München
e-mail: Angi.R@t-online.de

Harald Schmidbauer
MünchenSeminar für Ökonometrie und Statistik
Ludwig-Maximilians-Universität
Akademiestraße 1/I, D-80799 München
and
Yeditepe University
Đsk‚dar Kamp‚s‚
Istanbul

Christoph Schneeweiß
Lehrstuhl für Unternehmensplanung und Operations Research
Universität Mannheim
Postfach 103264, D-68131 Mannheim,
e-mail: schneeweiss@bwl.uni-mannheim.de

Hans Schneeweiss
Seminar für Ökonometrie und Statistik
Ludwig-Maximilians-Universität München
Akademiestraße 1/I, D-80799 München
e-mail: schneew@stat.uni-muenchen.de

Printing: Weihert-Druck GmbH, Darmstadt
Binding: Buchbinderei Schäffer, Grünstadt